UNIVERSITY OF ALBERTA
LIBRARIES

But Not in CANADA!

But Not in CANADA!

Walter Stewart

MACMILLAN OF CANADA

Toronto

ISBN 0-7705-1386-7

Printed in Canada for
The Macmillan Company of Canada
70 Bond Street, Toronto M5B 1X3

CONTENTS

ACKNOWLEDGMENT

This is the place where the blushing author knuckles his forehead and says that whatever is right in the book that follows is due to the unflagging aid of his friends, wife, contacts, and faithful dog, but that whatever errors occur are his responsibility alone. Well, to hell with that. This book would not have been written except for the nagging and bully-ragging of Douglas Gibson of Macmillan's, who had the original idea. If you enjoy the book, some of the credit must go to Gibson; if you want to throw ripe tomatoes, at least some of them should be directed his way.

This book is for Katie and Dusty Miller

CHAPTER 1:

GOOD OLD US

Canadians have, if they would remember it, a tradition for using reason, time and legality to solve problems as difficult as those faced by the Americans. They have a heritage quite other than the American.

James M. Minifie, 1960.

Williams Lake, British Columbia, 1966. An Indian girl met some youths in a beverage room, and they agreed to give her a lift to her aunt's place. Of course, they didn't take her to her aunt's; they took her to a garbage dump, where the three whites thought they would get a little free loving. Everybody knows about Indian girls.

Unfortunately, this girl didn't. She was found dead the next morning, naked and dead by the roadside. The youths, all of good families, admitted that they had wrestled her around some, got fed up with her, and pitched her out of the car into the cold April night. She died of a broken neck, but they said she was alive when they last saw her. What they did wasn't right, maybe, but it wasn't murder, either. A white jury agreed; two of the youths were convicted of assault, and fined $200; the charge against the third was dismissed.

The House of Commons, Ottawa, 1938. Premier Maurice Duplessis of Quebec had brought in a law, the Padlock Law, that permitted the seizure and closing of any premises suspected of being used to propagate communism. No proof was required, no defence was permitted, and "communism" was never defined. The law was used against all of Duplessis's political opponents. In Ottawa, J. S. Woodsworth, leader of the CCF, rose in his place in Parliament and, his voice shaking with emotion, declared, "Twice every day for six months the provincial police have carried out execution without judgment, dispossession without due process of law; twenty times a month they have trampled on liberties as old as Magna Carta." Woodsworth was shouted down. Ernest Lapointe, Minister of Justice, told him, "In spite of the fact that the words are so unpleasant to the honourable member for Winnipeg North Centre, I do desire to say that the reign of law must continue in this country, that peace and order must prevail."

Outside Vancouver, 1887. A mob of whites, disturbed that identured Chinese coolie labourers had taken jobs in the mines that God meant white men to have, rushed the Chinese camp and drove the workers out into the January night. There was a twenty-foot cliff behind the camp, and the coolies were driven over it; you could hear them going plump, plump, plump, into the freezing sea.

Toronto, 1945. E. B. Jolliffe, provincial leader of the CCF, charged that the Ontario Provincial Police were being used as political spies by the Conservative government, that a special squad was gathering private information for Premier George Drew, and that this information was being used to harass Liberals and CCFers. Jolliffe said the OPP was acting as a private "Gestapo" — an emotive word for that time. He had an impressive amount of evidence, including the testimony of Alvin Rowe, an OPP officer who had worked on the secret squad and who had come to Jolliffe because, he said, he was being used as a political spy, and didn't like it. A royal commission was called to inquire into Jolliffe's charges, but its terms of reference were so narrow that it was barred from conducting a real investigation. Then Alvin Rowe was killed in a plane crash; Jolliffe's party was badly punished at the polls.

Sydney, Nova Scotia, 1971. The Sydney police went on strike for higher wages. They had barely left their posts

2

when gangs of toughs took over the town and began drag-racing up and down the main street. Fights, looting, then a general riot broke out; the town was in a state bordering on anarchy until the strike was settled.

Near Seven Oaks, Manitoba, 1816. A disagreement arose between fur traders of the North West Company and settlers brought in by Lord Selkirk to found a permanent community. So the company arranged to have the settlement attacked, and twenty people were murdered. When Selkirk tried to exact justice, he was blocked by the political manoeuvrings of his opponents, defeated in court, and eventually driven into near bankruptcy.

Near Wymark, Saskatchewan, 1967. A man who had complained that the RCMP was slow in acting on his earlier charges that he was being harassed by obscene telephone calls was working in his pasture. An RCMP car pulled up, two constables piled out, and he was taken away and held for forty days, under the Saskatchewan Mental Health Act, without ever being charged, or convicted, or even told what he had done wrong.

During the forty days he was subjected to shock treatments and drug therapy and then, one day, he was turned loose as suddenly as he had been locked up.

Montreal, 1949. A university professor's house blew up, and his wife and daughter were killed, while he was injured. He was clapped into jail and held for three months under the provincial Coroner's Act. Police had discovered that he had had a mistress some time previously, and they assumed, without a shred of proof, that he had blown up his own house. He was not charged; he was simply held, while the press seethed with stories of his infidelity, his callousness, his savagery. Eventually, it turned out that the house had been destroyed by a natural gas explosion. He was released.

Toronto, 1974. An American sociologist, a controversial figure alleged to hold strong and wrong views on the subject of race, had been invited to speak at the University of Toronto. A group of left-wing students and teachers decreed that he was an inappropriate speaker; they stormed the lectern, staged a minor riot, and drove the sociologist away. His speech was never made. Months later, two students were suspended for their part in the affair; it can be argued that freedom of speech remains suspended at the university.

I am in favour of smugness, to a point; it rounds the figure, deepens the dimples, and aids the digestive process. I believe, too, that Canadians have a certain amount to be smug about; by and large, we have been a reasonable and prosperous people; by and large, we have avoided mass murder, organized tyranny, and the more public forms of corruption. However, since 1972, since Watergate, smugness has become a national religion, a national disease. Nothing that has happened on the North American continent since our side sacked Washington in 1814 has given Canadians such unalloyed pleasure as Watergate. While the Americans wallow in guilt and self-doubt, we bubble with joy and self-righteousness. Thank God, we say, for our British traditions and innate Canadian decency. There may be rot and racism, inequity and injustice, among those fractious, rebellious Yankees, but not in Canada.

Well, we have never had anything quite like Watergate, but that is a claim we share with most nations of the world. We have, however, had major political corruption involving our highest figures — remember Sir John A. and the Pacific Scandal, remember the McGreevy brothers, remember the Beauharnois Scandal, remember the Ontario Highways Scandal? — and we have had extensive cover-ups, political dirty tricks, payoffs, and — God knows — thousands of examples of the abuse of power.

A major difference between us and the Americans —

besides the size, the pervasiveness, the sheer bloody-mindedness of Watergate—is our diffidence. Except for the Pacific Scandal (after all, that was a long time ago), Canadian outbursts of corruption, venality, brutality, racism, and oppression have gone largely unrecorded. It's not that we don't want to hear about such subjects — we do — but we don't want to hear about them when they happen in Canada. During the spring of 1975, Canadians flocked to their theatres to see an American film about authoritarianism in the U.S., called *Hearts and Minds*. At the same time, they stayed away in droves from a Canadian film about authoritarianism in Canada, called *Les Ordres*. There are some things we would rather not know.

We view ourselves as a superior people, a sober, peaceable people, a people of extraordinarily decent instincts and firmly entrenched liberties, and we reject any contrary evidence. Thus, when our federal government comes along, as it did in October 1970, and throws 435 people into jail without charge or trial, when it makes it a crime ever to have belonged to a political organization that was legal five minutes before the law was passed, we are not shocked or upset; we applaud. If the government chooses to establish retroactive crime, our reaction is not to say that our civil liberties are in jeopardy, but that the government must have powerful reasons, secret reasons, reasons that remain secret to this day, to act so arbitrarily. Indeed, some officers of the Canadian Civil Liberties Association give their approval — although the Association itself does not. Because we know we are decent, reasonable people, because our government would never do anything really wrong, really suppressive, whatever is done must, of necessity, be reasonable and right. Indeed, some Canadians are still half-expecting the government to produce secret reasons, one of these days, that will explain the whole thing satisfactorily (just as some of us still wait around on Easter morn for a bunny to drop off a clutch of eggs).

One of the problems we face as a nation, perhaps in greater measure than other nations, is that we are held captive by the myth of the reasonable citizen. The Canadian as we see him, the Canadian in the mind of God, is a man who never gives in to extremism; he is a patient man (who shuns violence), a neighbourly man (who spurns racism), a democratic man (who supports free speech, civil liberties, and honesty in politics). He is, in short, all the things your average wild-eyed, gun-toting, bigoted, loud-mouthed, venal, aggressive, tyrannical bastard of an American is not. What is more, his history has made him the gentle citizen he is today. There have been blots on the copybook — things like the Winnipeg General Strike, the Regina Riot, the incarceration of Japanese Canadians during World War II—but these are minor slips, casually recorded or missed entirely in our history of ourselves.

Enough. Canadians, as a people, are no better and no worse than anyone else. We were slavers in the eighteenth and early nineteenth centuries, and our treatment of minorities, from Indians to Jehovah's Witnesses, is only marginally different from that of the Americans. We have staged some of the bigger and more bloody-minded riots on the continent, from the Bytown Riots of the 1840s ("Them Bytown days was fightin' days") to the Kenora race riots of 1974. We have not only passed, but applauded, viciously repressive legislation, and our gun laws, to take only one minor example of wrong-headed self-congrat-ulation, are in fact looser and dumber than those in most U.S. states.

What follows is an examination of the myth and reality of Canada's image — the way we see ourselves — a ranging back and forth over our history to examine incidents, some old, some new, some recorded, and some that have some-how slipped past the official record, that throw light on the kind of people we really are.

This is not an anti-Canadian book; I am, after all, a

Canadian nationalist. Rather, I hope, it is a gentle corrective, a reminder of who we are and where we came from, a look at our behaviour from a vantage point very different from that of the schoolteachers, historians, and politicians who have given us our present smug, distorted image of ourselves.

This is a very personal book, the result, not so much of the year's intense research that went into its preparation, but of the past twenty-three years that I have spent as a Canadian journalist. It has the weaknesses of the journalistic technique: the argument by example, the drawing of general conclusions from specific incidents, the willingness to make judgments on cases in which the last details may never be known. At the same time, I hope it has some of the advantages of journalism, chief among them the fact that, like most journalists, I have shaped my argument to a clear and discernible end. I am pleading for a cause. I would not have written this book if I did not care very much about my country, and its people, and its future.

CHAPTER 2:
A RIOTOUS TIME WAS HAD BY ALL

Canada is a live country, live, but not, like the States, kicking.
Rupert Brooke, 1913.

We were milling around the corner of the Grand'Allée and D'Auteuil Street in Quebec City, just down from the Quebec legislative buildings, just up from the Château Frontenac. We were wandering aimlessly back and forth through the gate in the wall around the old part of the city, waiting for something to happen. The place was jammed with kids, many of them sporting a chin-growth that gave promise of manhood. Every now and then, one of these kids would jump onto a light-standard and shout "Vive le Québec! A bas Ottawa!", and everyone would cheer. Or somebody would start to chant "Tick, tick, tick, tick, tick, tick, BOOM!" — a time-bomb, see? — and everyone would laugh uproariously. It was Saturday, October 10, 1964 — Nightstick Saturday.

The Queen was here for a royal visit. Weeks before her Canadian arrival at Charlottetown, P.E.I., the press had been full of concern for her safety. President Kennedy's assassination the previous autumn was still a raw wound, and a couple of grandstanding separatist leaders had attempted to head off Her Majesty with a warning that Quebec might become "another Dallas". The cops were having a fit from the moment the royal yacht heaved over the horizon. In Charlottetown—loyal old Charlottetown—photographers were ordered to put red tape on their rifle-like long lenses, for identification — or else. "Or else what?", somebody asked an RCMP briefing officer. "Or else you'll get shot," the Mountie replied. Also in Charlottetown, a seven-year-old boy carrying a toy pistol was frisked by the cops, and an old drunk who wandered onto the steps of the Memorial Building and sat down just before the royal arrival was snatched away so fast his poor, besotted head reeled.

That was for starters. By the time the royal party had come upriver to Quebec, by the time the royal yacht, *Britannia*, was anchored at Wolfe's Cove, and frogmen had assumed their underwater stations to ensure that no blackguard slipped a limpet mine onto the royal hull, by the time we reached that pass, all the official guardians were wound so tight that their nerves twanged like guitar strings every time they moved. The Quebec Provincial Police had ordered 2,000 24-inch oak nightsticks—brand new, never touched a skull before — just for the occasion, and they were looking for a chance to swing them in affirmation of the fact that Quebec was as loyal, dammit, as any other part of Canada. Or, more likely, to show that Quebeckers resented a reputation for lawlessness that had grown out of several bombing incidents in 1963.

The Grand'Allée on the morning of October 10, 1964, was not a very smart place to stage a demonstration, but then, demonstrators were not always very smart. I was mulling all this over when, around me, the crowd began to shift; word spread that something was going on down at City Hall, a few blocks away, so we all ran down that way. You couldn't see anything, just a bunch of men walking around with signs (I later discovered that they had been protesting the arrest of Reggie Chartrand, sometime boxer, full-time separatist agitator, who had been picked up earlier that morning in a scuffle). Then, the cops were with us; they had been waiting in busses parked all around the area, nursing their grievances and their nightsticks, and they came swarming out to vent the first and swing the second. The crowd began to push, to jostle, to try to get the hell out of the way, but the cops came right into us, swinging. They

9

seldom hit anybody — there was room to move out of the way. But I saw a fellow reporter catch the tail-end of a swing across the cheek. He was furious, and held up his press badge. "For Christ's sake!" he shouted, "I'm Press." The cop, who had rushed by, stopped, looked back, and swung again, narrowly missing. We left. It was not a time for arguing.

That was all for the moment. Then we were up at the gates to the Citadel, above Dufferin Terrace, overlooking the St. Lawrence. The Queen was there to open a new memorial to the Royal 22nd Regiment, of which she is Colonel-in-Chief. Inside, you could hear the clump, clump of booted feet, the blat of a bugle, the bark of commands, but outside, only the chants of the separatists — "A bas, Ottawa". (This was three years before "Vive le Québec Libre" became *de rigueur*.) Then the cops were with us again, pouring out of the rented busses, running across the grass, having a hell of a fine time swinging at anything that moved. Marc Shieffler, a freelance journalist from New York, screamed at a cop who had beaten a teen-age kid to his knees — trying to get him to stop beating the kid — and then there were five cops swarming all over Shieffler, backing him up against a wall, slashing at him while he tried to cover himself and scream, "Press! Press!" They hustled him off to a waiting van.

There was another brief respite, and then we were back at the old city wall on the Grand' Allée again, waiting for the Queen to come down to the Château for a spot of tea and a chat with Prime Minister Lester Pearson. The cops — the regular cops, not the special riot police who had been trucked in and revved up for the festivities — were standing around being kidded; youngsters were swarming all over the place, singing, joking, making their damn fool tick, tick, tick, tick noise. There was a motorcycle roar and, in the gathering dusk, the Queen swept by — a flash of black car, and that was all. The crowd began to boo — whether because they could see the Queen or because they couldn't, I never knew — and we started to move down the crowded Rue St. Louis, the extension of the Grand' Allée, towards the hotel.

This is the old part of the city, where all the streets are narrow, and all the sidestreets were fenced off with barricades. We were in a funnel, open at the top where the barricades had been swung aside for the royal passage. We walked on, past a containment line of soldiers, air cadets, and policemen. There were occasional shouts, but not much noise, just a kind of shuffle, shuffle, down the street. Whatever trouble we were going to have, I thought, was already over. Then there was another stir in the crowd (I learned later that, as the Queen's car turned into the hotel courtyard, separatists began to jeer, and somebody either threw something or looked as if he might). Behind us, the barricades were closed, and the cops moved in again. They had been parked in busses, trucks, and vans along the sidestreets, and out they bustled, anxious to justify the cost of their goddamn nightsticks.

This time, there was nowhere to run; youngsters were caught between the buildings and the barricades and hammered down. One youth, trying to dodge a swinging stick, fell over a wall, seven feet down to the cement below; he lay there stunned, and a cop promptly ran up and began beating him. The barricades gave way, the crowd pushed down past the Château, out along Dufferin Terrace, and disappeared into the night, and behind them pounded the cops, collaring any scruffy kid who ran, thumping any scruffy kid who didn't, while the rest of us pressed back, protected by our silence and our respectability (certified by our lack of beards and blue jeans) and simply watched. An American journalist to whom I had, a few hours earlier, explained the advantages of Canadian, over U.S., civilization — less violence, less repression, calm moderation in all things — swung me around and began to jabber in incoherent anger. "Listen," he said, "Listen . . . . Who the . . . who the Christ do you think you are?"

I am no longer very sure. Until Nightstick Saturday I had considered that as a Canadian, I was, by birth, a member of a superior culture, the beneficiary of what Sir Wilfrid Laurier defined as "a policy of Canadianism, of moderation, of conciliation". Since then, I have learned better.

A subsequent investigation of Nightstick Saturday, conducted by Quebec's newly-minted Minister of Justice (then a provincial Liberal, now a federal Conservative), found that everything that happened that day was regular and correct. Everything was the fault of the kids; the cops were merely doing their duty. Well, maybe; it didn't look that way to me, but I admit to being frightened and confused, not merely by the violence around me, but by the fact of the riot itself. Canadians don't riot, for Pete's sake; it's Un-Canadian!

I had been duped, as we so often are, by the record we keep of our history, as opposed to the history itself. Most of our reference books shun the word "riot"—try it out on any index. The *Encyclopedia Canadiana* slips demurely from "Riordan, Charles", to "Ripley, Ontario". The *Encyclopedia of Canada* recognizes nothing between "Rimouski River" and good old Ripley. The *Encyclopaedia Britannica* and the *Encyclopedia Americana* are not so shy; both carry long articles on riots and rioting. (The *Britannica* begins with the definition I have followed: "Riot, in general terms, is a temporary violent outbreak of civil disorder, falling short of an attempt to overthrow the government, and thereby distinguished from an insurrection or rebellion.") A chap could easily conclude that Canadian history is unmarked by riots, but in fact our past, like everybody else's past, is chock-a-block with them.

We have had economic riots and political riots and patriotic riots and conscription riots; we have had riots in French and English and Chinese and Italian and German and

Russian; we have had labour riots, racial riots, police riots, service riots, and religious riots; we have had riots to put people in jail, and riots to get them out; we have had riots in the name of peace and of war; we have had soccer riots, hockey riots, and a number of riots that, from today's vantage point, appear to have been held just for the hell of it, like the Toronto circus riot of 1855. We even had two hanging riots in Montreal in the nineteenth century; one when the authorities only strung up one victim after two were promised, another when the dangling body could not be seen clearly enough—the crowd stormed the place, tore down the offending barricades, and gawked to their hearts' content.

We have had early riots, such as the annual pitched battles that used to erupt in Halifax on Guy Fawkes Day during the 1740s, and such as the Bytown Riots, culminating in a "Stoney Monday" in 1849, and we have had recent riots, such as the rampage that did two million dollars worth of damage at a construction site on James Bay in October 1974.

Perhaps we have not had more than our share of riots, but we have had them aplenty, and they have been violent and deadly and savage and expensive, just like the riots of less privileged folk. From this rich motherlode of smashing and burning, of desperation, drunkenness, pillage, and despair, I ask you to consider only a representative sampling, culled from many candidates, to span the nation and our recorded history, and to reflect some of the many brands of riot recognized by aficionados.

A Political Riot, Montreal, 1849

During the "troubles" — nice word, that, for armed rebellion—of 1837-38, a sizeable number of people lost property through no fault of their own. Houses were looted and burned, cattle slaughtered, carriages confiscated, fences

13

smashed, bridges torn down — the kind of thing without which one cannot conduct a respectable revolution. In accord with the time-honoured principle that absolutely nothing is as important as property, the Province of Upper Canada moved, almost the moment the din died, to set up a commission to assess compensation for losses suffered in "the late unnatural rebellion". An enabling act was passed in March 1838. There were some moves towards a similar act in Lower Canada but, beyond a resolution—common to both provinces — signifying that only Loyalists would be recompensed, no business resulted.

Then the two provinces became one in the Act of Union in 1841. The first session of the new joint Parliament passed a bill to extend compensation in Canada West (the old Upper Canada, today's Ontario) to anyone, Loyalist or otherwise, who had lost property through the action of persons "acting or assuming to act on Her Majesty's behalf" during the unpleasantness. This act naturally stirred the embers of righteous greed on the far side of the Ottawa River and, in 1845, the united assembly petitioned Governor General Metcalfe to extend the same treatment to Canada East. Money was forthcoming in Canada West, but Metcalfe stalled on payments to Canada East. Then the Baldwin-LaFontaine administration came to power, and Louis Hippolyte LaFontaine introduced the Rebellion Losses Bill, which provided for an investigating commission of five members, and gave them £10,000 to divvy up, and extended reparations to all but the small number of rebels actually convicted or deported as traitors. This meant that a lot of rebels who had not been formally charged would receive compensation. The bill passed the assembly, then meeting in Montreal, by a 47-18 vote, but Lord Elgin, who had succeeded Metcalfe as Governor, put off signing it into law. He expected trouble — Montreal was already ringing with Loyalist cries of "No pay for the rebels"—and he was right.

14

Elgin believed in responsible government, however, and so, reluctantly but gamely, he announced that he would sign the accursed bill on April 25, 1849. That afternoon, the Loyalist—i.e., English-speaking Tory (I'm afraid that this is one Quebec riot which can't be smugly attributed to "those crazy excitable Frenchmen with their Gallic temperaments") — opponents of the bill swarmed into the parliament buildings in downtown Montreal and listened in truculent silence as Lord Elgin read the formal consent. Then they swarmed out again, and as soon as Elgin appeared, they began to pelt him with eggs and filth. In those days of slacker garbage-removal standards and ubiquitous horses, "filth" was always in rich, varied supply. At least one egg caught him square in the face, which surprised him almost as much as the fact that, as he later noted, many of the jeering, hooting pelters were "persons of a respectable class in society". Elgin sped away, filthy but unharmed, in his open landau.

That evening, there was a mass meeting on the Champs de Mars, where stirring speeches set forth the need to protect the righteous and punish the French, and whipped the crowd into a fair frenzy. They all took off for the parliament buildings. Stones flying through the windows alerted the fearless MPs, who beat a prudent retreat, and the mob took over, smashed the building, and set fire to it. When the fire engines tried to approach to put out the blaze they were stopped, in what has become a time-honoured riot tradition, and their hoses were chopped up. A portrait of Queen Victoria, no doubt under official protection from on high, and the parliamentary mace were all that emerged intact from the ruins.

That concluded the first part of the evening's entertainment. Then the mob descended on LaFontaine's house and, not finding him at home, clever chap, they wreaked their vengeance on his furniture and fixings, ripped all his feather mattresses apart, drank all his wine, and adjourned

15

with the righteous glow that accompanies the completion of a good job of work.

The disturbances continued for several days, and featured the stoning of Lord Elgin's coach when he was driving home from the Château de Ramezay (he was not hurt, but his brother was, along with many of the official escort), and general looting and hooliganism. Elgin went to ground at Monklands, the official residence, and the assembly, which had been meeting in temporary quarters at Bonsecours Market, was prorogued by a stand-in. Cooler heads eventually prevailed, and the crowd ran out of things to throw. Order was restored until later in the summer, when the government was rash enough to attempt to arrest a number of suspected rioters. That set off another riot, another attack on LaFontaine's house, and the death of a rioter, killed in the heat of action by persons unknown.

It was this performance that doomed Montreal's chances of becoming the national capital on a permanent basis, and opened the way for Ottawa to be chosen as the place where we all direct our curses at tax time. Elgin summed up his impressions of Montreal in a sentence that, for some reason, has been left out of the city's tourist literature: "Montreal is rotten to the core, and if all Canada be like it, the sooner we have done with it, the better."

Sorehead.

A Religious Riot, Toronto, 1858

Staid old Toronto has had its share of broken heads in the name of various causes over the years. In my first few days at university there, in 1949, I attended a freshman party; stimulated by supplies of illegal beer, for no particular reason the party developed into an attack on streetcars on the Bloor Street line. The damage was minor, but the riot squad arrived and chased us up and down Avenue Road for a while, before arresting a couple of students. One of these was a nephew of Tim Buck, the communist leader, and when he gave his name, quite correctly, as Tim Buck, he was promptly conked on the head and slammed into a paddy-wagon, for being a smart-ass. What impressed me about that mêlée, besides the fact that it blew up so quickly (I remember thinking that Toronto was going to be a hell of an exciting place to live), was the fact that not a murmuring word appeared in the newspapers. Certain subjects are not raised.

The city has been torn, from time to time, by racial battles and labour wars and May-Day riots. One of the strangest outbreaks was the Kosygin riot of 1971, when the police drove their horses into demonstrators who gathered outside the Ontario Science Centre to protest the visit of the Soviet Premier; much diligent effort went into the argument that this was a "disturbance" rather than a riot, but it sure as hell represented "a temporary, violent outbreak of civil disorder". Of all these, one of my favourites is the comparatively modest fracas that blossomed in Toronto on July 12, 1858.

The occasion was the annual Orange Walk, always a time for a cheerful exchange of views and stones between the city's Protestants and Catholics. The Toronto *Leader*, which covered the proceedings, reported that trouble erupted after a fight between an Orangeman and a Catholic near the corner of Queen and William streets. The *Leader* noted that "Shots were freely fired but, though the contents of the pistols took effect in some instances, they did not result fatally." The mayor's gardener was shot in the back, and "another man named King, of the opposite party" was shot through the cheek. The police piled into cabs and headed for St. Patrick's Market, where they cleared away the rabble, but another row broke out on Victoria Street, which the *Leader* insisted was "of a more trifling nature, though it is to be regretted that pistols were here also made use of." I think it is always regrettable when pistols are made use of.

And, of course, there were the damn kids: "The juveniles, as usual, amused themselves by setting off squibbs and firecrackers, sometimes to the no little inconvenience of ladies who paraded the streets with a rather extended display of crinoline." Served them right, the shameless hussies.

A Riot for Racial Purity, and Jobs, Vancouver, 1887

The Chinese coolies who had been brought in to kill themselves on the CPR and in coal mines in British Columbia were willing to work for less and put up with more than native Canadians. We will meet these people again in Chapters 3 and 14; they were a readily exploitable class of indentured labour, near slaves, and a blessing to railway owners and mine managers. They would labour for $1 or $1.50 a day, instead of the princely $2 demanded by Canadians; they would live in hovels and feed on slops and, although they grumbled to themselves, they remained outwardly stoic—and besides, who cared what they said in Chinese?

They were a threat, however, to Canadian wage-earners and the budding Canadian labour movement; they not only undercut the prevailing rates of pay, they could be brought in as strikebreakers. The newly-formed Knights of Labor took on the task of cutting back this "Mongolian competition to citizen labour", and agitation against the "Asiatic plague" became a popular west-coast sport in the mid 1880s. When a Royal Commission on Chinese Immigration was called in 1885, the Nanaimo Knights of Labor submitted a brief declaring that the Chinese were able "not only to live but to grown rich on wages far below the lowest minimum on which we can possibly exist. They are thus fitted to become all too dangerous competitors in the labour market, while their docile servility . . . renders them doubly dangerous as the willing tools whereby grasping and tyrannical employers grind down all labour to the lowest living point."

As it happened, it was the grasping and tyrannical employers who were in charge of things, so the obvious solution — raising Chinese wages to parity and providing decent living conditions — was ruled out. The Chinese problem remained and, fed by the ordinary mixture of bigotry and fear, blossomed forth into a full-fledged riot in January 1887. A massed crowd in downtown Vancouver was apprised of its duty by strident speakers, and started out, about midnight, for McDougall's Camp, on the city's outskirts, where the coolies lived. The Chinese, swarming out of their tents at the sound of the approaching horde (they were singing "John Brown's Body", of all things), took one look, and ran. Eric Nicol, in his excellent history of Vancouver, quotes an alderman's report of what happened to them:

> Perhaps, in the darkness, they did not know that the cliff, and a drop of twenty feet, lay in front of them; perhaps they had forgotten. Some may have lost their direction. The tide was in. They had no choice, and you could hear them going plump, plump, plump as they jumped into the salt water. Scores of them went over the cliff.

How many died? Who knows? Who counts Chinese? The next morning, the crowd descended on Chinatown and cleared it out. One Chinese was allowed to stay in each store, the rest were removed by force. Some were tied together by their pigtails to prevent them escaping (ho, ho) and they were all loaded on a steamer for Victoria. The provincial government in the capital was not pleased, and sent a force of special constables to Vancouver to prevent a recurrence, but no one was ever punished for his part in the riot.

Another riot, based on the same combination of bigotry

and economics, took place in 1907. This time Japanese as well as Chinese were the intended victims, but they fought back, greeting the mob that swarmed into the Oriental district with knives and flying bottles. Their "docile servility" was used up, and the whites lammed it out of there.

In the long run, however, the riots were successful; a policy of excluding Oriental labour became central to Canada's immigration regulations. It all goes to show what happens in Canada to those who take the law into their own hands and brutalize other people. They win.

An Economic Riot, Regina, 1935

In the spring of 1935, some of the thousands of Canadians who had been shoved into labour camps to sweat out the Depression earning 20 cents a day on public works projects said to hell with it. They began to leave the camps in the B.C. interior, and gathered in Vancouver; from there they would move eastward, gathering recruits as they went, until they could trek into Ottawa and lay their grievances before their rulers. After much brave speechifying, they piled onto boxcars and started east.

It was the fixed view of many Canadian politicians and much of the public that the trekkers were Bolsheviks, Anarchists, Communists, Reds — the names were interchangeable — who were bent on destroying the Canadian way of life. The notion was piffle, but it was so firmly held that the federal government — Prime Minister R. B. Bennett, Prop. — determined to bring the trek to a halt before it reached the Lakehead.

On June 14, 1,600 trekkers rolled into Regina, dismounted from their freight cars, formed in ranks of fours, and marched over to the stadium, their temporary campgrounds. Their behaviour was without blemish, but that didn't keep them from being branded as gangsters, thieves, and radicals by the press and municipal officials. When

5,000 townsfolk gathered to support the trekkers, it simply proved to the town fathers that civilization was tottering on its foundations. Squads of RCMP and special police were moved in to block the protesters' path to the east.

Jimmy Gardiner, the Liberal Premier of Saskatchewan, sent telegrams demanding that the federal government (which was Conservative) should at least listen to the strikers, and two federal cabinet ministers were dispatched to invite eight of the leaders to Ottawa. They went, but Bennett turned down all their demands, gave them a lecture on economics, and reviled them personally. The leaders came back west in a rage.

On June 28, after the trekkers had been in Regina for two weeks, a group of them tried to continue eastward by truck, but they were stopped, and five were arrested.

A mass meeting was called for July 1, and the government decided to use the occasion to arrest the leaders. They were to be charged with belonging to an unlawful association (under a 1918 Order-in-Council sanctioned by the War Measures Act, the government could, and frequently did, make illegal any organization to the left of the Girl Guides), so they might have been arrested anywhere, quietly. Instead, in the gathering dusk of July 1, while orators thundered and crowds cheered in Regina's Market Square, a phalanx of police swarmed out of the station, at one corner of the square, and began driving through the crowd to seize the leaders. At the same time, RCMP men, stationed in vans drawn up behind the podium, tumbled out and joined in the fray. The strikers broke up and dashed for fence posts, stones, and chunks of cement. A pitched battle broke out, with the police using tear gas, riding crops, and guns, the trekkers using sticks, rocks, and fists. Regina Detective Charles Millar, a plainclothesman, was beaten to the ground and killed.

The riot continued for three hours, and came to a climax when police fired into a group of trekkers who were attacking up a sidestreet with rocks and clubs. They broke and fled. More than one hundred citizens, police, and strikers were wounded, half of them seriously enough to require hospitalization. The trek was ended — which seemed to have been the government's aim—and most of the protesters left Regina five days later to return quietly to their camps.

The police made 120 arrests during the riot, but only enough evidence could be produced to indict 28 men, all of whom were charged with rioting (the charges against the leaders were dropped; none ever took part in the fighting). Emmett Hall, then a Saskatchewan lawyer, later one of Canada's most distinguished jurists, was asked to come down from Saskatoon to help with the defence. He accepted gladly. "It was obvious," he told me recently, "that this was a police riot. Until the police charge there wasn't the slightest evidence of wrongdoing or intended wrongdoing on the part of the strikers." The riot was an economic, not a legal, clash. "Instead of doing anything about the unemployed, the government slapped them into camps, and when they boiled over, a confrontation was provoked."

The trials lasted well into 1936. Five accused were acquitted, twelve cases were dropped for lack of evidence, and nine men were convicted and received sentences of up to eighteen months in jail.

But the protest was smashed, in a riot provoked and orchestrated by the state. It was exactly the sort of event you associate with a banana republic in South America — not with Canada.

A Riot of Frustration, Halifax, 1945

A lot of people knew it was coming, but that didn't help one bit. On V-E Day, Monday, May 7, 1945, there were 24,500 servicemen, including 18,000 sailors, in and around

Halifax, and another 10,000 merchant seamen in port. Nearly all of them were mad at the city. They were away from home, and had been away too long; they had nothing to do; the war was winding down, and everyone knew it; and they were fed up. They were fed up, mostly, with Haligonians — with crowded quarters, extravagant rents, jammed and over-priced restaurants, plundering cab drivers, and constant shortages. They were being fleeced by the locals, and they knew it; what made it worse was that the toffs of the city clearly regarded them as rabble, and the girls, except those who plied a brisk trade along the waterfront, treated them like dirt. Weeks before, months before, word had gone around that when the war came to an official end, the sailors were going to rip the hell out of Halifax. Committees were struck, plans laid, memos circulated, but the senior naval officer, Rear-Admiral L.W. Murray, RCN, took the loyal but optimistic view that his boys — "My citizen sailors", he called them — would heed the call of duty. So very little preparation was made for the big day, beyond a decision to close all the liquor stores, which may not have been a smart move.

At 10:30 a.m., word came through that Germany had surrendered. There was no official confirmation for some hours, so the city fathers decided to shelve any official celebration until the next day. In the meantime, all hell broke loose. Ship and factory whistles began to blow, church bells to chime, horns to honk. The townspeople began to pour into the streets, and they were joined by thousands of soldiers, sailors, and merchant seamen. When they got there, they found that there was nothing to do. Most of the restaurants were closed, and most of the stores, including all the liquor outlets, were locked up. The town had pretty much closed down; the store-owners had put up shutters and scuttled home. It was too early for the movies, and too late for calm reflection. The crowds began wandering up and down the streets, singing and swigging from bottles that had been set aside against this day, working themselves up.

The first trouble came just after 3:00 p.m., when members of a crowd outside City Hall began to lob eggs at a policeman on traffic duty; he took it with more aplomb than Lord Elgin did a century before and went on directing traffic.

The canteen of HMCS *Stadacona,* a shore training station, was stocked with 6,000 bottles of beer. They were soon gone. Bootleg rum was selling fast for $12.50 a bottle; the crowd was getting liquored up. Just after 9:00 p.m., when the *Stadacona* canteen closed, a mob of sailors attacked a streetcar on Barrington Street and smashed all its windows; they were cleared away by naval shore patrols. The local police—there were 90 of them to control a city of 80,000—had pretty well given up. A community singsong was hastily organized up on Citadel Hill, but your average sailor, with a bottle in his hand and rapine in his heart, is not easily deflected by the chance to sing "Rock of Ages" on a hillside, and the disturbances went on. A streetcar was rocked, toppled, then set on fire, and when the firemen arrived, their hoses were chopped up with their own fire-axes, and they found other duties to attend to.

Then it was time to smash into the liquor stores, and the looters made off with 1,280 cases of beer, 80 cases of hard liquor, and 80 cases of wine. Some of this was stashed (cemeteries were a popular spot), but most of it was consumed on the spot. Soon the rioters began smashing into other stores and passing out goods. A lot of these prizes were hidden away in garages and basements, more were wrapped up and mailed out to the folks back home in Orillia, or Brandon, or Calgary. When the police raided the post office after the riot, they confiscated hundreds of packages of booty.

All night long the mobs roamed the downtown area,

drinking, smashing, fighting, vomiting, bleeding, throwing things. A marvellous time was had by all. The next day, May 8, the authorities were sure the spasm was over, but it wasn't. More stores were smashed, and two were set on fire; the injured—more than 100 stretcher cases in the first 24 hours—were hauled off to hospital. There was a good deal of freelance fornication in the parks, on the lawns, in the churchyards, practically anywhere a space of six horizontal feet could be cleared in the startled city. Roving bands raged through the streets, smashing windows, hurling rocks, hassling bystanders. The cops, for the most part, lay low, and even some of the military police ripped off their identifying armbands and threw them away when the crowd got ugly.

Rear-Admiral Murray toured the city in a car equipped with a loudspeaker and ordered his men — his "citizen sailors" —back to their ships. A few — not many — went. Finally, the riot wore down, and when army troops marched in late on the second night to restore order, nature had already looked after the job. Downtown Halifax was full of broken glass, smashed furniture, sore heads, and spent vice, but it was quiet at last. Troops and police rounded up drunks and looters; police cells at City Hall and the local prison were soon overflowing, and an armoury was converted into an emergency jail.

The riot cost $3 million, and led to 211 criminal prosecutions. Stiff fines and jail sentences — one of five years, another of three years—were meted out to the most serious offenders, as the city took vengeance on its tormentors.

There were other disturbances on V-E Day in other cities; drunken miners, in Sudbury, Ontario, smashed into liquor stores there, too, and swarmed through the city drinking and fighting. But no other centre came close to the spree in Nova Scotia's capital. Fornicating in the churchyards! Halifax may never live it down.

A Hockey Riot, Montreal, 1955

Montreal is riot-prone; I'm sorry, but there it is. Racial and religious strife, labour troubles, French nationalism, English pig-headedness, strong and opposing views on the merits of conscription during the two world wars — all of these added to the troubles that accrue to any large city have kept the place in ferment for centuries. Montreal has had the historical advantage of being able to stage religious riots not only on July 12, when the Orangemen walked, but on June 24, when the St. Jean Baptiste Society took to the streets. In one of the early shindigs of this sort, on July 12, 1877, one Thomas Lett Hakett was shot and killed; in one of the most recent, on June 24, 1968, Pierre Elliott Trudeau sat in an open balcony while separatists hurled rocks and bottles at him, and other officials fled. The first incident helped to keep French-English relations unsettled, the second helped to elect a prime minister. The city even had a riot of relief, when the siege of Ladysmith, South Africa, was lifted during the Boer War. The mayor declared a half-holiday, and McGill University students, released from classes, went boiling into the streets. They found that some of their *concitoyens* were unable to feel the same fierce joy over news of a far-off British imperialist victory, so they smashed up the *La Presse* newspaper offices, then marched on Laval University for a pitched battle. A blinding snow-storm, more than any police action, cleared the streets and cooled the riot.

Perhaps the most spectacular Montreal riot—more spectacular than the conscription troubles — came in October 1969, when the police force walked off the job in a labour dispute, and bedlam reigned. One police officer was killed, downtown stores were looted, $500,000 worth of goods was stolen, and $2,350,000 worth of damage was done in a 16-hour spree before the Royal 22nd Regiment came clumping in and called the thing off. Then there was the racial riot at Sir George Williams University, also in 1969, which began with protests that a professor was biased against blacks and wound up in an attack on the university's computer centre which caused $4,000,000 worth of damage. And, of course, there was another labour riot in 1971, when *La Presse* was sacked again, this time by French Canadians.

One hurled wine bottle looks much like another, even if one is vintage and the other not; one smashed store on St. Catherine Street looks much like another on Peel, so I am willing to forgo examination of all these displays of verve and temper and come instead to a uniquely Canadian riot—the Richard Hockey Riot of March 17, 1955.

Maurice (Rocket) Richard was certainly one of the greatest hockey players ever to tie on a pair of skates; he was also a man of formidable temper, and at the time of the riot had been involved in more hassles with officials and had paid more fines than any other player in the history of the NHL. Because of his competitiveness, his temper, and his skill, he was the frequent butt of harassment by other teams. On the night of March 13, when his Montreal Canadiens were playing in Boston, he was high-sticked by defenceman Hal Laycoe, receiving a cut that took five stitches to close. Richard attacked Laycoe with his stick, and when linesman Cliff Thompson interfered, Richard attacked him in turn. He was thrown out of the game and fined an automatic $100, and the case was put to NHL President Clarence Campbell for final judgment. Campbell suspended Richard for the rest of the season.

At the time, Montreal was within one game of a league championship, and the decision was viewed by the English press as unduly harsh, and by the French as a deliberate racist put-down. Myself, I think that more season suspensions would do a lot to improve hockey, but assault and battery are so ingrained in the sport that perhaps it could be considered harsh to suspend someone on the trifling grounds that he slugs other players with his stick and tries

27

to punch out referees. In any event, Richard's suspension caused Montreal to work itself into a fine froth; Campbell's Montreal office was besieged with threatening phone calls, and a French weekly newspaper published a cartoon with Campbell's head on a platter, dripping blood, and the caption, "This is how we would like to see him." The NHL president also got a letter that said, in part, "You British criminal! Why did your vile ancestors set foot on our lovely land? Go back to where you came from — England and hell!" Another strand in the broad skein of French-English harmony.

In spite of all this, Campbell decided to go to the game on March 17, when Detroit came to play the Canadiens (without Richard) at the Forum. It was a bold but dim decision. He arrived at the game late—he had been out to dinner— and was greeted by catcalls, and a shower of rubbers, vegetables, and miscellaneous bric-a-brac. He stayed in his seat, grimly pretending to make notes on the play, and dodging missiles. The Canadiens were not at their best and at the end of the first period Detroit led, 4-1. The crowd decided it was all Campbell's fault, and descended on the box where he was sitting, to demonstrate its disapproval. One man smashed two tomatoes against Campbell's chest and rubbed them into his dark grey suit and smart white shirt. As the mob's temper rose, the police seemed to drift away, and just when it looked as if Campbell might be about to join Thomas Scott in the annals of English-Canadian martyrdom, somebody hurled a tear-gas bomb into an aisle near the ice surface. As the fumes spread, and the Forum organ played "My Heart Cries for You", the mob changed its mind about lynching Campbell, and headed for the exits.

Outside, they fell into the time-honoured pattern, marching up and down the streets, smashing into all the stores, setting a few fires, clobbering a few streetcars, beating up a few bystanders. They cut a fifteen-block swathe along St. Catherine Street, smashed most of the windows in the Forum, toppled over and set alight corner news-stands and telephone booths, and altogether put in a fun evening. Many of the rioters were hockey fans, but some were just riot fans, drawn by news reports of impending trouble. A policeman who arrested a rioting lumberjack from Chalk River, Ontario, commented that the rioter "must love Richard". His catch replied, "Richard? Who's he?"

The hockey game was called off (Detroit won by default), but the rioting went on until 3:00 a.m., when the partici-pants ran out of steam and missiles. The toll was not too high: twelve police and twenty-five civilians injured, sev-enty arrests, fifty stores smashed up, about $30,000 worth of looting and vandalism.

For Montreal, not much more than a brisk work-out.

A Riot Mainly for the Hell of It, Sydney, 1971

Nobody knows what sets off riots, why they occur some times and not others, although if you put together a room-ful of sociologists, they will give you a barrelful of explana-tions, most of them contradictory. My own suspicion is that a great many Canadians, like a great many other people, endure lives of quiet desperation and that, every once in a while, some spark sets them off; the quiet desperation becomes noisy, and they take the joint apart. For a nation that prides itself on its quiet, orderly, and law-abiding ways, it is interesting to note how quick we are to stream into the streets the moment we know the cops are out of action; it happened in Halifax in 1945, in Montreal in 1969, in Sydney, Nova Scotia, on August 19, 1971.

Sydney is not an attractive town, although the setting is lovely. It is a working town, dominated by steel mills and bathed in soot and cinders, a grimy and disheartened town that has known a good deal of labour unrest, heartbreak, and depression. On August 19, 1971, the fifty-six-man Sydney police force walked out. They had been bargaining for a pay-raise for eight months; a conciliation board had recommended a three-year contract with a thirty per cent pay-raise, to bring the annual salary of a first-class constable up to $8,100 a year. The city turned it down, and offered fifteen per cent over two years. So the police walked off the job.

Within hours, the downtown area was dominated by youngsters racing their hot-rods up and down the streets. The fire department was plagued by twenty-four false alarms, and one serious accident occurred when a firetruck speeding to answer a false alarm smashed into the back of a car. As evening drew on, the usual scenario unfolded; stores — beginning briskly, according to the rules, with a liquor store — were broken into, mobs roamed up and down singing, fighting, and having a hell of a time, and young ladies were taken in a number of unusual places and postures.

The next day, when it looked as if the performance would be repeated, the skeleton police staff — maintained to handle emergencies — was expanded. Then the provincial attorney general stepped in and the city fathers found their glasses and discovered that they could, after all, meet the police salary demands. In the end, the force got 38.5 per cent over three years, and went back to work. About twenty people were injured in the riot, most of them in traffic accidents caused by racing in the streets. The Mayor noted ponderously that "People with those Make-Love-Not-War slogans, that's the group that take advantage of a withdrawal of police", a statement for which there was not a scrap of evidence. Most of the rioters appeared to be young workers.

The riot had two results. In the first place, the nearby city of Truro, which was having trouble coming to grips with the bargaining demands of *its* police force, found that, by

Jove, those demands were not unreasonable after all, and it paid up. In the second place, the Halifax *Chronicle Herald,* one of the most resolutely cheerful papers in all creation, was moved to wonder whither we were drifting.

"Thursday night's riotous rampage by an unruly mob in downtown Sydney . . . was disgraceful," the paper rumbled. "It puts into question the premise that we are a mature, stable people."

Just so.

CHAPTER 3:

SEND ME YOUR RICH,
YOUR WHITE ANGLO-SAXONS...

Canadians have really been extraordinarily tolerant in accepting strangers within our gates.

Immigration Minister Robert Andras,
February 1975.

My friend Anthony Hughes made a terrible mistake. A Jamaican, he had been living in Canada for nearly ten years on a student visa, first while attending university—which is where I met him — then through the long process of becoming an accountant. His mistake was to apply for landed immigrant status, on his way to becoming a Canadian citizen. His application was summarily dismissed and he was ordered to leave the country within a few days. No reason was ever given, publicly, in line with government policy. But, after the launching of an appeal, and protracted negotiations between lawyers, the man who had signed the rejection was finally persuaded to give his off-the-record reasons. Hughes was a Jamaican, he said, and Jamaicans do not stand up well to the rigours of the Canadian winter; he was really doing him a favour by sending him back home. That was delicately put. There was another way to put it; Hughes was coloured—not black, rather a kind of tawny colour, but there it is—and persons of the coloured persuasion were not, are not, and never have been welcome in this country.

I was hurt, shocked, and surprised (this was in the 1950s, I was a young chap, still open to such reactions); I assumed, I had been told, dammit, in every history book, in every classroom, from every public podium, that Canada opens its arms to the world's wanderers. The Hughes case was settled, in what I discovered was the time-honoured way, by a little genteel blackmail. Hughes was put in touch with a Member of Parliament who specialized in immigration cases; the MP proposed to raise the issue as a matter of blatant racism, by way of a question in the House of Commons. He informed the Minister of Immigration of his intent. The deportation was stopped, landed immigrant status was granted, and Hughes, who has now become a full citizen, spends his winters battling through snowdrifts and wondering if that immigration officer didn't have the right dope about Jamaicans and the Canadian climate.

Incidentally, the lawyer-MP explained that this kind of case was common, and carried its own ground rules; that is, the question in the House of Commons must be *threatened*, not asked. Once the question is asked, the government will always stand on its right to deport whomever it chooses, and sucks to you. But that route is fraught with the danger of public disapproval (Canadians don't mind having a racist immigration policy, they applaud it; but they do mind having it pointed out). So a trade-off is always possible, as long as the potential deportee realizes that his bluff may be called, and he may be whisked out of the country faster than you can say, "Welcome, stranger."

Since the time of the Hughes case, I have given a good deal of time to studying Canada's immigration policies, both the public ones, which are so generous and free from any taint of racism, and the private ones, which are, well, just about like any other nation's. I don't think Canadian immigration policy has been any more selfish, narrow, and bigoted than that of other lands. South Africa is not setting any new marks for tolerance; the Australians, until recently, always screened visitors for a taint of colour; the British were in favour of open immigration until the wrong kind of people began to arrive; the Americans had barely

33

finished scratching "Send Me Your Poor" on the Statue of Liberty when their government set out to make a mockery of that noble invitation; some of the emerging African nations have framed blatantly racist laws (the fact that they are against whites or Asiatics makes them different, but no better). We are no worse than the others; a credibility gap opens only when we try to insist—as we do—that we are better.

Canadian immigration policy has gone through a number of cycles; there have, indeed, been times when our gates were opened wide for the right class of foreigner. But, by and large, policy has been dominated by the nation's narrow self-interest, as defined by the government of the day. When it was smart to bring in foreigners to battle the bush, to open the West, or to take on the sort of jobs Canadians shunned, the welcome mat went out; when racism, unemployment, or dogma suggested a change, the mat was whisked away and the door slammed; and when, as now, world opinion demanded the appearance of tolerance and the reality of restrictions, well, our governments have been able to oblige.

Our earliest immigrants — next to the Indians and Eskimos—were brought in by the English Lords of Plantation to settle the place. (The French did not see North America as anything but a giant fur-farm until it was too late; with occasional exceptions — such as Louis XIV's novel idea of sending over a boatload of brides for settlers—colonialism received little support from France.) These Plantation Lords set a worthy precedent by issuing invitations and promises that were never to be honoured. A typical proclamation from the London Gazette of 1749, noted in Thomas Raddall's history of Halifax, promised fifty acres of land to every qualified settler, plus arms, ammunition, and materials to help clear and farm the land. The welcome was selective; what was really wanted was a supply of soldiers to drive away the heathen savage (heathen because he insisted on choosing his own gods, savage because he took unaccountable exception to having his lands snatched away by whites). Army officers were to be lured with more land than civilians, on a scale according to rank, from 80 acres for non-commissioned officers to 600 acres for majors.

The advertisement in the *London Gazette* that laid down the offer also promised, "That all such as are willing to accept of the above proposals shall, with their families, be subsisted during their passage, also for the space of twelve months after their arrivals." In short, a free trip on the American plan, with meals included. And, besides that, "They shall be furnished with arms and ammunition as far as will be judged necessary for their defence, with a proper quantity of materials and utensils for husbandry, clearing and cultivating the lands, erecting habitations, carrying on the fishery, and such other purposes as shall be deemed necessary for their support." Who could resist?

These lavish promises did bring responses from some soldiers, but much more from the poor of London, who saw in them a chance to break out of the bondage of their drunken, dirty, diseased slums. The promises were seldom kept. The immigrants were brought out, lied to, cheated, frozen, half-starved, and, on suitable occasions, scalped by the heathen savage. Within three years, most of the original contingent from London's slums had either died or vanished, but there were lots more where they came from, and for 150 years the lower classes of Britain supplied the bulk of settlers on Canada's east coast.

That coast also became a refuge for the religious disaffected of Europe, such as the sturdy German Protestants who settled the Lunenburg area along Nova Scotia's south shore in 1753, under the sponsorship of George II, who as a Hanoverian had strong German links.

Like the cockneys, these immigrants were not so much welcomed to the country as laid on it; the issue of whether we wanted them or not never occurred to anyone (except to the Indians, whose objections were overruled by force).

So, too, with the United Empire Loyalists and the other Americans who came pouring into the country during and after the American Revolutionary War in search of a haven, the solace of monarchical government, or a quick buck. They simply arrived, spread out, and took over. In 1767, Governor Guy Carleton had written: "Barring Catastrophe shocking to think of, this Country must, to the end of Time, be populated by the Canadian [by which he meant French-Canadian] Race." Within twenty-five years, the influx from the American Revolution had given the nation an English-speaking majority and a North American outlook, for the first time; but that was not a matter of immigration policy, it was an accident of war.

Indeed, when we did get around to establishing an official policy, it was designed to restrict the flood of Americans. After the War of 1812, Upper Canada, miffed at the Yankees for sacking York, decreed that no American could hold land here until he had been a resident for at least seven years. In effect, this barred U.S. citizens from the farmland that was then opening up and ended any significant flow across the border until late in the nineteenth century.

While we were shutting out the Yankees in Upper Canada, however, we were welcoming in the British through the ports of Lower Canada. We sought out the poor and homeless, because their transfer to this country would serve a dual function. First, they would provide a handy surplus of labour, not so much to augment the native-born in such tasks as knocking down trees, digging up canals, building roads, and breaking sod, as to compete with them. There was always the danger that, in a labour-short market, our ancestors might have to pay decent wages. A steady flow of hungry immigrants ended that nonsense. Secondly, encouraging emigration to North America would get the poor, dumb, diseased, and despairing off the parish registers and out of the pockets of those

better favoured by God and economics in the old country—
and would make way for sheep, or deer, or grouse, or
factories, or whatever the local landowner preferred to
raise on his land. For most of the first half of the nineteenth
century, we were not so much a haven as a dumping
ground.

Between 1815 and 1839, 431,089 immigrants were landed
through the port of Quebec, and Lord Durham noted in his
famous report that, had they known what awaited them,
most of them would never have come. Gustavus Myers,
never one to mince words, put it plainly in his *History of
Canadian Wealth*: "Reduced to pauperism by the results of
centuries of plundering, extortion and exploitation of the
ruling class at home, these emigrants were herded in foul
ships and packed off to Canada under the most inhuman
and horrible conditions." If you're a fourth-, fifth-, or
sixth-generation Canadian whose ancestors came from
Scotland, England, or Ireland, the chances are that Myers
was talking about your family. Not many of us are descended from dukes.

They were jammed into the ships' holds like a catch of
fish; they had little to eat, little water, little air, little exercise. The only thing readily available was disease, and they
had that in God's own plenty. The British *Blue Book on
Affairs Relating to Canada* quoted a doctor as noting that,
because of the foul conditions on board, the immigrants
"fall into a state of debility and low spirits . . . and on their
arrival here I find many cases of typhus fever among
them."

Not only typhus, of course; the savage cholera epidemic
of 1832, which killed 3,800 in Quebec City and at least 4,000
in Montreal, was born in the jammed hold of *The Voyager*
which limped leaking into Quebec harbour on June 7, 1832.
Two years later, the British government tried to palm off a
boatload of diseased and disabled veterans and their
families on Nova Scotia. They were outpatients of Chelsea

Hospital, and the Colonial Office sent them over with a straightforward request that they be established on land; by the time they arrived, cholera had broken out on board, and there were some deaths before they had been ashore a week. With the compassion and hospitality for which Canadians have always been famous, the colony simply packed the survivors up in another ship and sent them back to Britain, along with a bill for expenses.

If disease didn't get them, poverty did. They were exploited by a group of ship-owners and masters compared with whom, says Thomas Raddall, "The seventeenth-century buccaneers were a company of philanthropists." The captain normally told the emigrants before they left Britain that they should provision themselves for a three-week journey. The average passage, in fact, took six weeks, and many voyages lasted two months; as a result, the passengers were soon out of food. Then the captain would break out his own ample supplies, which he had providentially stacked on board before sailing, and sell them for a markup of up to 400 per cent. This meant that even those who started the voyage with a good supply of money seldom had anything left by the time they landed in Canada.

Or were landed. It became the custom to dump the immigrants off anywhere and let them shift for themselves — especially after it became obvious that they were not welcome in the established ports. Sometimes they were de-boarded at gunpoint; sometimes they were herded off onto Grosse Isle, in the St. Lawrence, to survive as best they could in drafty "fever sheds" while waiting for a period of quarantine to pass, or a bout of disease to subside, or until they died and thus neatly solved the problem of what to do with them. Eventually, the good burghers of Quebec set up an Emigrants' Fund, which would pay up to five shillings to each new arrival to keep going. The motto was "Welcome Anywhere — Anywhere But Here".

Every year when the ice broke up and the river opened, Quebec City dwellers would catch, first, the stench of the arriving ships and then the sight of the emigrants, abandoned and hopeless, stretched out for a mile and a half along the banks of the St. Lawrence. The river bank stayed crowded until the river froze over again; for every new arrival who moved off — or was carted off — a new one would come to take up his post.

This influx from the old country coincided with a much smaller flow from the U.S. When the British Parliament abolished slavery in the Empire in 1833, American blacks began to flee into Canada. Although our mythology has us welcoming these dark strangers, these refugees from *Uncle Tom's Cabin* (remember Eliza crossing the ice floes to Canada and Safety?), it was only a tiny minority of Canadians who were either involved in, or approved of, the Underground Railway. The prevailing sentiment was voiced in the Ontario legislature in 1857, where Colonel J. Prince pronounced the blacks "the greatest curse ever inflicted upon the two magnificent counties that I have the honour to represent".

In addition to a flood of British and a trickle of Americans, we had, towards the end of the century, a modest stream of Chinese. Between 1881 and 1884, 15,000 Chinese were brought in through British Columbia. They were never intended as permanent settlers; rather, they were indentured to work in the coal mines of B.C. and on the building of the Canadian Pacific Railway. Their role was to take on those tasks — including such unsavoury ones as getting blown up by carelessly laid dynamite charges—that Canadians were content to leave for others. These coolies were, to all intents and purposes, slaves; they were sold under contract by Chinese companies to white railwaymen or miners. The *Report* of the Royal Commission on Chinese Immigration of 1885 contained a memorable description of their living conditions: "The Chinese live, generally, in wretched hovels, dark, ill-ventilated, filthy and unwholesome, and crowded together in such numbers as must utterly preclude all ideas of comfort, morality or even decency." And of their food: "I have never yet known an English or French gentleman from the old countries who would feed their [sic] dogs upon the food consumed by the ordinary Chinese labourer."

The official government attitude was laid down in the Electoral Act of 1885: "'Person' means a male person, including an Indian, and excluding a person of Mongolian or Chinese race." However, these non-voting non-persons were welcomed by one class of people — the employers. Professor Chester H. Rowel wrote approvingly of the Chinese in 1909 that "He will transform less food into more work, with less administrative friction, than any other animal."

The cheapness and the docility of Chinese labour made these immigrants ideal fodder for the workforce, but, as we have seen in the previous chapter, they were fiercely resented by whites, and their employment led to riots, strikes, and other diversions, culminating in the 1885 Royal Commission on Chinese Immigration. The result of that commission was a poll tax of $50 imposed on every Chinese person entering the country; this tax was eventually raised to $500, a staggering sum for those involved.

To make assurance doubly sure, British Columbia passed a law in 1900 under which every immigrant in the province was compelled, when so ordered, to write an application to the provincial secretary in a European language. Those who did not, or could not, were subject to fines, imprisonment, and deportation. The federal government disallowed this law after protests from the Japanese ambassador to Ottawa, so B.C. passed the same law again in 1902, 1903, 1905, 1907, and 1908. It never did stick, but it certainly let the heathens know where they stood.

Readers from further east who are shaking their heads about those bigots in B.C. should know that Saskatchewan, Ontario, and Quebec all passed various forms of restrictive legislation against the Chinese; in Saskatchewan's case, the peril was posed by a grand total of 57 Orientals in the province, most of them farmers. Provincial law prohibited white women from working in restaurants, laundries, or other businesses owned by the slant-eyed rascals, proving that Saskatchewan knew a lot about the mythology of the Chinese, and nothing about their practice.

At first, the restrictions seemed to work; only 77 Chinese entered Canada during 1905, but then, partly because of the aid of employers anxious to use Orientals to break B.C. strikes, the total began to rise again, and 7,145 Chinese entered through the west coast in 1913. We couldn't have that, so the federal government reacted; stronger and stronger legislation was locked in place until, in 1923, the Chinese Immigration Act (a nice, uncommonly straight-forward name) effectively ended the inflow. Between 1923 and 1947, only 44 Chinese entered Canada legally.

The Japanese received a similar welcome here; although they were not barred entirely from entering, they were subject to a quota of 150 adult males—plus their families—per year. That quota was worked out by Mackenzie King when he was Deputy Minister of Labour, in 1908.

You will note that the drive to exclude Orientals was at its height during the years when our history books tell us Canada opened her doors to the world, the great immigration years of 1896-1914. Clifford Sifton, the immigration minister who launched the open-door policy, wanted to populate the prairies with "peasants in sheepskin coats". He meant the Ukrainians, Austro-Hungarians, and Central Europeans who were being crowded out at home, and who looked like ideal settlers for our wheatland. They were lured to Canada with assisted passages and glowing promises, and they were given an official welcome. So were the British, as usual, and some Americans. Not all Americans; not, for example, black Americans.

The northern flow of slaves and ex-slaves came to a halt with the American Emancipation Proclamation in 1863, but when the Canadian government offered free land to U.S. settlers in 1911, blacks began to look to us, again, as a land of hope. A party of blacks from Oklahoma was organized to take up the land offer, but when word of their impending arrival spread in Canada, press and public reaction was so swift and virulent that they decided they would be better off, in the long run, to stay put. As usual, the explanation for this *de facto* exclusion was that it was for the blacks' own good. In its April 11, 1911 issue, *Saturday Night* magazine explained that, while Negroes could be "fairly successful" labourers under the right conditions—i.e., white control— they lacked the initiative for farm life. Your average black, said *Saturday Night,* no doubt after long and patient study, is "indolent, prodigal and shiftless. In other words, he is by nature unfit for carving out for himself a home in the wilderness."

Saturday Night had some wholesome thoughts for Jewish immigrants, too, in an item forthrightly titled "No Jews", which commented that "Without them, there will be no filthy slums, in which they now teem, and without them our courts and our jails would have some measure of relief."

This, I repeat, was at the time when our doors were said to be open wide. Even those who did slip past the screens of selective prejudice found themselves under attack on arrival. As historian Kenneth McNaught comments, "Both the Europeans and many of the English faced a strident Canadian nativism expressed principally by ex-Ontarians who occupied most western positions of influence."

The signs went up — "No English Need Apply" — the epithets rolled out — "Polack" and "Square-head" and

"Hunky" and "Dago"—and the sermons rang forth—"To make this country a dumping ground for the scum and dregs of the old world," said one Canadian servant of God, "means transplanting the evils and vices that they may flourish in new soil."

While much of the reaction reflected racial bigotry, it was buttressed by hostility to immigrants in general. Thus the "No English Need Apply" signs, erected by men with names like Smith and Brown, underlined the fears of Canadians that any newcomers represented a threat to their jobs, their homes, their comfortable stations in life.

It was, then, into this atmosphere of official openness and practical prejudice that the *Komagata Maru* sailed in 1914. Whenever I hear an immigration minister expand on the friendly welcome that awaits the foreigner in Canada, whenever an after-dinner speaker leans across the remains of his chicken-à-la-king to warble the usual malarky about our open hearts and open doors, I think about the *Komagata Maru*, and the poor, dumb bastards who thought they could ride her into Canada.

She was a Japanese-owned passenger ship of 3,000 tons, and she sailed into Canadian waters on May 21, 1914, in a brave attempt to crack Canada's race barrier. Her passengers were Sikhs from India, 371 men, 2 women, and 3 children, all dressed in their Sunday best, slicked down, brushed up, and waving to the crowd that gathered along the shore near the immigration station at Victoria, B.C. Nobody waved back. These Sikhs were British subjects, and Canadian law, so handy against the Chinese, could hardly bar British subjects; but a cunning regulation had been devised in 1910 to fit the case. It said that all immigrants to Canada must arrive "by continuous journey and on through tickets" from their homeland. There was no direct service from India, so that 1910 regulation effectively barred Indians without ever saying so. However, an unruly Sikh named Narain Singh landed in Vancouver with

43

thirty-five countrymen, contested the regulation, and had it declared *ultra vires* by the courts. Gundit Singh, another Sikh and another troublemaker, decided to take advantage of this legal victory because, as he wrote in the ship's log, "When I came to Hong Kong in 1914, I could not bear the trouble of those who were in the [Sikh] temple waiting to go to Vancouver.... I resolved to take them to Vancouver under any circumstances."

Singh had made some money in the contracting business in Malaya; he used this to charter the *Komagata Maru* for six months and, with the Japanese Captain Yamamoto at the helm, sailed for Canada with his shipload of hopeful immigrants. The Canadian government replied to this initiative by enacting three new regulations to replace the failed measure of 1910, specifically barring the entry of Asians. So, when the *Maru* cleared Victoria Harbour and sailed into Burrard Inlet off Vancouver on May 23, 1914, she was greeted by a special detachment of police and an order to anchor 200 yards off shore. In addition, two guards were placed on board to make sure nobody sneaked ashore and defiled the land.

The Sikhs sat in the harbour for two months, while their ship grew fouler, their tempers shorter, and their food and water scanter. No one fooled around about the reasons for their exclusion. "We must keep the country a white man's country at any cost, and a British country if possible" was the verdict of the *British Columbia Magazine*. A Vancouver minister, thundering against the insolent Asians, was overcome by a momentary fit of Christian charity. "It is our duty to explain to those men in the harbour that we do not despise them as dogs," he said. One of his parishioners thundered back, "But we do!"

A protest meeting was called in Vancouver, and, under the guidance of the mayor, it demanded that Ottawa force the foreigners to leave at once, as "hurtful . . . from the standpoint of citizenship, public morals and labour conditions". When two men at the meeting sought to speak on behalf of the Sikhs, they were dragged down by members of the audience and marched off by the police, perhaps for their own protection.

Canadian immigration law required the setting up of a board of inquiry in such a case, to render decisions according to a strict timetable, and to oversee the enforcement of those decisions. The Sikhs were anxious for that process to begin; they felt that, in any court of law, they were likely to win (since the real reason for their exclusion — naked prejudice—is hard to defend). So the law was simply ignored. A board of inquiry was convened, but it only heard six cases in a month, and refused to hand down any decision, since that could be appealed. H. H. Stevens, the Vancouver MP, and a leader of the battle against the Sikhs, drew up a plan to shanghai them aboard the *Empress of India* and send them home. He wired Ottawa for approval, but that was going too far, and the idea was dropped.

Instead, a test case was finally brought to court, and the ruling went against the Sikhs. By this time, they had decided not to appeal — which had been their original intention — because they were slowly forming the notion that they were not welcome here. So, they said they would stay put until the government came up with enough money to allow them to get home again.

We weren't having any of that, either. On Sunday, July 19, the tug *Sea Lion* chugged away from the Vancouver shore bearing 120 policemen and 40 immigration officers, led by the redoubtable H. H. Stevens. Their plan was to swarm aboard the *Maru*, quell the Sikhs, and set the Japanese crew — who had been prevented from sailing home, as their owners requested, by the angry Sikhs — back in charge. Then the *Sea Lion* would tow the pest ship out to sea and to hell with her. A brilliant plan, with one minor flaw. The *Sea Lion*'s deck was a full fifteen feet below the *Maru*'s; swarming was out. When the cops came puff-

45

ing alongside, the Sikhs — most of them veterans of the British Army in India, all of them ready for battle—greeted them with salvos of garbage, chairs, scrap metal, coal, and driftwood. The *Sea Lion* beat a retreat for shore, where eight of the officers were hospitalized for cuts and bruises.

Canadian dignity had been offended. HMCS *Rainbow,* a battered but serviceable cruiser, was brought around from Victoria, her crew augmented by eighty sailors from the HMCS *Niobe* (the other half of the Canadian navy of the time), who had been rushed over from Halifax by train for the next big sea battle. The *Rainbow* trained three powerful firehoses on the *Maru* and invited her to leave. The Sikhs finally gave up, after extracting a promise that their financial claims would be looked into, and that they would receive some provisions. They got the provisions, but no money (a commission found, later, after they were safely out of the way, that the money put up on their behalf had been intended to forward "seditious motives", and need not be repaid). On July 23, two months after she sailed into Burrard Inlet, the *Maru* sailed out again, tailed by the redoubtable, but leaking, *Rainbow.* Another page had been turned in Canada's guest book.

Rumbles of the *Maru* incident were still in the air when World War I erupted, and brought immigration to a halt. The post-war years, while busy, saw nothing like the massive infusions of the early 1900s. The average immigration during the 1920s was about 123,000 annually (compared to 400,000 in 1913, when Sifton's peasants in sheepskin coats were pouring in); the emphasis in the '20s was, as usual, on British immigrants.

The Depression made it possible for people to be perfectly miserable without leaving home, and the flow dropped to a meagre 16,000 per year. At the same time, the practice of deporting any foreign-born character who caused trouble was stepped up. Deportations for cause had always been part of Canadian law, and between 1903 and

1928, an average of about 1,000 immigrants were turfed out each year, usually for violations of Canadian law. However, as economic conditions grew harsher, and political protests arose, deportation became a handy weapon to use against any trouble-maker who criticized the government, and who happened not to be native-born—even if he had become a Canadian citizen. In 1931, the incredible number of 7,000 "undesirables" were deported, most of them without any but the most perfunctory hearing. In October 1931, the Melville Island barracks at Halifax were turned over to the RCMP to be used as a detention centre to aid this cleansing process.

There were occasional complaints from the Canadian public—as occurred, for example, when a Winnipeg man was rushed off to Halifax for deportation, and managed to prove only at the last minute that he had been born in Canada — but it was generally accepted that the victims were communists, or at least radicals, and not worth bothering about. Canada's welcome mat had not only become smaller, it was developing a tendency to skid under the feet of the ungrateful, namely anyone who didn't just sit tight and shut up about any injustices he saw around him.

Then came World War II and the end of the Depression. At war's end, we were going to leave all our foibles behind and welcome the world's swarming, homeless, displaced poor to the land of opportunity. Alas, it didn't work out that way; although we did receive immigrants, racism and political discrimination were still built into our policies. Indeed, during the anti-communist witch hunts of the 1950s, even a hint of wrong-thinking was enough to bar a foreigner from this country, or earn the deportation of a landed immigrant.

In 1954, Mrs. Shirley Brent, a native of Buffalo who had married a Canadian and settled in Toronto, applied for permission to remain in Canada with her husband (she was

47

here on a visitor's permit). For reasons that were never disclosed, but apparently on the basis of a bum tip that suggested her politics were suspect, her request was refused and she was arrested and informed she was to be deported to the U.S. at once. Friends — and a lawyer — intervened, and, after a battle of several months, she was allowed to stay. But she never did find out what she had done to arouse our official wrath.

In another 1954 case, Shing Lee, a Chinese-Canadian born in this country, went on a visit to China with her parents; they stayed, and she attempted to return to Canada. It took her five years to get back in; our immigration experts refused to believe the birth certificate she kept showing them was real. Presumably, she had been contaminated by those rascally Reds.

Our policy was at least consistent. J.W. Pickersgill, when he was Immigration Minister, summed up his views in a 1955 speech: "I don't believe that any immigrant, no matter where he comes from or how good he is, is as good as another Canadian baby, because the immigrant has to learn to be a Canadian and the baby is Canadian to start with." Under Pickersgill's Law — still widely supported in this country—bank robber Red Ryan was one up on, say, John A. Macdonald, and we would rather clasp a Lucien Rivard to our bosoms than a U Thant. What Pickersgill really meant, of course, was that we would continue to screen out the lesser races and those of the wrong political persuasion. We used the word "selective" rather than "discriminatory", but, as Pickersgill said, "I do not understand there is any real difference between the words selection and discrimination."

Even selectively, we were accepting a lot of immigrants. Between 1946 and 1964, 2,357,262 came to Canada. They were divided, by policy, into four classes. Preferential treatment was given, as always, to those from Britain, Australia, New Zealand, the U.S., and France; next came

Germans and Dutch; then came Italians; and, finally, "all others".

The "others" included all the coloured races, who were allotted places on a quota system. In the mid-1950s, when 20,000 East Indians were pressing for Canadian visas, the quota for Indians was set at 150 a year; we had a 133-year supply lined up before the process was fairly started. There were few Canadian objections to this discrimination. When the Conservatives succeeded the Liberals in power, and Richard Bell became Immigration Minister, he made the same point as Pickersgill: "If we adopted an immigration practice that was truly non-discriminatory, it wouldn't last longer than a year — and the government that set it up would be defeated."

As blatant racism went out of style, our policies were adapted to the demands of public relations. Of more than three million immigrants who arrived between 1925 and 1965, only 17,206 were blacks, but blacks were no longer being refused on racial grounds. It was the climate. Thus yet another Immigration Minister, Walter Harris, in 1954: "It would be unrealistic to say that immigrants who have spent the greater part of their life [sic] in tropical or semi-tropical countries become readily adapted to the Canadian mode of life which, to no small extent, is determined by climatic conditions." An interesting argument could be made whether it is harder to adapt to snow in Saskatchewan or starvation in Ethiopia, and as this line became harder and harder to defend, successive governments retreated into a shell of secrecy. We would simply refuse people entry, and to hell with reasons; if they persisted, we would simply wait them out. The case of Leong Hung Hing shows how the system worked.

Leong was a Chinese cook in Vancouver. In 1951, when he was 67, he received his citizenship papers, and that entitled him to bring over his eighteen-year-old son, Leong Ba Chai, whom he hadn't seen since Ba Chai was a little boy. Leong applied for his son's entry but, after two months, he was told that the boy was not eligible. No reason was given, but Leong, though frail, was a persistent cuss and finally managed to worm the reason out of an immigration officer. Ba Chai was born of a concubine; even though he was legitimate under Chinese law, and even though Leong had supported the boy and his mother from Canada, he was just a Chinese bastard. Once he knew the reason, Leong had something to go on — that, indeed, is why reasons are not given — and he went to a lawyer. In March 1952, the B.C. Supreme Court held that if Ba Chai was legitimate in China, he must be regarded as legitimate here; the department was ordered to reconsider the application. The government took the case to the B.C. Appeals Court, lost again, and went to the Supreme Court. That takes time, and money.

Leong finally won his case for good in December 1953, but by that time his health was failing, his savings were gone, and now the department announced that, before it could consider Ba Chai's revived application, it would have to investigate him in Hong Kong, to make sure he complied with all immigration requirements. The investigation was never completed, although it dragged on for a year. In December 1954, Leong died of a heart attack. Now, for once, the government moved swiftly. Since the boy no longer had a Canadian sponsor, he no longer qualified as an immigrant. His application was rejected, the case closed, and Canada was saved once more from the Yellow Peril.

A certain odour was beginning to arise from our immigration policy; throughout the 1950s and early '60s, a number of attacks were made on the department and its policies. Our views were changing. In 1962, for the first time, Canada announced that "any suitably qualified person from any part of the world can be considered for immigration to Canada entirely on his own merits, without regard to his race, colour, or the country from which he comes." After 95 years of nationhood, and decades of blather about open doors, we were at last to have a policy free from prejudice. This radical notion was warmly applauded in Parliament, and quietly shelved.

We had worked out a new wrinkle; while even coloured folks could apply, we wouldn't make it easy for them to be accepted. Thus, while we have twenty immigration officers stationed in four cities in the United Kingdom, there are only four in all of India, all of them stationed in New Delhi. An immigrant from England can get through the red tape in three months; for Asians, the waiting period is counted in years.

Until 1967, the effect of our bold new stance was negligible. The number of coloured immigrants went up from about 3,000 annually to about 5,000 annually—from a drip to a trickle. We were still safe. But in 1967, that giddy centenary year, the government passed new regulations based on the White Paper on Immigration of 1966. That White Paper was an extraordinary document; short—less than 60 pages — concise, clear, and liberal. Canada, it proclaimed, "will need as many well-qualified immigrants as it is likely to be able to attract during the foreseeable future." Newcomers were a boon and a blessing, and if they came from a number of races, so much the better, since the mix would "buttress our position of independence and our ability to follow a course of friendly co-operation with like-minded countries of the world."

In place of all the quotas, blocks, and barricades, the 1967 legislation provided for a point system, under which potential immigrants were to be assessed in terms of such matters as education, training, occupational demand, and whether they had relatives already living in Canada. Many problems remained; for example, immigrants could be asked to post a cash bond as a condition of entry, and this device was used as a racial screen. Toronto lawyer Rewachand

51

Sainaney reported to the Canadian Civil Liberties Association that, of 5,000 immigrants he catalogued at Toronto International Airport, 2,000 were required to put up a bond. "In none of these cases was such a requirement made of a European. All persons subjected to this requirement were non-Europeans — mostly Asians and South Americans and West Indians." Sainaney took up the cases of 300 immigrants who were ordered deported from Montreal International Airport for failure to post a bond. "All of these persons are non-Europeans."

But at least now their cases could be taken up, because the most unusual aspect of the 1967 changes was that immigrants, once they managed to get a toe-hold on Canadian soil, were allowed to appeal their rejection. This clause meant that immigrants could come in illegally, be rejected, appeal, then disappear, or else hang on long enough to get married or otherwise qualify for admission. Immigrants who followed the regulations and applied from home were at a disadvantage, while the appeals procedure was jammed with people who had jumped the queue. This was not only unfair, it threatened to turn Canada into, God save the mark, a multi-racial nation. In 1966, more than three-quarters of our immigrants came from Europe and only 6 per cent from Asia; by 1973, the number of Asians had risen to 23 per cent, and the European portion had dropped to 39 per cent (most of the rest were Americans).

The result was inevitable; we had blacks, Orientals, Tibetans, Sikhs, South Americans, and God knows who else walking around the country breathing white air, using up white space, and even drinking from the water fountains. It couldn't last, and we have been in the grip of a racial backlash ever since. What is intriguing about this backlash is that most commentators react as if racism in immigration were new, probably an infection caught from those nasty Yanks, when in fact the only real aberration in our policy came during the liberal years of 1967-73.

In early 1975, after eighteen months of fretful cogitation, the government brought down another paper on immigration. It was called a Green Paper this time, as opposed to the 1966 White Paper. (The difference is alleged to reflect the fact that a White Paper presents government policy, while a Green Paper is only policy-in-making, and open to revision.) In place of the clarity and brief simplicity of the 1966 paper, we got four volumes of bumph, circumlocution, retreat, and reaction. An early draft of the paper had contained a direct racial reference to "the absorptive capacity" of the nation to accommodate non-whites. This was toned down to, "In the circumstances, it would be astonishing if there was no concern about the capacity of our society to adjust," which was translated for *Time* magazine by a senior government official: "What this means is that we are worried like hell about the influx of coloured people and want to clamp down."

Gone was the optimism, the economic argument, the idealism of 1966; in their place were murky worries about "exploding migration demand". Gone was the notion that immigrants bring new jobs, new skills, new tolerance, new opportunities; instead, "Canada, like most advanced nations, counts the costs of more people in terms of congested metropolitan areas, housing shortages, pressures on arable land, damage to the environment — in short, the familiar catalogue of problems with which most prosperous and sophisticated societies are constantly endeavouring to cope."

Before the 1975 Green Paper wound its way through four volumes, the open-door policy of 1967 was in shreds. Then the government took the paper on a road-show tour, ostensibly to glean public reaction before settling on a new, firm policy. In fact, as most of us who talked to immigration officials in Ottawa discovered, the road-show was designed to educate the public, not to seek its views. The decision to adopt a much more restrictive approach was

53

firmly in place long before the public charade began. Predictably, the hearings, which continue as I write this, have attracted the attention of a gaggle of radical groups, anxious to hammer the government for racism, a handful of serious critics — like the Civil Liberties Association — and a broad range of right-wing loonies, who want to send all the lesser races back where they came from. A study released in September 1975, of 1,200 letters to the government on immigration, showed Canadians calling for more restrictive policies by a ratio of ten to one, with comments like "exclude all non-whites" and "prevent racial pollution". The government, having already accepted the loony thesis, though not its rhetoric, should have fun drawing up a new set of rules onto which future immigration ministers can clamber, like Robert Andras, and tell the world what a warm and welcoming bunch we have always been.

CHAPTER 4:

FREEDOM OF SPEE . . !

Democracy implies liberty, something of which Canadians are so
sure that they never mention it.

George M. Wrong, 1938.

Land-a-mercy, we are smug. We are smugger than a Bap-
tist preacher with his hands on the keys to every liquor
closet and chastity belt in town. We are so sure that the
rights of free speech, self-expression, and open assembly
are safe in Canada, that our smugness cannot be disturbed,
not even by midnight raids through broken doors or the
bundling off of innocent people to jail with never a charge
or even a formal arrest.

I was not there, thank God, when the Russian tanks
rolled through Budapest to crush the spark of freedom
among the Hungarians in October 1956, but I was certainly
there when the army trucks rolled into Ottawa in October
1970, and the men in green uniforms hopped out and slung
their automatic rifles around their shoulders and marched
off to take up strategic positions.

Oh, no, it was not the same; they were our troops, not
foreigners, they were embarrassed and polite, not rudely
truculent, they didn't kill anybody — except one poor sol-
dier who tripped jumping down from a truck and shot
himself—and they didn't beat anybody up. But the principle was the same, the attack on civil liberties and free
expression was the same. The state, for reasons that were
never satisfactorily explained, was determined to bring
gunpoint justice to Canadian streets; hundreds of men and
women were rounded up and herded off to jail; their homes
were invaded, their families harassed, even their books

were seized and burned, a nice neo-Nazi touch. Years later, when Prime Minster Trudeau was questioned about the arrests, it was pointed out that, as a university professor, he might have been so raided, and his books might have been burned. Would that have made him angry? Yes, he replied, but not against the state, against the people whose behaviour made such repression necessary. There were no warrants, no questions, none of that claptrap; the victims were simply slapped into the slammer without formalities. Of the 497 persons rounded up in 1,624 lightning raids, only 62 were ever charged, and only 2 were ever convicted of violations of the regulations that had been invoked to justify the raids.

And Canadians cheered; we went berserk with delight. We lined up for the pollsters and wrote letters to our papers and clambered aboard the open-line radio shows to pour out our jubilation that the government, at last, was clamping down, that our boys, our very own boys, were just as willing to hurl people of the wrong political persuasion into the coop as any Russian commissar. At York University in Toronto, students held a large, noisy demonstration *in favour of* the repression.

The government made wrong thinking a crime, and they made it retroactive. One day it was perfectly okay to belong to the Front de Libération du Québec — not nice, or even smart, but legal — and the next it was a crime *ever to have belonged*. It was a crime to have the wrong books on your shelves, the wrong thoughts in your heart, the wrong friends. The regulations were so broad that, as Walter Tarnapolsky points out in his study, *The Canadian Bill of Rights*, any reporter who ever covered a meeting of the FLQ could be charged and convicted, just for having been there. And we cheered. Land-a-mercy.

What fools us, I think, is the fact that we are washed over so often by the traditions of British justice and the pap of American TV that we fall into confusion. We think their rules, so often proclaimed, apply to us. Well, they don't. *Habeas corpus* is a marvellous instrument of British law, but it is automatically suspended by the War Measures Act. It is available except when it is most needed. The Canadian Bill of Rights guarantees the right of *habeas corpus*, but the War Measures Act overrides the Bill of Rights, and no appeal launched on the basis of the habeas corpus section has ever been successful. (*Habeas corpus*—literally, "you are to bring the body" — is the legal procedure used to determine whether one person—usually a police force—is entitled to retain custody of another. It is the key defence against unlawful imprisonment, and its emasculation by the War Measures Act deprives Canadians of a right that dates back to the fourteenth century.)

Nor do we possess some of the American rights so widely broadcast on TV. When, just before the brassière ad, Ironside advises the thug he has collared of his rights, we think Canadian police do the same; they don't, and they are not required to. When Kojak reluctantly allows the bad guy to make his sacred phone call, we think our boys follow suit; sometimes they do, and sometimes they don't. In the overwhelming majority of cases, as Martin L. Friedland pointed out in *Detention Before Trial*, Canadians accused of serious crimes are held in custody before trial, and make their first court appearances without ever talking to a lawyer. Americans may whine, "I wanna see my lawyer", and watch the fuzz slink off snarling, but not in Canada. As Law Professor Walter Tarnapolsky notes, "There is no obligation on the part of the police to inform the accused of his right to consult with counsel before submitting to questioning or testing, as is the case in the United States." Even if the accused is smart enough to demand a lawyer, without being informed, he may be refused and questioned anyway. Ironside's writs do not run in Canadian courts, only in our living rooms.

It is hard to work up much indignation, of course. We all

know that if we behave in a decent, law-abiding fashion, all this simply won't affect us; everybody knows that it is only punks and hoodlums and hippies who are hassled by police, only freaks, French Canadians, and other weirdos who have their rights trampled on; those characters deserve what happens to them — it couldn't happen to us.

But it could and it does; perfectly normal, law-abiding Canadian citizens are arrested, hassled, and terrified; people who hold views only slightly off-centre are squelched. Civil liberties are not something we can take for granted in Canada, they are something that have to be fought for, over and over again. And if we have a tradition in this line, it is a tradition of stepping on the rights of anyone whose views stray too far from the centre of consensus.

Take Robert Gourlay, who, in 1818, issued an address in the form of a pamphlet, *To the resident landowners of Kingston*, complaining about the Family Compact and its abuse of power in Upper Canada. He was promptly arrested and brought to trial on a series of charges, but juries at Kingston and Brockville refused to convict. So he was rearrested and found guilty of sedition, under a little-used clause of the Alien Act of 1804 (he was an immigrant from Scotland). The punishment was banishment (a neat solution from the Family Compact's point of view), but Gourlay refused to go, so he was slapped into prison and kept there for five years, by the end of which time he was quite satisfactorily insane. Our history books always tell us about Joseph Howe's successful defence of free speech; why do they never tell us of Gourlay's failure, or that during World War II it was against the law to "advocate the principles of Jehovah's Witnesses in speech or print".

Or take good old George Brown, that staunch reformer and proprietor of the Toronto *Globe*. In March 1872, his printers went out on strike—the greedy fellows were after a fifty-four-hour week and wages of $10—and Brown, digging through old law books, found that Canada had never abolished the Combination Acts passed by the British Parliament in 1792 and 1800 (although Britain had repealed the legislation herself). These laws made it illegal to belong to any "combination" designed to "lessen or alter the hours of work, to obtain an advance in wages," or "to quit work before the work is finished." So Brown had fourteen of his printers bunged into jail for joining a union, which is nothing if not a combination to obtain an advance in wages. They were held in prison for weeks until political pressure —there was a federal election coming up—brought about their release. They were never brought to trial.

Or take Gerald Dealtry, whose crime was that he dared to attack the Ku Klux Klan when it came wandering into Canada, trailing its blood-stained sheets, in 1927. Dealtry was not a particularly nice man. He worked as projectionist in a Saskatoon movie house and, on the side, ran a scandal sheet called *The Reporter*, which dug up gossip and rumours about local notables. But Dealtry was a tough egg, and when the Klan hit town and the established press treated it with shy circumspection or, in some cases, with welcoming enthusiasm, he waded in with all adjectives firing.

The Klan came to Saskatchewan ostensibly on a moral crusade, to clean up crooked politics, cat-houses, and patronage; but in fact it was the same old Klan, pushing racism, hatred, and dissension. Instead of attacking the blacks, as in the southern states (which were better supplied with blacks than Saskatchewan) the Canadian Klan was after Catholics, Jews, and aliens—any aliens. Its motto was: *One flag. One race. One religion. Racial purity and moral rectitude.* This line went down well in the Saskatchewan of the late 1920s, where economic conditions were worsening, where political patronage was rife, and where uneasy citizens were looking for scapegoats (those who were not looking for, and finding, cat-houses). Many of the provincial Conservatives, including party leader W. T. Anderson, used the Klan as a weapon against the ruling Liberals who had been in power since 1905; prominent citizens joined or supported the crusade or, if they opposed it privately, held their peace in public. The KKK attained a certain respectability.

Dealtry, of course, was a stranger to respectability, and when J. J. Maloney, a Klan organizer from Ontario — the home of tolerance — rolled into town, *The Reporter* greeted him with a blast of headlines: WELL-KNOWN HATRED BREEDER COMES TO TOWN, and EX-CATHOLIC CLERIC SPREADS LIES AND ILL-FEELING and (my favourite, for eloquent simplicity) HE IS A LIAR. Dealtry did not believe in pussy-footing. The Klan, he said, was "founded by fakers and financed by fools"; it was also "unBritish". Maloney, who doubled as editor of a virulent anti-Catholic paper called *The Freedman*, was "a liar and a man in whom little or no trust should be placed".

This was strong stuff, and invited a libel suit, but Dealtry was not sued; instead, the Liberal provincial government decided to have him charged with criminal libel. It was not *Maloney* vs *Dealtry* on the court lists of spring, 1928, but *Rex* vs *Dealtry*. The editor was to feel the full force of the state's wrath for his impertinence.

Dealtry went to Emmett Hall — later Mr. Justice Hall of the Supreme Court of Canada — a well-known Catholic as well as a well-known lawyer, and Hall took on the case. The defence was straightforward and futile; it consisted mainly of readings from Maloney's paper, *The Freedman*, whose outpourings, in Dealtry's stern but defensible view, were the product of "a polluted and twisted mind". Maloney noted that there were 27 priests in the federal Department of Immigration — obviously a plot to undermine Wasp purity; he discovered that a campaign to make "O Canada" the Canadian anthem (yes, even then) was designed "to Romanize our songs"; he contended that the Catholic church had been a "degrotary [sic] influence wherever it existed."

60

The defence was brushed aside; hating Catholics was one thing, attacking prominent visitors another. Dealtry, neither prominent nor Catholic, but a hell-raiser, was convicted. He got off with a $200 fine. Hall, for his role in defending him, was burned in effigy at a public meeting in Saskatoon.

It was really too bad that Dealtry was such a miserable squirt, and was never invited to join anything; he might have been sifted away under Section 98 of the Criminal Code, a law that went on the books in 1919 and remained until 1936. (Even when the House of Commons struck it out five times, the Senate stuck it right back in again.) The section was a catch-all to define as an "unlawful association" any group aimed at bringing about a change in Canadian government, industry, or economy, by force, or any group that defended the use of force for such an end. It was illegal to sell, write, or publish anything on behalf of such a group, to wear its badge or motto, or to contribute to its upkeep. For any of these breaches of the peace, you could get up to twenty years in the hoosegow. If it could be shown that you had ever attended a meeting, spoken for, or distributed literature on behalf of such a group—even if you didn't know it was illegal—you were presumed to be a member. You were guilty, and the burden of proof was on you to wiggle out of it, or bid friends and relatives farewell.

(It was this broad law that allowed the government to arrest Tim Buck and eight others for belonging to the Communist Party in 1932. The party was not illegal, but the court found it to be so retroactively, convicted the men, and sentenced them to jail terms that, in Buck's case, ran to eight years. Later, during a prison riot at Kingston Penitentiary, shots were fired into Buck's cell, apparently by his jailers.)

This all-embracing statute went even further; it allowed the state to seize any printed material in which any statement appeared that it was ever, anywhere, justifiable to use force, or to have used force, to accomplish a change of government. Strictly speaking, the Crown could have jailed most historians who have written about the American Revolution.

And how did we react to this repressive measure? We lapped it up; indeed, almost every area of Canada set out to create a little regional repression of its own. The police in Toronto decided in 1929 — when communism was still technically legal in Toronto—that they were going to stamp it out. When communists tried to hold open-air meetings, they were refused permits; when they met on street-corners, they were charged — and readily convicted — for obstructing traffic, creating a disturbance, or vagrancy. When they tried to hire halls or theatres, the police called on the owners and persuaded them that the principle of free speech was not as important as the principle of staying in business. The city set up a Red Squad, and sent the members off to New York and Chicago to study the strong-arm methods in vogue there.

Why am I indignant over what happened to the strange and twisted men who made up the Canadian communist movement of the 1920s and 1930s? For two reasons. First, because there is some evidence — chiefly in their own writings — that it was the persecutions, more than any internal cohesion, that kept them together and helped them grow. For a time, the communists were not only martyrs, they were the outstanding defenders of free speech and free association in this country—and there is an irony to rot your socks. But there is a more important reason; I am haunted, as any member of my generation must be haunted, by what Martin Niemoller, a Protestant clergyman, had to say about his experience of Hitler's Germany:

First they arrested the Communists — but I was not a Communist, so I did nothing. Then they came for the

Social Democrats—but I was not a Social Democrat, so I did nothing. Then they arrested the trade unionists—and I did nothing because I was not one. And then they came for the Jews and then the Catholics, but I was neither a Jew nor a Catholic and I did nothing. At last they came and arrested me—and there was no one left to do anything about it.

For a time, it went that way in Canada; from harassing the communists, it was a short step to harassing anyone who was not an anti-communist. In 1930, a peculiar group of idealists formed a Toronto chapter of the Fellowship of Reconciliation, an international body which had taken on the awesome task of sorting out all international misunderstanding. These optimists rented the Foresters' Hall in downtown Toronto; they were disturbed by the treatment that had been meted out to communists in the city, and they invited the police chief, Brigadier Dennis Draper, and a member of the police commission to speak on the subject of free speech and free assembly. The invitations were refused, but the Fellowship decided to go on with the meeting anyway. Then the Foresters' Hall was withdrawn, so they rented the Empire Theatre. That, too, became unavailable after the head of the Red Squad called on the manager.

The meeting was never held, but sixty-eight professors at the University of Toronto were foolhardy enough to write a letter to the Toronto newspapers, supporting the principle of free speech:

> The attitude which the Toronto police commission has assumed towards public discussion of political and social problems makes it clear that the right of free speech and free assembly is in danger of suppression in this city. This right has for generations been considered one of the proudest heritages of British peoples, and to restrict or nullify it in an arbitrary manner, as

has been the tendency in Toronto for the last two years, is short-sighted, inexpedient and intolerable.

Hard to argue with that, right? Wrong. At once, a howl arose for the sacking of the sixty-eight professors. The Toronto *Globe* commented: "This matter of 'free speech' which is agitating the Fellowship and has brought forth the 'protest' of sixty-eight college professors is but a 'red herring' across the trail. Why is the cause of a group of revolutionary agitators to be preferred to the welfare of a loyal, Christian nation?"

The *Telegram* wanted the pinko professors bundled off to Russia: "If a few of Varsity's teachers were sent to Russia, not as tourists personally conducted by Soviet agents, but as toilers in Soviet wheat fields and Soviet factories, they would return to their Canadian jobs with a restrained admiration for the privileges that go with free speech theories put into practice."

Although the university did not dismiss the sixty-eight, its chancellor, Sir William Mulock, was all for it; he, like the *Telegram*, wanted them flung out of the country.

Montreal, never a city to be left out of such doings, joined in. When the Unemployed Council of Montreal — a Communist Front organization — applied for a permit to hold a protest meeting, it was refused, and when the group went ahead anyway, it was broken up by flying squads of police, wielding truncheons. Then the Canadian Defence League — another Red-tainted group — held a meeting of protest over the first meeting. The police raided that one, too, and arrested a number of speakers. Yet another meeting was attempted by the Unemployed Council, and the cops waded in once more and arrested three men on charges of distributing posters in a public place.

Those charged generally got short shrift in the courts. One Pete Mazapa — obviously a foreigner — was charged with "attempting to incite others to fight the police". He asked for bail and the judge told him, "You are in a good country and we do not want your sort. You are dangerous and therefore I refuse to grant you bail." This, of course, was before he had been tried, or a shred of evidence had been adduced against him.

The deepening depression brought more unrest and more suppression. As we saw in Chapter Two, the leaders of the On-To-Ottawa Trek, when they were arrested in Regina, were charged with belonging to an unlawful association under the notorious Section 98 of the Criminal Code, and their protest was smashed.

There was some easing off after that, at the federal level, but, to fill the gap, Alberta passed a Press Gag Law, or, to give its proper title, "The Alberta Accurate News and Information Act of 1937". It was a law that would have delighted Richard Nixon and Spiro Agnew. It provided for the licensing of the press, compelled reporters to disclose story sources, and made publishers print official replies to any articles deemed to have been inaccurate or unfair—the deeming to be done by the government. Fortunately, neither the Canadian public nor Parliament got to rule on this law — there is no evidence that either would have disapproved — because the Supreme Court held it to be beyond the powers of Alberta, and it died aborning.

By the time that was worked out, it was time to take after the commies again, and the Province of Quebec complied with the Padlock Law. This was one of the first laws passed by Premier Maurice Duplessis after his rise to power in 1936. It received the unanimous consent of the provincial legislature. "An Act Respecting Communist Propaganda" gave sweeping powers to the Attorney General — a post filled by Duplessis himself — to close and padlock any premises where, in his judgment, communist propaganda was being prepared or distributed. Communism was never defined in the Act, an omission that allowed Duplessis to use it against anyone, including, in the memorable phrase of one of his Cabinet members, "the thousands and thousands of people who are Communists without being aware of it".

The Padlock Law remained in force until 1957—that is, for two decades. Under its rules, Red Squads censored CCF election pamphlets, raided the office of the provincial Liberal leader (Liberals, too, you see, can be communists without knowing it), arrested members of the Social Credit movement, and jailed Labour Progressive Party (as the communists became when the old name was outlawed) candidates for election. Hundreds of houses were broken into, ransacked, and locked up. Thousands of books — including the Bible — were burned on the spot by police raiders or taken to headquarters for burning later; newspaper offices, printing plants, and cultural centres were put under lock and key and left that way, because Duplessis suspected they might be breeding grounds for "moral contagion". Whenever a house or apartment was padlocked, the inhabitants were simply evicted, sometimes in the dead of night; and they could not return, even to gather their clothing.

In no case was there a trial, an accusation, or a conviction; all that was necessary was a suspicion, and down came the Red Squad, padlocks at the ready, and, slam, you were out of your house or apartment, with only the possessions you could grab on the way out. This law, said Duplessis, was "a safeguard of liberty, because it attacks in an effective manner, under the care of our courts, the worst enemies of liberty and democracy."

Protests were few and ineffective. In the House of Commons, J. S. Woodsworth declared: "Twice every three days for six months the provincial police have carried out execution without judgment, dispossession without due process of law; twenty times a month they have trampled on liberties as old as Magna Carta."

The Minister of Justice, Ernest Lapointe, replied, to thumping applause: "In spite of the fact that the words are so unpleasant to the honourable member from Winnipeg North Centre, I do desire to say that the reign of law must continue in this country, that peace and order must prevail."

The Padlock Law held. There was not even any way to bring it to court—because no charges were laid—until, on January 27, 1949, a ten-man police squad burst into the apartment of John and Iris Switzman on Park Avenue in Montreal. Every room was ransacked, every book, magazine, and paper gathered up and burned. The Switzmans and their twenty-month-old daughter were evicted and their home was padlocked. But the Switzmans were not your ordinary left-wing pushovers; they were both war veterans — a strong point, in those days — and they were outraged enough to bring a lawsuit for damages against the raiders. The police defence, of course, was the Padlock Law; at last, it went to court. The Switzers lost at every level of court in Quebec, but managed to carry their appeal into the Supreme Court, where, in 1957, the Padlock Law was finally killed. The Court held that it had never been legal.

Why, over the twenty years it was in force, was there not more protest over this iniquitous law? I suggest it is because, despite our mythology, Canadians have never been particularly concerned with the issue of free speech as long as its violation affected only unpopular minorities, and our concern for freedom of speech vanishes entirely at the first onset of apprehended danger—from communists, fascists, Jehovah's Witnesses, Doukhobours, spies, or strangers. When two university professors, George Grube and Frank Underhill, persuaded a Toronto CCF riding association to pass a resolution condemning Canada's entry into World War II, the cry for their scalps went up in almost every paper in the land. Opposition leader George Drew joined Premier Mitch Hepburn in framing a provincial resolution to have the men fired from their posts. That step was blocked by the inconvenience that the provincial government couldn't do the firing, and the university wouldn't (two members of the board of governors, a prominent Conservative, J. M. Macdonnell, and a Liberal, J. S. MacLean, stuck up for the beleaguered professors). The public was apparently all for throwing them out.

As a people, we are, in the words of Alan Borovoy, General Counsel to the Canadian Civil Liberties' Association, "decently authoritarian". How else can we explain the War Measures Act?

This law, which most Canadians seem to believe is recent, and rarely evoked, was in fact passed in 1914, and Professor H. Marx, author of *The Emergency Power and Civil Liberties in Canada*, has calculated that we have been living under the regulations of this Act, or its transitional variations, for forty per cent of the time since its passage.

Its provisions are, on the face of it, horrendous. The Act declares that, at any time the federal Cabinet deems this nation to be in a state of "war, invasion or insurrection", whether it is real, or merely "apprehended", the Cabinet can take any measures — any measures — necessary for "the security, defence, peace, order and welfare of Canada".

All the ordinary rules of law are swept aside. The government's powers—without any reference to the courts— include those of censorship, arrest, detention, exclusion, and deportation. Control of all harbours, all transportation, all trading, production, and manufacturing may pass to the Crown, which may also seize and dispose of any property it chooses.

And the Act is not an idle threat; we keep it limbered up. During World War I, thousands of people deemed to be "Enemy Aliens" were rounded up and herded into internment camps, without trial. In 1917, after the Russian Revolution, thousands of Russian-Canadians were interned, even though they could not be classified as enemy aliens, because we were not at war with Russia. They were just interned because the law said they could be and their internment seemed a good idea to the government. In preparation for the 1917 vote on conscription, voting rights were stripped from anyone who had emigrated from anywhere in either the Prussian or Austro-Hungarian empires, on the ground that as possible secret enemy sympathizers they might vote against conscription. Many of those who lost their right to vote on these grounds were fighting in the Canadian Armed Forces.

In World War II, the act was used to establish press censorship, to clamp down on any speeches that might "prejudice recruiting" and to make it illegal to belong to any of several dozen organizations. The banned groups included not only fascists — who were presumably the enemy — but communists — who were alleged to be our gallant Allies. Jehovah's Witnesses, because they were pacifists, were outlawed; most members of the Montreal Italian community were interned, the Ukrainian-Farmer-Labour Temple, which was regarded as a communist front, was declared illegal and its 108 meeting halls were seized. This was all done, of course, in the name of liberty.

It was the War Measures Act that was used to uproot 23,000 Japanese Canadians, some of whom had been citizens for generations, from the coast of British Columbia. Just after Pearl Harbor, the notion spread that the wily Orientals might sabotage Canada's war effort, so they were simply rounded up and moved inland. Three quarters of those who wound up in detention camps scattered across the interior of B.C., or spread out across the nation wherever they could be dumped, had been born in Canada. It didn't matter a bit. No Japanese Canadian was ever charged, much less tried and convicted, on a count of espionage or sabotage. Nobody cared. Their houses were seized, their businesses sold, their fishing boats turned over to their white competitors for a fraction of their worth. Those interned were used on road-building projects, and paid a net salary—after deductions for room and board—of $7.50 a month.

All of these moves were applauded in Vancouver, where most of the uprooted Japanese came from. The issue wasn't discussed in the rest of Canada until after the war, but even then, nobody cared. In December 1945, long after the surrender of Japan, three Orders-in-Council were passed under the War Measures Act to deport Japanese immigrants, and even Canadian citizens of Japanese descent; in all, 3,964 of them were hustled out of Canada and dropped into war-torn Japan.

The repression continued, incomprehensibly, for four more years. Japanese Canadians could not travel more than fifty miles without an RCMP permit, nor work on crown lands or in mines, nor take up such professions as pharmacy and the law. They could not go back to the coast or reclaim any of their property or lands and, needless to say, they could not vote.

The War Measures Act is still there on the books, ticking away like a timebomb under the civil liberties of any Canadian.

After the war, it was time for another Red scare, and while we never reached the zany heights of the U.S. Un-American Activities Committee (the very name tends to produce a superior smile), we were certainly quick to step on rights to prove our loyalty. University professors were drummed out of their jobs for holding wrong views and "subversives" of all sorts were deported, or refused entry. During the spy scare set off by the revelations of Igor Gouzenko, who had served as a cipher clerk in the Russian embassy in Ottawa, the War Measures Act was trotted out again to suspend *habeas corpus*, and to allow dozens of suspects to be seized, held, and questioned without warrant, charge, or counsel. This all went down well.

The RCMP, which had always been in the spy game with its Security and Intelligence Directorate, had a field day throughout the 1950s and early '60s, trampling on the rights of privacy, free speech, free association, and even the right to have the wrong relatives. Among their triumphs were the discharge of one Gordon Knott of Cowichan, B.C., from the Navy, on the grounds that his uncle was a communist (in fact, he was not; the RCMP got the wrong uncle); the discharge of Eric Petersen of Victoria from the Navy because his father had once been a communist (though he was not then); the interrogation of a Saskatchewan university student who took part in an anti-nuclear demonstration in Regina (people who favour peace have always been regarded with suspicion in this country), and the hassling of the family of a fifteen-year-old Winnipeg boy who wrote a letter to the paper suggesting that Santa Claus must be a commie, because he wore a red suit and gave away presents, which was bound to undermine the free enterprise system. The boy's parents were warned —I'm not making this up, it happened in 1964—to curb his "dangerous beliefs".

I talked to the then Commissioner of the RCMP, C. W. Harvison, about these incidents in 1964. He explained that his men sometimes made mistakes, but if you're going to keep subversives in line, "if there are any errors, they must be on the side of safety." But could a guy be lifted out of the Navy for having a wrong relative? One of Harvison's deputies answered that one: "If a man has relatives who are known subversives, he has a disability, though it's not his fault."

No, this was not Washington in the McCarthy era; it was Ottawa in 1964. And protests were few.

What all this suggests is that we do not have a long tradition of free speech, free association, and freedom from repression. We only *think* we have. By and large, those who suffer from the rigours—or the errors—of oppression are people outside the mainstream of Canadian life, and therefore of no account. Only when someone safely middle-class and square gets caught up do we see how frail our liberties really are.

In October 1971, while Stan Roach, a freelance cartoonist in Montreal, was having a cup of tea with his wife Sheila and playing with his four-year-old son and seventeen-month-old daughter, the Montreal cops came calling. They had a tip—quite wrong—that a suspected bank robber was living at 6258 Anger Street—Roach's address. Sheila went upstairs and happened to look out the window and see a group of uniformed men, most of them with submachine-guns, fanning out around the house. She called her husband, who told her to take the two children and lie on the floor under the bed. They all started crying. Roach then went to the back door and was ordered to come out at once with his hands over his head. He did that. Then he was frisked, and told to lead the way back into the house. He told the cops they were not going into his place with those guns, and a cop replied, "If you don't go into the house right now, I'm going to shoot you here." He went inside, with a gun at his back.

His wife and children, hysterical now, were rousted out and for forty-five minutes the police ransacked the place, tearing open drawers, turning over furniture, ripping up rugs. They found a plastic submachine-gun, a typical four year old's toy, and were sure they had hit paydirt; Roach was jammed up against the wall while the cops checked out the gun and found it innocent. The Roaches still didn't know what was going on, but Sheila Roach, a spirited lady, had had enough; she said she was taking the kids and leaving, even if they shot her. She retired to a neighbour's. By this time, the police were coming around to the notion that they might have the wrong house, so they clumped out, leaving a gawd-awful mess behind. Contacted by a

72

puzzled press later, an official police spokesman had no apologies to make; Roach was not, after all, a bank robber or suspect, but the raid had been carried out, "in the only way possible".

So much for the presumption of innocence; so much for the sanctity of the home.

How about the sanctity of the person? On May 11, 1974, flying squads of police burst into the Landmark Hotel in Fort Erie, Ontario, intent, as they later said, on catching marijuana users. The possession of marijuana is a minor offence. The police thoughtfully took along with them an RCMP officer with a writ of assistance. This is a writ, issued under the Narcotic Control Act, that allows any member of the drug squad to conduct any search without a search warrant; all he requires is a reasonable belief in the possibility of the presence of proscribed drugs. All of the Landmark patrons were lined up and searched. Among them were thirty-six women, who were marched into the hotel washroom, stripped, and subjected to searches of the vagina and rectum. As Norfolk County Judge J. A. Pringle later commented, "Not one female was ever given the benefit of the doubt that she was not acting as a cache for drugs by concealing them on her person."

In the end, the police found a few ounces of marijuana—none on or in females; indeed, as the Canadian Civil Liberties Association pointed out, "a drug as normally bulky as marijuana is not likely to be stored in such regions."

The police were rebuked by a royal commission in the Landmark case, but the law governing writs of assistance remains firmly in place. Another such raid could take place anywhere, at any time; all that is required is for the police to suspect that the drug law, or one of the provincial liquor laws, is being tampered with, and the civil liberties of Canadians go out the window.

Frankly, I am not much impressed by rights that work only when the sun shines, any more than I am impressed by people who think freedom of speech should be reserved for like-minded folk. When Mulford Q. Sibley, an American radical, was invited to make a speech in Winnipeg in the late 1960s, he was blocked at the border, and Canada's left-wing students raised hell. When radical spokesmen of the left were hassled, pelted, and, in some cases, manhandled by the right-wing Western Guard in Toronto in the early 1970s, the same students, and their professors, were apoplectic. Then, when Edward C. Banfield, an American sociologist considered to be a right-winger, and branded as a racist, was invited to speak at the University of Toronto in March 1974, left-wing students stormed the stage, threatened Banfield, and generally kicked up such a rumpus that the speech was never made. (It was rather dull, actually; the title was *Adam Smith: The Cassandra of Commercial Society*. Although the ostensible reason for silencing Banfield was his alleged racism, his speech contained not a word on the subject.) A *Globe and Mail* reporter asked one of the university teachers who had led the charge against Banfield how he, the prof, would feel if a left-winger had been silenced. The intellectual freedom-fighter responded that the issue didn't come up, because there weren't enough right-wingers at the university to raise a really good mob.

Canadian civil liberties, in short, are just as much in danger from the left as the right, and just as likely to be undermined by smugness and neglect as by tyranny. In times of calmness and tranquility, we have nothing to worry about. But as soon as the going gets rough, our liberties go up like a lift-bridge, and we are subjected to exactly the same kinds of hassles as other peoples elsewhere in countries whose lack of freedom causes us to shake our heads in regretful sympathy. Our freedom of speech is subject to recall, free assembly depends upon with whom we want to assemble, and even freedom of thought is subject to seasonal variations. This is not a new state in Canada; it is part of our heritage, like pea soup and cold winters. Nor are we more oppressed than other people —in some ways we are better off, in others worse off, than U.S. citizens.

But my point, the point of this entire book, is that we have nothing to be so damn smug about.

And, before we leave the subject, one final reference to that damn War Measures Act. Shortly after it was proclaimed in October 1970, a jeepful of armed soldiers screeched into the small, dead-end street where I lived in Ottawa. Not surprisingly, we all sprang to our windows. The jeep came for our place like an arrow, pulled into the driveway, then backed out and pulled away. Obviously, the driver hadn't realized this was a dead-end street, and needed somewhere to turn around. That morning, I had said some rude things about the Act on the radio, and most of my neighbours thought the troops had come for me. Some of them, as I learned at a party afterwards, were indignant, and some thought it was about time I was squelched, *but not one of them was surprised*. In Canada, in modern times, picking up a loud-mouthed reporter for saying the wrong things seemed a perfectly natural thing to do.

CHAPTER 5:

JUST TRYING TO MAKE A BUCK

The rights of the minority must be protected, and the rich are always fewer in number than the poor.

John A. Macdonald, 1865.

One of Canadian history's more delicious japes is the notion that we are somehow less aggressive, less greedy, less commercial than, say, the Americans. They had Robber Barons, we had Merchant Princes. It is a matter of record that their businessmen go to work with knees up and elbows flying; it is a matter of myth that our tycoons hang shyly back. Whenever a Canadian firm loses a contract to an American competitor, we receive sly hints in the business press that the Yankees were not only bigger, slicker, pushier, and richer, but dirtier, and that's how they got the work. We have made a warm place in our homes and hearts for the quality folk who sell us goods — the Eatons and Burtons and Woodwards and Molsons—as if they were not out there scratching for a buck just like Goodyear or Kodak or anybody else.

In point of fact, in business as elsewhere, Canadians are much like their brothers around the world; all the rannygazoo about good fellowship and fair play is saved for the Rotary Club luncheon; when it's divvy-up time at the pay-window, our chaps are up there kicking and gouging just like everybody else. In fact, we have something of an international reputation for tough dealing and tricky ways. The man who actually framed the interesting financial arrangements that led to criminal charges being laid against U.S. wheeler-dealer Robert Vesco was a Canadian, Norman LeBlanc, who faces similar charges. When Interbank

— a spectacular but unfortunate banking venture on the tax-haven island of Grand Cayman—went belly-up in the spring of 1975, it was another Canadian, Jean Doucet, who wound up in the hoosegow. Two of the most famous media emperors in England have been Canadians — Lord Thompson and Lord Beaverbrook—and both trailed reputations as formidable and tough-minded entrepreneurs. (In a CBC interview, it was pointed out to a prominent British journalist that both these men were Canadians. Did he regard that as a coincidence? "No," he replied, "a disaster.")

Let's say it once and for all: in business, we are not nice guys, and, of course, it has always been that way. Our rich heritage of skullduggery and skull-bashing for money goes back to the foundations of this nation. Look at what they did to good old Marie La Tour.

Marie was the wife of Charles Amador St. Etienne, Sieur de La Tour, a French nobleman who claimed monopoly fur-trading rights in the Bay of Fundy. He got his monopoly from the French crown, and paid for it, but, by one of those errors in book-keeping that crop up wherever things are sold, another monopoly covering the same area was given to Charles de Menou, Sieur d'Aulnay Charnisay, a palpable rogue. The two men set up shop right across from each other; La Tour built a fort on what is now the waterfront of Saint John, New Brunswick (you can still spot a small green mound under the Harbour Bridge), and Charnisay built one at Port Royal, just across the way. Then they settled down to snarl at each other and see who could cheat the Indians more.

In 1643, Charnisay decided to get rid of his rival in a straightforward manner; he sailed across and attacked Fort La Tour. The boss was not a hell of a lot of use in this battle, but Marie, who had been an actress back in France (a toughening profession, even then), rallied the troops and personally hoisted the family flag. A doggerel poem, written later, described the fort's defenders as they raised a cheer to the rising flag, then noted Charnisay's reaction:

"The dark-brow'd d'Aulnay heard it as he paced his deck
  in pride,
And cursed the sound, and cursed La Tour, and cursed
  the adverse tide."

You don't hardly get poetry like that any more.

When the first rush failed, Charnisay set up a seige, but Marie and Charles, in a tiny boat, slipped past his pickets and got to Boston, where they raised a fleet of their own. When it heaved over the horizon, the rascals from Port Royal knew the jig was up. Exit Charnisay, stage left, muttering curses.

Later that year, Marie went to France to enlist aid among the Huguenots of La Rochelle (she was a Huguenot, although her husband was Catholic). Charnisay, who was back in Europe himself, had her proclaimed a rebel by the Queen Mother, and obtained a letter of arrest for her. Marie, however, escaped to England, chartered a vessel, and started for home. Charnisay intercepted her ship off the coast of Acadia and searched it, but Marie was hidden in the hold, and escaped once more. When the ship eventually reached Boston, she sued the captain—he had dawdled, she claimed, along the way—and collected, too. She got £2000, which she spent outfitting three small ships for Fort La Tour. She arrived home with her supplies in 1644.

Alas, Charnisay was persistent and, in February 1645, when Charles was away cheating Indians, he attacked again. After four days of battle in which Marie, wearing a steel breastplate and helmet, again played an active role, it became clear that the badly out-numbered garrison could not hold out much longer. When Charnisay promised to spare all the inhabitants, Marie surrendered to him. She should have known better; once inside, Charnisay hanged every man in the place, and forced Marie to watch with a rope around her neck.

The authors of *An Historical Guide To New Brunswick* would have us believe that "the shock was too great for her, and her noble spirit was completely broken. In three weeks she died and was buried near the scene of her heroic fight." If you'll believe that, you'll believe anything; Marie was not the wilting type, and the archivists at the New Brunswick Museum harbour a dark suspicion, which I share, that Charnisay did her in.

Charnisay drowned in 1650. (Served him right, too. An Indian, who happened to be on the river-bank when Charnisay's canoe dumped, had little love for the Frenchman, who once had him whipped; the Indian leapt to the rescue and towed Charnisay to shore — but with his head under water.) Once the coast was clear, Charles La Tour came home again. He married Charnisay's widow — setting a pattern for future industrial mergers — and solved the monopoly problem.

Rough stuff was part of normal business practice throughout Canada's early years. Ask Thomas Douglas, 5th Earl of Selkirk. Early in the nineteenth century Selkirk got the bright idea of founding a colony of distressed Highlanders and Irishmen on the banks of the Red River. The Hudson's Bay Company ran that end of the country, and the Colonial Office would not interfere with that giant, so Selkirk turned his attention, temporarily, to two colonizing ventures in eastern Canada, one around Orwell Bay, Prince Edward Island, in 1803 and the other at Baldoon, near Lake St. Clair, in 1804. The Baldoon Settlement failed, but the P.E.I. venture succeeded, and Selkirk was emboldened to try again out west.

This time, he did it the business way and, with friends and relatives, bought a substantial share of the Hudson's Bay Company. The company duly awarded him a tract of 116,000 square miles in the district of Assiniboia, and Selkirk put up Fort Douglas there in 1812. Fur traders of the rival North West Company took exception to this permanent settlement, which threatened their livelihood, and expressed themselves in the forthright way of our early entrepreneurs by inciting the Indians and Métis to murder Selkirk's governor, Robert Semple, and 19 of his men, at Seven Oaks, near the fort, on June 19, 1816. Selkirk in turn seized the North West Company's headquarters at Fort William, but the Nor'Westers had powerful political allies in Montreal and Selkirk was assessed £2,000 for false arrest after a long, drawn-out trial that depleted his resources and ruined his health. In 1819 he died in France, a broken man. Two years later, the North West and Hudson's Bay companies were merged, to form the most powerful monopoly this nation has ever known.

And this monopoly was run, not by a man of vision and compassion who wound up broke, like Selkirk, but by George Simpson, the "Little Emperor". Simpson ruled as governor of the Hudson's Bay Company (and therefore as governor of more than one quarter of North America) for nearly forty years.

He ran his empire with brisk efficiency, swooping back and forth across the continent in swift-travelling canoe convoys on inspection tours. He was always preceded into camp by a Highland piper in full fig, who made the pines ring with his squalls and must have set the Indians to pondering furiously about the white man's music.

He was successful, but he was not nice. He described the Canadian voyageurs, on whom so much depended, as "Mongrel half-gentry and Northwest renegade ... the very dross and outcast of human specie ... but a useful class of people if kept at a respectable distance." He wrote of his suppliers: "A little rum, you know, operates like a charm on the Indians. They cannot resist the temptation and if the affair is properly managed, every skin may be had from them."

He entered into liaisons with a number of Indian or half-breed women, and scattered illegitimate offspring across the west. When one of his "wives" became pregnant, Simpson, then off on a trip, instructed the post factor, "Pray keep an Eye on the Commodity, and if she bring forth anything in the proper time and of the right colour let them be taken care of, but if anything be amiss let the whole be bundled about their business."

Simpson's contempt for the Indians set a pattern that was followed by many Hudson's Bay factors until well into this century. The company plied the natives with rum, cheated them in trade, beat them, starved them, and even, on occasion, had them executed. A Select Committee on the Hudson's Bay Company in 1857 took the testimony of one John McLaughlin, who said that he had seen an Indian hanged by the company at Pembina. He was asked if he did not know that the company was prevented by law from such an act, and replied that he did.

> Q: How is it that the Colonists resident on the spot did not remonstrate against this execution?
>
> A: It is impossible for them to remonstrate there; they are too much under control of the Company; the Company would stop supplies.

Hudson's Bay ran a rigid monopoly, and if an Indian sold furs to a settler (instead of to them), the company would seize the furs and imprison the native. Indians who ran afoul of any of the dozens of HBC regulations were cut off from supplies — some of them died in consequence. A Salteau chief testified before the Select Committee that "The Traders have never done anything but rob us and keep us poor. . . . We have many things to complain of against the Hudson's Bay Company. They pay us little for our furs, and when we are old we are left to shift for ourselves. We could name many old men who have starved to death in sight of many of the Company's principal forts."

Indians were even prevented from trading with other

Indians, or doing anything that would lessen their dependence on the company. In one case, a factor at Penetanguishine forbade the Indians to gather cranberries for a white man who was willing to pay them; if they persisted, he said, they would receive no support during the coming winter. The object was to "prevent the Indians learning that there was another pursuit whereby they would become independent of the Company, and cease to be its hunters", according to a witness before the Committee.

Another witness, a surgeon who had worked for the company for three years at Moose River, testified that when two nearly starving Indians came aboard a company boat to beg for food, "The Governor took an Oar and beat them most unmercifully, saying, 'I'll teach you to go aboard without my leave.'" The company even cheated on the meagre prices it paid for furs by shortening the measure of its own goods, so that a pound of powder traded for pelts was shaved to weigh fourteen ounces.

Out of all this fun, huge fortunes were built for the whites, while the Indians were reduced to dependence and then starvation; then the HBC went into the history books as a paragon of entrepreneurial virtue. (And Governor Simpson, who presided over and perfected this system of fleecing the Indians, was rewarded with a Knighthood. He died in Lachine, Quebec, full of honours, in 1860.)

Fleecing the Indians was a major industry in Canada for most of our developing years, and when we ran out of Indians to cheat, we turned our attention to the half-breed Métis, and stole them blind. The Canadian Pacific Railway, seen from one angle, was a triumph of industry and persistence against great odds; seen from another angle — that of the natives of the west — it was the greatest land-grab in history. Those who could be suckered into treaties were swindled, and those who could not be so suckered simply had their land taken away from them.

The CPR has been the subject of more earnest study than the sex-life of the teenager, and I do not propose to tell its story again here, except to note the overwhelming consensus on one point: most of those involved in the financing of the venture were rogues and thieves. The only real debate is over whether roguery and thievery were so much a part of the business ethic of our early days that it is not fair to criticize. Perhaps there is something in that argument; when Alexander Tilloch Galt, Canada's first finance minister, was chief land agent for the British American Land Company — which worked land swindles through the Château Clique in Quebec — he wrote, "I consider the interests of the Company and of the country to be identical. . . . my views are all for objects of material advantage." (At least our forefathers were frank about these things; during the debate on the bill to grant the Grand Trunk Railway a charter in 1853, Tory Opposition leader Sir Allan McNab told the Legislative Assembly, "Railways are my politics." He was, at the time, president of the Great Western Railway.)

At the other end of the attempts to gain "material advantage" were the workers. For them, the price paid was not only in lousy wages, but in confinement, beatings, and death. Servants for the Hudson's Bay Company, for example, were imprisoned, lashed, and starved for the crime of trading on the sly with Indians, and one man, named Pilgrim, starved to death in a HBC post while under punishment. In British Columbia, in the profitable coal mining industry, the accident mortality rate was staggering. Out of a work force of about 4,000 men, 11 were killed in explosions and cave-ins during 1879, 65 in 1881, 23 in 1884, 148 in 1887, and 75 in 1889. The injured came to several times that many, and there was no compensation except by charity. Attempts to get decent safety regulations were brushed aside, and when the workers tried to band together to improve their lot, they were often fired out of hand. James Dunsmuir, owner of some of the biggest and most profitable mines — and later Lieutenant Governor of the province — was queried on this practice before a Royal Commission on Industrial Disputes:

> Q: Have you not, when you became aware of a man belonging to the union, got rid of him?
> A: You mean, fired the heads of the union?
> Q: Yes.
> A: Every time.

We know from the novels of Charles Dickens, from Charles Kingsley's story about young chimney sweeps, and from numerous horrible historical records, that child labour was used extensively in Victorian England, and indeed into the early years of this century. How different things were, you say, in the free, uncrowded air of our home and native land, far from the crumbling slums of Europe. Well, not quite. In Canada, we, too, used children as a form of cheap labour in the 1880s and '90s. They worked ten, twelve, fourteen hours a day in sawmills, factories, and mines, and were often crippled or killed in industrial accidents. They were whipped when they were deemed to need it, and were liable to be fined for so many petty offences that they wound up at the end of the week owing their employers money.

In the cotton mill at Hochelaga, Quebec, children who failed to show up at 6 a.m. (after working until 9 p.m. the night before) were fined. Employees worked all holidays except Christmas and New Year's, and lost two weeks' wages for failure to show. Charles Lipton, in his book *The Trade Union Movement of Canada*, chronicles the case of a fourteen-year-old boy who worked all week for $1.60, was fined $1.75, and ended up owing the boss fifteen cents.

A Royal Commission *Report* of 1882 looked into the conditions under which women and children worked in Canada:

The employment of children and young persons in mills and factories is extensive. ...As to obtaining with accuracy the ages of the children employed, we found some difficulty inasmuch as the employer had no record thereof, having no interest or obligation in doing so . . . . We were sorry to report that in very many instances the children, having no education whatsoever, could not tell their ages, some being found as young as eight or nine years. It must be borne in mind that the children invariably work as many hours as adults. . . . They have to be in the mill or factory at 6:30 a.m., necessitating their being up at from 5:30 to 6 o'clock for their morning meal. . . . This undeniably is too heavy a strain on children of tender years, and is utterly condemned by all except those who are being directly benefitted by such labour. . . .

Female labour is very extensively employed, not only in mills and factories, but also in private houses and what may be described as workshops which are very difficult to find, sometimes in the attic of a four-storey building, at others in a low, damp basement. . . .

Profits were often high, but wages were always low. In the tobacco industry, centred in Montreal, skilled workers earned from 80 cents to $1.25 a day, while children were paid as little as $1 a six-day week. Another Royal Commission (nothing much happened after the first one), which reported in 1889, contained this exchange:

Q: Have you seen little girls whipped?
A: Yes, sir.
Q: Why were they whipped?
A: Because they talked among themselves while at work.

It was customary for the factory owner to have a punishment room. Montreal tobacco manufacturer J. L. Fortier made a practice of stuffing unruly apprentices into a tiny, unheated cell in the basement. A young boy who refused to stay after working hours to sweep up was beaten unconscious by Fortier's foreman, and Fortier himself beat an eighteen-year-old girl with a cigar-mould—a plank about thirty inches long and six wide. He saw nothing wrong with this; the overseer's job, he said, was to act "like a schoolmaster . . . lightly touching the children with the ruler or his hands to correct them."

Every year between 1859 and 1889 the Macdonald Tobacco Company cut its wages during the winter months; when company president William C. Macdonald was asked why the wages should go down when living costs went up, he explained that there was a surplus of labour in the wintertime, and that he did not work for charity: "I am in business for the purpose of business."

After the 1870s, both Ontario and Quebec had laws prohibiting the employment of children under the age of twelve, but they were often ignored. Children of ten and eleven were common in the tobacco industry, and some of them worked all night in the Montreal glass works.

In the Maritimes, it wasn't even illegal to work children; ten-year-old boys routinely worked sixty-hour weeks in the Nova Scotia mines. At a large cotton mill in Moncton, New Brunswick, sixty-five children worked six days from 6:30 a.m. until 6 p.m. for $1.50 a week. (It was not uncommon, at this time, for the industry to pay dividends of twenty-three per cent annually.)

That was in the "regulated" industry. In the sweatshops, not large enough to qualify as factories, conditions were worse. In *Faith, Sweat and Politics*, Doris French described these establishments as "wretched little places . . . where women worked like serfs in perpetual bondage". The sewing sweatshops, the heart of the garment industry, paid piece-work rates of about $1 a week, and the women had to buy their own thread and put in a month's free labour "to learn the job". In most of the shops, the owner was a sub-contractor, working for a large company under commission. There were generous profits for everyone but the people who did the work.

It was an age when profit explained everything and excused everything—an age much like our own—and a man like Newfoundland's Abram Kean was regarded as a public benefactor. Kean was the acknowledged leader of the Newfoundland sealing fleet, and his crew earned an average of $29 a season for a life of danger, hardship, and incredible squalor. It was dangerous because the floating, wheeling icefields frequently caught and crushed the wooden ships that nosed around them looking for seals. On board the ships the men fed mainly on hardtack; their clothes afforded little protection on the windswept ice where the seals were killed and cleaned; and, as the ships' holds filled with seals, even their crude bunks disappeared and they flopped down at night atop the bloody, half-frozen pelts.

In their book, *Death on the Ice*, Cassie Brown and Harold Horwood describe how in March 1914, Kean abandoned 132 sealers on the ice off the Newfoundland coast, in the face of an oncoming storm. Even today the facts aren't clear, and Kean seems to have thought that their home ship was closer than it was. Anyway, for two hellish days and nights the men wandered over the floes, fell through the ice, huddled together to keep warm, and died. Conditions were terrible; one man froze his lips biting ice off his comrades' eyelids.

By the time they were picked up, seventy-eight men had frozen to death, and all the survivors were in serious condition, many of them crippled for life.

Kean (who had cheerfully ordered them off his ship into the storm with instructions to head for their own ship for shelter) learned of the tragedy from two other ships that came across the exhausted survivors. He stopped long enough to pick up a few bodies — *then went back to the important business of sealing.* He finally broke off from that only in the face of a near-mutiny among the sealers.

A public inquiry turned up a catalogue of ignorance, callousness, cupidity, and stupidity on the part of all the sealing masters and shipowners, but no damages were ever paid to the families of the dead sealers, nor to the men who lost limbs, health, and livelihood through the ordeal. Indeed, the only damages ever paid came in the form of an award of $100 for libel paid to Abe Kean because a St. John's newspaper attacked his role in the debacle. Kean sailed and sealed for another twenty years, killed more than a million seals, and in 1934 was awarded the Order of the British Empire.

That same year brought more evidence about Canadian business practices in the Parliamentary Committee on Price Spreads, chaired by H. H. Stevens, the same chap who worked so hard to keep the Sikhs out of Vancouver (see Chapter 3). His committee detected a pattern common to many industries in Canada — one or a few firms would seize control of a market, undercut suppliers by dropping their prices (a dress manufacturer would get locked in to selling most of his production to the company, then suddenly face a price drop; he would either lose money, or fold up, or find himself bought out by the big company), drive down wages, and walk off with the profits.

In 1933, forty T. Eaton Company directors received an average of $35,000 each—some of them for attending a few meetings—while their 25,736 employees averaged $970 for a year's hard work. The Committee was not fond of Eaton's:

> Its influence on Canadian industry and trade since it has attained monopolistic proportions has been disastrous; and . . . its operations, particularly during the past years of depression, have been one of the chief

contributing factors towards the degradation of labour in practically all lines of the production of consumer goods and the ruination of manufacturers and independent retailers.

Strong words, but based on some horrifying evidence. A Miss Nolan, who worked in Eaton's sewing department, talked about the results of a drop in piece-work rates from $3.60, for making a dozen dresses, to $1.75: "Well, you had to work so hard, you were driven so fast that, it just became impossible . . . and you were a nervous wreck. The girls cried. I was hysterical myself. It almost drove me insane."

> Q: Was that condition general, or did it happen only to you?
> A: It was general. All the girls were the same.
> Q: And did you break down by reason of it all?
> A: Yes, I went into hysterics several times and I had to go to the hospital and the nurse said, "What is the matter? You girls are always coming here."

It's nice to think that while good old Eaton's may have been causing "the degradation of labour" and "the ruination of manufacturers and independent retailers", it was providing work for the hospitals at the same time.

The girls were sent home for working too slow, locked out if they arrived five minutes late, and bullied by their supervisors. When a group of them tried to form a union to better their conditions in 1934, they were locked out of the place forever. Eaton's employees still have no union.

The tobacco industry was also closely managed. In 1932, Imperial Tobacco held off bidding for the crop, and other firms followed the giant's lead. Within three weeks, the price to growers dropped from forty cents a pound to twelve. Many farmers were wiped out. From 1929 to 1933, in the trough of the Depression, Imperial president Gray Miller received an annual salary of $25,000, plus bonuses ranging from $32,000 to $61,000; clerks in the Imperial-owned United Cigar Stores were paid $25.45 for a fifty-four-hour week.

The story was much the same in the meat-packing industry. Canada Packers, formed in 1927, had annual profits averaging close to $1 million throughout the lean years, and paid its workers as little as nineteen cents an hour.

The Stevens Committee stirred up a lot of controversy, but nothing happened. We have had many reforms since those days, but none have been voluntary. Decent wages came from the force of the unions; safety standards were imposed by public demand and government regulation; proper working conditions came, as often as not, as the result of bloody strikes. Where there was no outside force, and business was left to its own devices, there were no reforms.

For example, the fluorspar miners of Newfoundland worked for decades in circumstances that were, quite literally, deadly; more than 100 died as a result of conditions in the mines at Lawn and St. Lawrence, conditions that were public knowledge in the 1940s. It was not until 1960, when the Aluminum Company of Canada took over the last operating mine, that the oft-repeated warnings of doctors, miners, and even a provincial commission were heeded, and ventilation was installed. One of the major issues in the Asbestos Strike of 1949 was the health hazard in the Quebec mines; one of the major issues in the 1975 strike in the same mines was the very same hazard.

Money explains it all. In 1968, I went to Sarnia, Ontario, to investigate pollution problems in that smug, bustling, industrial city in southwestern Ontario. I wandered into a small shoe-repair store and asked the proprietor, a thick-set middle-aged man, whether air pollution presented him with any problems. "You could say so," he replied, "I buried two children with bronchitis."

He went behind the counter, fumbled in a drawer, and emerged with a much-handled newspaper clipping. The pretty face of a dark-haired teenage girl stared out above terse paragraphs describing her sudden death two years earlier.

"She was fifteen," the shoemaker said. "The other one was eleven."

I went directly from his shop to the office of a vice president of Polymer Corporation (a crown company which has since become Polysar, the jewel in the crown of the Canadian Development Corporation). Polymer was the city's single largest employer and, through a coal-fired plant then a quarter of a century old, a generous contributor to the garbage in the air. It was possible to cut down the plant's daily output of grit, fly-ash, and sulphur dioxide, the vice president admitted, but it would be "very expensive".

Money talks; in Sarnia it coughs some, but it still talks. The city had the highest weekly wage-rate in Canada at that time, a per capita income seventeen per cent higher than nearby Brantford, and an incidence of respiratory illness, asthma, bronchitis, and pneumonia twenty-seven per cent higher than Brantford. The director of the county health unit told me, "There is unquestionably a link between the air pollution and health problems in Sarnia"—but nobody wanted to hear that.

Another doctor, a specialist in allergies, organized a medical committee to investigate the city's air problems, and produced a report in which he lambasted industry for indifference and his fellow doctors for inaction. He got action, almost at once. The committee was disbanded, and he was cited before the local medical society for making unauthorized statements to the press. When I talked to him, Dr. William van Hoogenhuize had given up and was trying to sell his practice and move away.

But he had created a public relations problem, and a watchdog committee was set up to consider the air pollution question. It was called the St. Clair River Research Committee, and it turned out to be composed of one representative from each of the major industries in the area, so it had the distinction of being the accused, expert witness, and jury, all rolled into one. This committee sniffed the air and released an impressive-looking report that declared, "We believe that our levels [of air pollution] are well within the standards outlined today. We believe, too, that pollution is under control in this area."

The committee arrived at its conclusions by using standards for sulphur dioxide — the telltale for most air pollution — that had been established as safe for crops, not humans, and industrial standards applicable to an eight-hour shift, not to the problem of living in polluted air. The committee also said that "In spite of a nominal increase, sulphur dioxide levels in Chemical Valley have been stable over the years." In fact, the committee's own figures showed a jump of nearly 100 per cent in four years. When I protested to Dr. Rodney Morton, a DuPont chemist who chaired the committee, that this could hardly be called "nominal", he replied generously, "You can take out 'nominal' if you like."

He also said, "We're fighting to hold our own," but when I pointed out that a 100 per cent jump in four years was not "holding our own", he replied, "Well, you've got the figures. We think we're doing a hell of a good job."

Your definition of what is a hell of a good job in Sarnia is likely to depend on where you live. Thousands of Sarnians live in the shadow of Chemical Row, with the day-and-night, sick-sweet smell of its refineries, and the soot and stink of chemical manufacturing, while the quality folk live in the city's north end, or along the lake, or in comfortable suburbs, all blown clear by prevailing winds, and wonder what the fuss is all about.

And everywhere in Sarnia, when the subject of pollution comes up, the answer is the same; everybody agrees that something should be done, but to act would cost too much money, cut into profits, cause layoffs, or offend the city fathers. One day when a school teacher asked her pupils to copy notes off the blackboard, none of them could do it; they had been playing outside at recess, and chemicals in the air left them all with streaming eyes. The incident went unreported in the local paper, which regards all talk of pollution in the area as "hysteria".

I have written in detail about chemicals in Sarnia because I spent some weeks there, but the same principles apply elsewhere in Canada. Near Kitimat, B.C., in 1964, Indians were being poisoned by raw sewage that was being poured into the river by the town. The sewage clung to the fine nets the natives used to catch oolichan—a small fish—and two women were hospitalized and nearly killed as a result. I went to the town fathers, who explained that it was a matter for the province; the province said anything to do with Indians came under the care of the federal government; the Indian Affairs branch said I should talk to the Fisheries Department, and the Fisheries Department explained that they were powerless to act, because the sewage was affecting people, not fish. "If we could show it was harming the fish population, we would be in a position to act." They suggested I talk to the provincial department of health.

The first reports of mercury poisoning began to come out of the Dryden, Ontario, area in the mid-1960s, and the problem was traced to chemical and pulp plants in the area. A decade later, with the fishing almost destroyed and some of the people showing symptoms of mercury poisoning, we were treated to a visit from Japanese experts who were familiar with the problem in their own country. They were upset by what they found here, and their visit produced a great deal of bad public relations for the Ontario government and the companies. Any day now, we are assured, the problem will be licked.

In the meantime, the Indians have been advised not to eat the fish — although the alternative, for some of them, appears to be starvation.

Similarly, when it was discovered that the fallout from a smelter at Sudbury was making the small town, called (ironically) Happy Valley, uninhabitable, the solution proposed, and accepted, was to close down the town. Gluck in the air made the area around Sudbury a wasteland for years, so much so that you'll remember U.S. astronauts visited the place to stage a warmup for conditions on the moon. Eventually the pressure got so heavy that the order went out to install taller smokestacks. Now Sudbury's pollution count is comfortably down, but the junk is falling over a much wider area — sometimes as far away as North Bay, 78 miles to the east.

Driving south one day from Saskatoon to Regina, my wife and I noticed a massive pall of black smoke drifting slowly across the peaceful farmland. After some miles, we were able to spot the source — the Interprovincial Steel and Pipe Company mill outside Regina. The next day, I asked an aide to Premier Allan Blakeney if the province — which owns 20 per cent of the company — had received many complaints about it. "Oh, sure," he said, "it's been an issue around here for years. At one time, when the complaints got heavy, they just opened up the roof, so you got steam belching out with the smoke, and it didn't look so black." He said action was being taken to correct the situation, "as soon as we can afford it".

We live in the middle of an equation; on the one hand are money, profits, and jobs, and, on the other, health and good working conditions. Unless they are prodded, pushed, and shackled by regulations, our captains of industry plump, almost every time, onto the money side of the scale. Like old William C. Macdonald, they are in business for the purpose of business.

Perhaps that is only natural; they are urged on, after all,

by the mottoes of free enterprise—Every Man For Himself, Devil Take The Hindmost, and Up Yours, Jack. As long as they don't try to kid me about their noble impulses, as long as they don't try to pretend that Canadian businessmen are more public-spirited and less grasping than their American rivals, I can accept their foibles as the inevitable outcome of their historical development.

But what really upsets me is when the Canadian government takes on the same set of standards. I am speaking of the way we sold nuclear technology to India — and are now selling it to other and more dangerous nations; how we learned to stop worrying and flog the bomb.

It began innocently enough in 1956, when we gave India a CANDU (for Canadian Deuterium Uranium) reactor for research purposes, partly as a generous gesture to a fellow member of the Commonwealth, and partly to show off the Canadian system for generating nuclear energy. No safeguards were attached to that reactor — called CIR, for Canada–India Reactor—because no one dreamed, then, that it could be used to produce weapons. But the key point about a nuclear reactor is that the materials and technology required are very much the same as those used to build a bomb, and by 1960, when CIR was in operation, experts in the Canadian Atomic Energy Control Board began to worry about what we had done.

In 1964, India built a uranium separation plant. Most of the uranium in a CANDU reactor is non-fissionable U-238; less than one per cent consists of the isotope U-235, which is fissionable, and provides the energy. When U-235 is split, it produces neutrons, which are absorbed by the surrounding U-238 in a process that creates plutonium, which makes dandy bombs. The plutonium is produced in small amounts, and to get good bomb material, it must be separated and refined. News that India had built a plant capable of doing that very job set off a jangle of international alarms; more were set off when, in the mid-1960s,

India made it clear that she would not sign the Nuclear Non-Proliferation Treaty. That treaty distinguishes between nations that already have the bomb — who are allowed to go on making and stockpiling the weapon — and those who don't, who are not allowed to get into the business. India said the treaty was discriminatory; she would sign a treaty that banned all bombs, but not one that left the great powers armed and the lesser powers unarmed.

It was now clear to the dimmest intellect that India was going to build a bomb, and Pakistan, a nation that had been at war three times in the past 17 years with India, made direct and forceful complaints to Canada to this effect. We brushed them off. A second nuclear deal for two more CANDUs (they were to be bought, this time, not given) was under way. These two units — called RAPP I and RAPP II, for the site at Rana Pratrap Sagar — would produce power, not merely research, and part of the deal included the training of 271 Indian scientists in nuclear technology. It was by far our most precious gift; nuclear materials can be obtained elsewhere, but know-how cannot.

During the RAPP negotiations, a quarrel erupted among the Canadians who wanted to demand more safeguards from India and those who were anxious to see the CANDUs sold, and to hell with safeguards. The salesmen won. RAPP I and RAPP II were placed under safeguards to be enforced by the International Atomic Energy Agency, a UN body centred in Vienna. Unfortunately, the safeguards have a megaton-sized hole through the middle of them. The IAEA rules cover the transfer of nuclear equipment (clearly defined) and materials (less clearly defined), but say nothing about nuclear technology. What is worse, there is no provision for enforcement of the provisions, or punishment for their violation. They provide symbolic reassurance, nothing more.

In January 1971, when Prime Minister Trudeau stopped in Pakistan en route to the Commonwealth Conference,

President Yahya Khan told him personally about his fears that India was making a bomb with the aid of Canadian technology. The Prime Minister said he was satisfied with the safeguards (what safeguards?) imposed on India. A series of statements from Indian Prime Minister Indira Ghandi indicating that her nation felt it had the right to build atomic weapons led to questions in the House of Commons, but these were always brushed off with assurances that everything was under control.

But it wasn't, and we knew it wasn't. In October 1971, Trudeau wrote directly to Mrs. Ghandi, expressing his "concern" on the subject. She replied telling him politely but firmly to buzz off. The letters were suppressed, but we did begin to cut back on nuclear aid to India.

Finally, on May 18, 1974, India set off an atomic explosion. Officially, Canada expressed shock and alarm and amazement over a development that we had been warned about, both by outside observers and our own experts in the Atomic Energy Control Board, for ten years. Sure enough, it turned out that the material for the bomb came out of good old CIR, our original gift to India. External Affairs Minister Mitchell Sharp called the whole thing "most regrettable".

But that did not stop us trying to sell reactors; if anything, the pace has increased. We have concluded a sale to South Korea, and are trying to deal off reactors to Iran, South Korea, Denmark, Argentina, Finland, Rumania, Japan, Mexico, and Italy, although any reasonably astute ten-year-old can see the lunacy of spreading around the potential to destroy the world. A number of these nations have refused to sign the Nuclear Non-Proliferation Treaty, including two of the zaniest, South Korea and Argentina. That hasn't slowed us down a bit; we are prepared to accept their word that they won't do anything wrong, and we are also prepared to accept the inspection system of the International Atomic Energy Agency. We know — because our own experts have told us—that this inspection system will not stop any nation that wants to from building a bomb with our aid. We also know that South Korea—a nation run by an apparently paranoid dictator — is already dickering for a uranium enrichment plant, just as India did. (Perhaps our minds are easier now that Indira Ghandi has apparently given democracy the heave-ho in India; we seem to feel more comfortable with iron-fisted rulers.)

But the Canadian position has not changed; we are out to sell all the reactors we can. A senior official of Atomic Energy of Canada (the crown agency that handles the deals) told me, "The Canadian taxpayer has spent all this money and if he can get it back, he deserves it . . . . If we don't sell these reactors, you can be damn sure somebody else will, and maybe under even worse conditions."

The then Energy Minister, Donald Macdonald, made much the same point in an interview with the *Washington Post* shortly after the Indian explosion. He said that atomic safeguards were "an international problem, not a Canadian one". And he asked, "After developing a very viable system, should we not sell it internationally?"

This is the gun salesman's argument ("Lissen, you want me to get stuck with all these sawed-off shotguns?"); it is an argument bereft of morality, common sense, or any logic beyond the insignificant and unsuccessful philosophy of snatch. There is money to be made, and we are going to make it. What if South Korea's dictator, Chung Hee Park, who has already announced that his country will have to develop its own nuclear weapons if there is no United States' nuclear protection for it, cooks up a bomb and drops it on his enemies in North Korea? Will there be anyone around afterwards to call that "most regrettable"?

It is a bitter pill for any Canadian to swallow that we sold the Americans over $1 billion worth of weapons to use in South Vietnam—although we were members of the International Control Commission, charged with, among other things, keeping arms out of Vietnam—but it is far bitterer to find that we appear to be in the business of arming other nations with weapons capable of destroying all mankind.

And what is bitterest of all is to find that we are doing all this for no loftier motive than the one that sent Charles de Menou across the Bay of Fundy more than 300 years ago— we're just trying to make a buck.

CHAPTER 6:

CLASSLESS US

We have here no traditions and ancient venerable institutions;
here, there are no aristocratic elements hallowed by time or bright
deeds . . . here, every man is the son of his own works.
Thomas D'Arcy McGee, 1865.

A friend of mine, who had the good fortune to graduate
from the University of St. Andrews in Scotland, was asked,
not long ago, to help the old alma mater out in a finance
drive. He was glad to do it. His role turned out to be
assisting the Duke of Hamilton, flown over for the occasion, to put the bite on Canadians. The way it worked was
this: starting with lists of likely suckers, the finance committee invited suitable Canadians to meet the Duke of
Hamilton at the Granite Club in Toronto for a bit of tiffin
and tea. They could get to shake the noble hand, look into
the peer's eyes, and hear words of wisdom from the blue-
blooded lips (actually, I gather he was a very charming
man, and chatted pleasantly with everyone). They lapped
it up, and were duly creamed for substantial donations.
What dazzled my friend was that Canadians—democratic,
anti-snobbish Canadians—would flock to have their arms
twisted as long as the twisting was done in the form of a
handshake by a real, live, registered, four-square, genuine
member of the Privileged Classes.

But there is no mystery in this; Canadians are as class
conscious as anyone else, although we share with Americans a distaste for admitting the fact. Have you ever noticed
that most of the major newspapers in this country carry the
works of two gossip columnists? One writes about people
who *do* something—and the column is called *Names In The*

News or *People* or *Personalities* — and the other writes about people who *are* something, and the column is called *Society* or *On The Scene* or *About Town*. In the first, you meet actors, tycoons, media biggies, and newly-minted millionaires; in the second, you meet quality folk, blooming hostesses, and fading princesses.

Toronto, always in the vanguard, is able to support three full-time society name-droppers, two of whom — Zena Cherry and McKenzie Porter—have been at it for decades, and display a flatulent zeal in buttering up the well-connected that is positively awesome. Their folk go to Bishop Strachan School, or Branksome Hall, Trinity College School, or Upper Canada College, they marry at Timothy Eaton Memorial Church, hold their receptions at the Toronto Club or the Granite Club, dine at Winston's, holiday in Spain or the South of France, are divorced with the aid of a lawyer from Blake, Cassels and Graydon, and are buried back at Timothy Eaton. They do not come in touch with ordinary mortals except at the end of a sneer. And Toronto sneers defiantly back at them, class by snobbish class, from Cabbagetown to Don Mills. The same rituals, the same snobbery, the same sneers are repeated from coast to coast, from the Province House crowd in Halifax to the nobs who live in British Properties in West Vancouver. We are a nation that lives, like any other, behind class barriers; we have always done so.

Our ancestors arrived here neatly sorted out by class, and worked to keep it that way as long as they could. The Mess Book of settlers who came to Chebucto, Nova Scotia, with Governor Edward Cornwallis in June 1749, carefully listed all the arrivals under Name, Quality, Servants, Children, and Regiment or Ship. Thus, we find, on the roll of the frigate *Charlton,* that Richd. Jackson, a Perriwigmaker, had two male servants, but no children; Alexr. Ross, a bachelor husbandman, had neither kith nor servants, while Willm. Joyce, with the quality of First Lieutenant, had five male and two female servants, though no wife or children. Quality, not quantity, was what mattered.

The battle for responsible government that took up so much of our early history was a brutal class battle with religious overtones; the idea was to keep the lower orders and Catholics the hell away from the levers of power. When brawling democratic pressure led to the establishment of a "house of representation" in Nova Scotia in 1757, care was taken to ensure that it represented the right sort: "No person shall be chosen as a member of the said House, or shall he have the Right of Voting in the Election of any Member of the said House, who shall be a Popish Recusant, or shall be under the age of Twenty One years, or who shall not, at the time of such Election, be possessed in his own right of a Freehold Estate."

Slavery, of course, was the ultimate class barrier, and we certainly had slavery. The Indians made slaves of conquered neighbours, and the first French explorers accepted some as gifts. They were called *panis*, a name derived from the Pawness tribe, who lost a lot of battles, and supplied much of the luckless fodder. Because labour was short in New France, Louis XIV authorized the importation of black slaves; in the British colonies to the south, the slave trade brought workers to the burgeoning plantations. When the Articles of Capitulation were signed between the French and English in 1760, they included a clause specifically guaranteeing that "Negroes and Panis of both sexes shall remain in the possession of the French and English Canadians to whom they belong."

The British conquest modified, but did not end, seignorial tenure, a legacy from feudal days, in what is now Quebec. The seigneur, in return for a grant of land, paid homage and fealty to the crown, as well as performing military service on demand. He was required to build a grist mill for his *censitaires*, (who actually preferred to be called *habitants*,) who in turn, owed two sets of dues — *cens*, a nominal annual payment of homage (hence *censitaires*), and *rentes*, which cost a substantial share of the crop — to the boss, and worked free for him on his lands and roads. The seigneur had legal and administrative control over his habitants, and if they tried to sell out, could collect a special fee called *lods et ventes* which was generally stiff enough to persuade them to forget the whole deal. You will recognize this system as remarkably similar to the one that provoked the French Revolution.

In time, especially after the arrival of those damn democratic Yankees who flocked over the border pretending to be Loyalists on the heels of the Revolutionary War, there was a softening of class divisions. A softening, but not an erasure. A traveller to Niagara Falls in the early 1800s noted that it made his "blood boil" when he was set at the same table —although at the other end—as some servants at the local inn. Writers of that era found that there was a noticeable division in occupation by race, nationality, and religion in Canada. The Scots, for example, tended to be merchants, and Catholics were generally what John Godley called "the Pariah class—they are the porters, carters, waiters at Inns, etc." Blacks worked in hotels, too, and did the whitewashing, plastering, cooking, baking, and entertaining. The upper classes, white, Anglican, and "thoroughly English", visited each other, married each other, and snubbed anyone who could not produce a letter of introduction to the governor, bishop, or other social big-shot.

Slavery continued, although it was increasingly frowned on, after the turn of the nineteenth century. A newspaper ad from just after 1800 announced to Haligonians: "To be sold—a healthy, strong Negro woman, about thirty years of age, understands cooking, laundry and the taking care of poultry. N.B. She can dress ladies' hair. Enquire of the printers."

Not only were there black slaves, there were white ones, too, men and women who bound themselves to employers

103

for years to pay their passage from England or Ireland, and orphans who were sold into bondage. A Kingston newspaper item on May 7, 1836 announced the impending arrival of "70 boys and 30 girls" who had been "trained to habits of industry and instructed in moral and religious duties" (including, presumably, the duty not to sass the boss or eat too much). They could be had for a payment of "Ten dollars per annum, Seven of which to be invested in the Savings Bank, for the future benefit of the child". A kid who survived ten years of indentured labour could have a whole seventy bucks to live on for the rest of his life.

Kingston, like other early towns, took a dim view of anyone stupid enough to be born poor, and set up "Houses of Industry", described as "Suitable buildings for the reception of the Poor and Indigent, and of the Idle and Dissolute . . . where they shall be kept diligently employed in labour".

These people were at least a cut above the slaves, but after slavery was abolished when Mother England made it illegal in 1833, they slipped down to fill the need for an absolutely rock-bottom class, along with domestics, voyageurs, half-breeds, and Indians. We have always had someone to look down on, and someone to look up to, and inheritance has always played a major role in the division. Sir Francis Bond Head was on firm ground when he affirmed—in 1837, yet—that "the people of Upper Canada detest democracy." Oh, yes, there was a fuss about the Family Compact in Upper Canada, and the Chateau Clique in Lower Canada, but Head explained the position of the oligarchy in terms of merit, not privilege:

The Family Compact of Upper Canada is composed of those members of its society who, either by their abilities and character have been honoured by the confidence of the executive government, or who, by their industry and intelligence, have amassed wealth. The party, I owe, is comparatively a small one; but to put the multitude at the top and the few at the bottom is a radical reversion of the pyramid of society which every reflecting man must foresee can end only in its downfall.

It has become fashionable to laugh at old Head and to salute his enemy, William Lyon Mackenzie, but the aristocrat spoke for many more Canadians than the democrat, as Mackenzie found when he put the issue to a test of arms. Head's notion that merit and character determined entrance to the ranks of power was, and remains, one of the beguiling fairy tales of our society. As today Eatons beget Eatons, so in the 1800s did the elite beget the elite. The Compact, like its Quebec counterpart, the Chateau Clique (named for the Château St. Louis, residence of the Governor in Quebec City), was a narrow group of families, mostly Anglican, English speaking, and mostly connected to the military hierarchy. This group managed land-grabs, bank charters, canal charters, and all forms of patronage, high and low. They were joined together by a common background and an unwritten "code" whose components are described by historian Michael Cross as "the correct attitudes on social and political questions, and the indefinable attributes of a gentleman". A "sense of honour" was important, and that included the willingness to fight a duel over an insult to oneself or a lady friend.

Front was what counted, not merit. John Langton, one of the original settlers of Sturgeon Point near the present city of Lindsay, Ontario, wrote home to England in 1833:

> On Sturgeon Lake you will find six settlers. Certainly this is not many, but then four of them have been at an University, one at the Military College at Woolwich, and the sixth, though boasting no such honours, has half a dozen silver spoons and a wife who plays the guitar.

Dread democracy did, in the long run, do in both the Family Compact and the Chateau Clique, but as the nineteenth century advanced, class distinctions were merely blurred, not eliminated. It remained the lot of the lower classes to go uneducated, untrained, and unwanted; public funds were used to educate the scions of the rich, but no tax moneys were spent on the schooling of the poor. Egerton Ryerson's report calling for open education was published in 1846, but there was no free general education in this country until 1871. Throughout Canada's history, a rich relative has been infinitely more precious than the greatest brain, the purest heart, and the most industrious hands in the Empire.

Women were the special victims of economic discrimination in the 1800s; unless they were well-born or well-wed, they could look forward to lives of domestic drudgery either at home or in the homes of others. Leo Simpson Johnson, writing in an excellent new study, *Women At Work*, comments:

> Necessary, but despised, not slave but required to be always subservient, the house servants of the nineteenth century found themselves in an unenviable position .... Children of the servant class became servants at an early age, and could expect to remain servants for life, rising, if they were successful, to such skilled occupations as butler, cook or housekeeper.

For the masses, there were few schools, little pay, and such long hours that there was no time to improve themselves. Left-wing writers call this system "exploitation", but that is a harshly pejorative term; let us simply say that the class system proved remarkably convenient for those at the top and remarkably inconvenient for everyone else.

It was harder to keep the lower orders in place on the opening frontier of the Canadian West—indeed, that was one of the lures of the West for many of our ancestors—but no one can say our gentry didn't try, in such places as Cannington Manor. Cannington Manor was the brainchild of Captain Edward Mitchell Pierce, a gentleman of impeccable antecedents but questionable finances, who came to Canada in 1882 after a bank failure in his native England. He had a letter of introduction to Sir John A. Macdonald, and used it to wheedle a grant of land in southeast Saskatchewan (near the site of what is now Moose Mountain Park). Pierce proposed to erect a settlement there in the style of English manor houses, and he very nearly brought it off.

He founded an agricultural college, where he proposed to teach farming to young men of good breeding for a paltry £100 a year; he set up the Moose Mountain Trading Company, a grist mill—whose flour once won first prize at the Chicago World's Fair—a general store, and a paint business. The gentry flocked to the site, and brought their maids, their monocles, their tennis raquets, and their riding-habits with them. They bowled and sipped tea, rode to hounds, played cricket, and looked down their noses at the surrounding Canadian settlers, whom they regarded as unfit to share a cricket pitch with their own offspring.

Pierce died in 1888, which is perhaps just as well, because his manor was doomed. The railway, which was to have provided permanent prosperity and an easy access to market, arrived late (in 1900) and in the wrong place (ten miles south of the Manor). Today, Cannington is a provincial park, with a museum, church, pioneer homestead, and a reconstructed version of one of the grand homes of the colony, which provides a sharp contrast with the homestead. The museum includes, among other treasures, photos of the swells disporting themselves, and the hide of Bessie, the first cow ever slaughtered on the scene.

Cannington Manor was not unique. During the 1880s and '90s, the small Saskatchewan town of Whitewood boasted no fewer than four authentic French counts. In his book, *The Road Across Canada*, Edward McCourt describes them as "haters of French republicanism and heavy taxation" who hoped to recoup their fortunes in the new world. "They brought with them retinues of servants from France, they imported the best of food and wines and they drove over rutted trails in costumes and equipage — tall hats, white gloves, dog carts, coaches—unlike anything seen on the prairies before or since." But they failed to make their fortunes and left, with the prairie ladies still swooning behind them.

These experiments failed in part because the caste system did not work well on the western plains—you could not go racing off after foxes in the middle of the wheat harvest and hope to make money. But that didn't mean that Canada lacked a caste system; it meant that, as time went by, we adapted the codes of class to our own needs. Those codes are visible to anyone who cares to look for them, in the paddock of the Queen's Plate, in the panelled drawing rooms of Calgary's Petroleum Club, the Vancouver Club, Toronto's York, Toronto, or Albany Clubs, Ottawa's Rideau Club, or the St. James or Mount Royal Clubs of Montreal. Our upper classes know which are the right schools — Upper Canada College in Toronto, Trinity College School in Port Hope, Ashbury College in Ottawa, and Ridley College in St. Catharines, draw the scions of our swells from coast to coast. They know the right church — Anglican — the right politics — Liberal — the right restaurants, caterers, architects, interior decorators, and all the other purveyors of goods rare enough and expensive enough to be beyond the reach of the teeming masses. At the other end of the scale, Canada's working classes know their own milieux in the slums of Montreal and Toronto, the skid rows of Halifax and Vancouver, the poolhalls of Saint John and Inuvik.

The myth of Canadian classlessness, the notion that our castes have almost equal opportunities for advancement, was dealt a severe blow, in 1965, by John Porter's *The Vertical Mosaic.* Porter showed, with impressive documentation, that Canada was ruled by a self-perpetuating elite, mainly Wasp, and mainly raised along the St. Lawrence River valley. This ruling caste was bound together by old school ties, family relationships, and interlocked company directorships.

Porter's findings came as a cold shock to many of his fellow sociologists, but never mind, they said, the research was based on old data, some of it reaching back to 1951. Since then we have become more enlightened, more democratic. Anyone Can Still Make A Million, just as Morton Shulman (a millionaire) has written. Opportunities, if not exactly equal, are moving towards equality. Right?

In a pig's eye. Wallace Clement, a sociologist, like Porter, brought the pioneer work up to date in 1975 with a book called *The Canadian Corporate Elite.* By the Corporate Elite, Clement means the men (for the top rung of power is reserved almost exclusively for males) who dominate the nation's economic life and decision-making processes. He found, contrary to myth, that "family-controlled firms still have a prominent place" among the country's power-wielding corporations, and he cited "The Burtons of Simpson, the Molsons, Eatons, Woodwards, Westons, the Bronfmans of Seagrams [and] the Jefferys of London Life". Again contrary to myth, the ownership of Canadian business is not widely spread; only one Canadian income-earner in ten owns as much as a single share; the top ten per cent of our income-earners hold three-quarters of all the shares held in this country, and the top one per cent hold more than half of that. That is, one per cent of the people own more than a third of all the shares. Most of our top corporations are inter-linked; the 113 dominant corporations in Canada have 1,848 interlocked directorships and the men who hold these directorships are also directors in 41 per cent of the next 175 largest corporations. (By "dominant corporations" Clement means "those . . . powerful enough to establish the 'tone' and direction of particular segments of the economy and together the general direction of the entire economy".)

There isn't really a hell of a lot left for the rest of us, and the barriers are getting higher, not lower. Porter found in his 1950s study that the upper class, representing between one and two per cent of Canada's population, held half the positions in the corporate elite; Clement found that they now hold nearly sixty per cent. Private schools are even more the symbol and preserve of the powerful. In Porter's study, 34.2 per cent of the Canadian-born elite had been to private school; in Clement's study, the figure had risen to 39.8 per cent. Porter shredded the comfortable notion that the rich get rich by their own efforts; he found that only 7.6 per cent of the elite had pulled themselves to the top. Today, Clement says, the figure is less than a third of that— 2.2 per cent.

For real wealth and real power in Canada, inherit it, or marry it, or forget it.

The ring of privilege that Porter described—a ring that sealed out most foreigners (except Americans), most Catholics, most French Canadians, and nearly all women—has become a wall of steel. New Canadians represent 26.7 per cent of our population, and 5.4 per cent of the elite; French Canadians make up one third of the population, and one eleventh of the elite; Catholics represent 46.2 per cent of the population and 12.7 per cent of the elite; half of us are women, and that sex holds .6 per cent of the elite positions.

As in, say, the Court of St. James, the Nobs are mostly pals. A Canadian textile magnate, the director of several other corporations, told *Executive* magazine, "They all know each other or of each other. It's really like a small community where there are no strangers, although they might live far apart. Nowadays, that doesn't matter.

They're linked together by telephone and jet." Beats page-boys and carriages.

The educational system, which in our mythology provides a road out of the caste system, has in fact bent itself to serve that system. Less than one Canadian in ten attends a university, but four out of five of the elite attend. University is heavily subsidized by the taxpayer; everyone chips in to support institutions which, by and large, only the middle and upper classes ever attend. Socialism for the rich, free enterprise for the poor.

Children are streamed, from the time they enter school, by class, language group, and ethnic origin. This is not how it is supposed to be, just the way it is, and always has been. The conditioning is so much a part of our heritage, we are seldom conscious of it. When J.S. Woodsworth was a young preacher in Brandon, Maniotoba, in the early part of this century, he noted in his diary that he had had a long talk with a man named Hughes, who was "of comparatively uneducated class — narrow and bigoted and jealous of upper classes . . . . They forget, or rather cannot comprehend the different attributes—the quality as well as the quantity." The difference between J.S. Woodsworth, who went on to spend most of his life working for a more egalitarian Canada, and the rest of us, is that he survived his education in snobbery. Most of us aren't even aware that we had such an education, until something triggers our consciousness.

When we lived in Ottawa, our son Craig (a fairly bright lad, all things considered) on entering Grade Seven was put into a class of lunkheads and failures. They were nearly all children of immigrants, with a scattering of poor kids and a couple of genuine middle-class dunces. We were told that Craig and two others had been shoved in (although "boys of his type are generally in better surroundings, ha-ha") to help leaven the loaf. It was an experiment; generally, the school system was content to leave the immigrant kids, the poor kids, and the dummies in a sodden mass under the school's dimmest teachers. What was the point of wasting time and talent on them? They weren't going anywhere, anyhow.

Sometimes the hiving off of the chosen few for streaming into university and the lumpen proletariat for sacrifice to the community college system or the work force is the result of deliberate planning by a local board of education; sometimes it merely reflects a teacher's prejudice. Two bright Italian-Canadian high-school students in Toronto, who felt they were being downgraded because of their ethnic background, tried an experiment. One submitted an essay in her own name, the other a nearly-identical essay in the name of a Wasp friend, to the same teacher. The Wasp paper received a much higher mark than the Italian one.

Immigrants are not supposed to be so pushy; there is a job for them to do, and they should do it. A headline in the *Toronto Star* for April 1, 1975, read:

CLEANING HELP HARD TO FIND AS IMMIGRATION TIGHT-ENS.

While there are toilet bowls to scour, kitchens to scrub, and floors to wax, Italian girls should forget about essays and bend to the work God and precedent set for them. If we are going to have this bumptious crossing of class lines, we won't know — as Lord Goddard once remarked in an English courtroom — whether we stand on our heads or our feet — and pretty soon Canadians will hesitate to fork out good dough to shake hands with a Duke.

CHAPTER 7:

GENTLE US

Canada is the product of understanding, not conflict; we are the trustees of reasonableness, not violence.

Prime Minister Trudeau, 1969.

Standing on the porch of a cottage on a sideroad back of Piedmont, Quebec, I paused only long enough to wonder what a nice boy like me was doing in a place like this, screwed up my courage, sucked in my breath, and knocked. I had heard footsteps inside while I was advancing to the door; they ceased at once. There was the creak of a board, then silence. I knocked again. Nothing. I spotted an open window, just to the right of the door, so I stuck my head in there and announced, in quavering French, that I was a journalist, *un bon type,* that I was working on a story about André Durocher, and that nobody had sent me. The interior of the room was dark, after the bright sunshine outside; I could make out a table, some chairs, and a small closet, closed off by a curtain. I could hear somebody breathing. Aha, I thought, he's in the closet. I told the closet, ''Je suis journalist.'' More silence.

I began to brood. This was a mobster hide-out; André Paquette had stayed here, and Lucien Rivard, and André Durocher. This guy in the closet, maybe he wasn't keen on talking to journalists, good types or not, maybe he was going to take umbrage, maybe if I stuck my head in one more inch, he was going to hit it with something heavy and drop me in a lime pit. I tipped my hat—a little politeness never hurt anybody — withdrew my head and left at an impressive rate of knots.

On the way back to Ottawa, I got to thinking about André Durocher, the subject of my research, and about his place in history. After all, he had brushed with fame, but nobody wrote about him — certainly not in English Canada. That seemed wrong; Durocher is as much a part of our culture as Jean Sutherland Boggs or Sir Ernest Macmillan; the only difference is that he represents a strain we prefer to forget about, the segment of our society where people hit people with blunt objects, or shoot or stab or otherwise inconvenience them, to earn their daily bread.

Durocher was a second-generation gangster; he slipped into that twisted world the French call *le milieu* as naturally as a doctor's son might aspire to his father's practice, or a lawyer's son take to the law. His father, William Durocher, was a minor figure in the Montreal underworld until November 1943, when he was arrested for the murder of a nightwatchman, Patrick Campbell. Campbell had been bludgeoned to death in the course of a robbery, and Durocher came home with his watch. Mrs. Durocher ratted to the cops, and he was charged with murder. He hanged himself in his jail cell while awaiting trial. André was six at the time, an impressionable age.

He did not do well in school and dropped out after grade seven to bum around and drive a truck. In 1955, when he was eighteen, he was arrested for auto theft, and served a month in jail. In 1958, he was arrested again for theft, and received a three-year sentence in penitentiary. Do-gooders are always complaining that our penitentiaries serve no purpose; it is not so. Durocher, like so many others before and since, put his time to good use, making underworld contacts, learning the subtleties of his chosen craft. In 1961, just out of jail, he was picked up for theft once more, but escaped with a fine. Then, rounding into manhood, he hit his stride and, during late 1961, 1962, and early 1963, he took part in seventeen thefts, robberies, and hijackings. As his career began to ripen, he settled down, married, and produced a handsome son. Knowing what is expected of the rising executive in the way of symbols, he bought a Cadillac.

Then he hijacked a tobacco truck, but got caught, convicted, and sentenced to five years in penitentiary. He launched an appeal, but was refused bail, so he was sent to Bordeaux Jail in Montreal to await his next hearing. There he met Lucien Rivard.

Rivard was at the height of his fame. The 49-year-old "resort owner" was awaiting extradition to the U.S. on charges of drug-trafficking. Efforts to obtain bail for him, which involved bribery and corruption at the highest level of Canadian politics, had plunged the nation into the noisy fracas of the Dorion inquiry. Rivard thought it would be nice to be away from all that, and Durocher thought so, too.

At 6:20 p.m. on March 2, 1965, Durocher, who had been given the task of looking after the prison skating rink, asked for permission to water it, with Rivard as his helper. Despite the balmy, 42-degree Farenheit weather, guard Noel Bonneville agreed, and the three men went to the prison boiler room to get a hose. There, Rivard produced a home-made gun — fashioned of wood, coated with black shoe polish — and they tied up the guard. Pausing only to slug another guard patrolling the prison wall, they slid down the watering hose and escaped. On the street, they commandeered a passing car (Rivard gave the driver $2 for cab fare) and headed for a hiding place in east-end Montreal. There, Rivard put in a phone call to his old friend André Paquette.

Paquette — "le P'tit" — was the kind of underworld big-shot Durocher aspired to become; executive vice-president in charge of planning. He had managed to stay out of jail since 1960 and, in 1964, pulled off his greatest caper, the Great Mail Robbery. Paquette had learned that every evening at 9:15, a mail truck left the St. James Street post office in downtown Montreal for the three-block ride to the railway station. It was always loaded down with material drawn from "the cage" — the post office security area. The truck drivers went unarmed, on the theory that unarmed men in ordinary vehicles were less likely to draw the attention of hoods. For several nights during March 1964, the evening run was shadowed by Paquette's men and then, on March 31, the trailing car simply forced the post office truck to the curb, and seven armed men piled into it. They got away with $1,400,000, the contents of ten bags of registered mail, including $600,000 in cash. The gang reconvened in a north-Montreal apartment to split the loot, and then the gang members were individually escorted to their homes by an off-duty Montreal cop, in uniform, laid on for the occasion. You can't be too careful when carrying money on Montreal streets.

Despite its careful planning, the Great Mail Robbery was not a complete success. Ten men were rounded up, charged, and convicted (the off-duty cop got eight years). About half the loot was recovered, but nobody ever caught up to André Paquette. He was in hiding in a cottage near Piedmont, about forty-five miles north of the city, and when Lucien Rivard, still panting after his escape, called and asked for a hiding place, Paquette extended the hospitality of the house. To accept it, Rivard and Durocher would have to get past the ring of police patrols which the frantic radio was announcing had been set up to recapture them. Durocher decided to disguise himself as a woman, and when he emerged from the Montreal apartment, it was as "Bébé", a thick-set but not unattractive brunette, stylishly clad in a tailored lady's suit, frilly blouse, brown wig, and stylish glasses set with rhinestones. Underneath were a false front, a girdle, and nylons. Alfred Cadieux, Rivard's chauffeur and bodyguard, opened the car door, Rivard and Durocher piled in, and they set out for Piedmont with all three in the front seat. They were stopped by a police patrol, but passed on after Durocher planted a kiss on

116

Cadieux's lips. "Please, Bébé," he protested, "people are watching." The embarrassed cop waved them by.

At Piedmont, Durocher was introduced and welcomed warmly by Paquette and his mistress, Alice Rioux. He was even invited to gangland meetings in the parking lot of a nearby dancehall. He was not a gracious guest. One evening when Paquette had driven into St. Jerome, fourteen miles away, to conduct some business, Durocher raped Alice Rioux. Hell, a chap has to have something to do to while away the hours. Alice complained to Rivard, who was furious, and called in a friend of Paquette's, Vincent "le boeuf" Blais, a hefty Montreal nightclub manager. Rivard told Blais to take Durocher back to Montreal.

Durocher was glad enough to go; not only did he have an inkling that he may have worn out his welcome *chez* Paquette, he wanted to get back to the city to bask in his new fame as a celebrity, the man who escaped with Rivard. He teamed up with another hood named Conrad Brunelle, took a new nickname — "le meilleur", literally "the best", but really more like "Mr. Big" — and went back into the crook business in Montreal and the Eastern Townships between April 16 and May 11, 1965.

But he kept thinking about Paquette and the mail robbery loot he knew must be stashed somewhere around the cottage. Changes had been made at Piedmont; Rivard had moved to a new hiding place, and Paquette and Alice Rioux were alone. One night, Durocher and Brunelle drove up there, tortured the couple to find out where the money was hidden, killed them, and made off with $17,000. The bodies were later buried in a shallow grave and covered with lime.

When Vincent Blais went to call on Paquette and discovered that both he and his mistress were missing, word was passed to Rivard in his new hiding place that something had gone wrong, and that Durocher was probably responsible. On June 4, thirteen days after Paquette disappeared, the Montreal morality squad received a tip — presumably from someone connected with Rivard — and swooped on an apartment on St. Christophe Columbe Street, in the north end of the city. They scooped up Durocher, his wife, and $2,200 in cash, some of which could be traced to the Great Mail Robbery. In turn—this is a tit-for-tat business—Durocher told the police they could find Rivard by tailing his bodyguard, Alfred Cadieux, who was still being seen around Montreal. They did that, and Cadieux led them straight to Rivard, who was captured, extradited to the U.S., and sentenced to twenty years in jail (he served less than ten).

The police didn't know about the murders of Paquette and Alice Rioux, but, over the next few months, Durocher told them about his other endeavours with Conrad Brunelle. Brunelle was arrested, and became convinced that Durocher would not only talk about the killings, but that he would try to pin them on his partner. So he hanged himself in his jail cell, but thoughtfully left behind a note that said, among other things, "I know it was André Durocher who killed Paquette." (Paquette had been shot with a .38 calibre pistol, Rioux with a .22, so it seems likely the chores were shared.) Durocher did, in fact, try to pin the murders on Brunelle, but the note made that awkward; he was found criminally responsible in the deaths of André Paquette and Alice Rioux by an inquest in St. Jerome on June 1, 1966. Two nights later, he hanged himself in the shower room of Quebec Provincial Police headquarters in Montreal.

I started on the trail of Durocher because, frankly, I was fed up with the glamorous sheen that had been laid on Rivard. He was lionized in the press (indeed, when he returned to Canada in January 1975, he was still being lionized with extensive newspaper "colour stories".) On information received, as the police say, I had reason to believe the Durocher story would throw new light on the underworld through which he moved, and so it proved, as you have just seen. There was no honour among thieves, no high life, just treachery, savagery, and thuggery, slightly relieved by the low farce of a thug in drag.

There is a fair sprinkling of thuggery in our background, although it is not much celebrated in our conventional history. Perhaps this is fair enough; a frontier society is a violent society, and we may not gain much from knowing that our ancestors were accustomed to hanging the poor for stealing a loaf of bread, that in 1810 there were over 100 offences for which a felon could be hanged, that bloody murder is as much a part of our national upbringing as, say, biculturalism or a tendency to rely on resource-based industries. Our history books normally gloss over the fact that seven of our countrymen who were rash enough to side with the Americans in the war of 1812 met a fate that we associate with the dark side of mediaeval Europe. As W. R. Riddell's research papers for the Ontario Historical Society show, seven men—after due process of law—were hanged, drawn, and quartered on Burlington Heights, Upper Canada, on July 20, 1814.

The mass murder of the feuding Donnellys in Biddulph, Ontario, in 1880, has been much celebrated, because it provided all the classic ingredients of drama. On the night of February 3, 1880, a mob of about forty men with faces blackened descended on the Donnelly homestead at Whalen's Corners. They killed Jim Donnelly and his wife, then despatched their young niece Bridget, and killed their son Tom—who had been handcuffed, bludgeoned, and stabbed—by striking off his head with a spade. They set fire to the house and left for the other Donnelly farm nearby, where they shot and killed John Donnelly. Then they went home, content that they had put in a busy and eventful evening's work.

Although there were a number of eyewitnesses to the murders, no one was ever convicted. The reason was simple; in those days Biddulph Township was much like Tombstone or Dodge City of the bold, bad West—a place of blood feuds, violence, and intimidation. A word out of place could lead to a beating, a beating to a barn-burning (that happened almost every week), a barn-burning to the maiming of cattle or horses, the maiming to a murder. In these circumstances, witnesses tended to develop leaky memories, and juries tended to stretch the benefit of the doubt beyond recognition.

The Donnelly case has come to us in folklore, in drama, and in books like Orlo Miller's *Death To The Donnellys*, and we tend to think of it as unique, but, in fact, mayhem was common coin among our ancestors, as anyone can see from a look back through old newspaper files in the National Library at Ottawa.

In February 1819, a man named De Benyon threw his thirteen-year-old stepson out of their cabin near Whitby, Ontario, because he was irritated. When the boy crawled back in, half-frozen, a short time later, De Benyon tied him in front of the fireplace, and roasted him to death. When the neighbours found out, they lynched De Benyon.

Hanging, as we noted in Chapter 2, brings out our taste for violence as a spectator sport. In 1861, a double hanging was scheduled for the delectation of the public at the Montreal prison, but the sentence of one of the victims was commuted at the last moment, and the crowd, feeling that they had been cheated of half of the expected double-header, attacked the sheriff, priests, and hangman, then went on a rampage along St. Mary's Street, smashing windows and wreaking havoc. Ten years later, when a murderer was hanged in the same prison, public executions had been banned, but invited guests received black-bordered tickets. The trap was duly sprung, and the murderer dropped, but some ass had encased the lower part of the scaffold with boards, so his death struggles were partly hidden from sight. The crowd surged forward and ripped off the offending boards to get a better look.

In September 1877, a Weston, Ontario brickmaker named John Williams beat his wife to death — taking some time about it—and then advanced the argument that a man is entitled to correct his spouse. He was convicted of murder, but the jury brought in a strong recommendation for mercy.

Well, they were rough days. Nobody knows how many died in the gangland wars of Bytown from 1828 to 1843. The best estimates suggest that at least fifty men were beaten to death, stoned, shot, or simply thrown into the Ottawa River off the bridge to Hull and drowned. The chief combatants were the Shiners (Irish workmen who had been brought over to build the Rideau Canal — where many of them died in brawls, in construction accidents, or of disease —and found themselves with nothing to do on its completion; they took to cutting oak-trees, thus "cheneurs", thus "Shiners") and French Canadians, most of them raftsmen. Peter Aylen, a well-to-do Bytown entrepreneur, organized the Shiners into a terrorist mob with a view to muscling in on the rafting trade. Aylen's lieutenant was a man called Jimmy the Wren, whose speciality was throwing rocks with uncanny accuracy; his bodyguard was Martin Hennessy, an ill-tempered giant whose specialty was barroom brawls, and another of his sidekicks was Bobby Boyle, whose specialty was setting fires. There were others with such sidelines as cutting off the ears of the horses owned by the mob's opponents.

Shiner gangs set traps for the raftsmen when they hit town with their great floats of pine logs; they were waylaid, beaten, robbed, and sometimes killed in the brothels and bars and along the back alleys of Bytown. Then the Shiners would take over the rafts for delivery — and payment — downstream. This was not such a smart technique as it seemed, because from Bytown down, the Ottawa River banks were in French-Canadian hands; at suitable points the rafts were boarded and the Shiners removed, not gently.

Although his business methods were somewhat crude,

Aylen did have one legitimate complaint to make on behalf of his Irish followers; they had been denied the vote in municipal elections. On January 2, 1837, Aylen and his mob stormed into a Bytown Council meeting with a demand that the Irish be given the vote post-haste. This would have given them control of the town, and of the juicy monopolies —on flour milling, saw milling, tavern-owning, etcetera— that made such stalwarts as Nicholas Sparks and Thomas Mackey into millionaires. The demand was refused, and Aylen embarked on a four-month campaign of terror that included beatings, arson, and gang fights. Things got so bad that the local economy threatened to grind to a halt, until someone hit on the bright idea of boycotting the Shiners. They were unable to find work anywhere in the timber trade, and they began to drift away. The gang wars continued, fired by language differences, but were not so well-organized. After a final flareup, on "Stoney Monday", in 1849 (when one man was killed and thirty injured in the Ottawa rendition of the Rebellion Losses Bill Riot mentioned in Chapter 2), they began to peter out. Aylen moved across the river to his mansion on the Quebec side and there, in 1847, he tacked up the proclamation of the town of Aylmer. He founded the Aylen Academy and died, suitably saluted and much mourned, in 1868.

The story of Bytown's gang wars went virtually untold until Lucien Brault included a brief account in his history of Ottawa, published in 1945. The Irish Benevolent Society petitioned the city to stop giving away copies of Brault's book to visitors because of this unseemly reference.

This instinct to sweeten our past by retroactive editing has been given free play in Canada. We all know that the days of Prohibition were, in the U.S., days of gangland war, corruption, and killing. In Canada, we are treated instead to sly stories about the bravado and dash of rum-runners, minor heroes of a zany age. In fact, bootlegging here was accompanied by the same corruption and violence, though on a lesser scale, as in the U.S.

Perhaps our most famous bootlegger was Emilio Picariello, who operated out of Fernie, British Columbia, and delivered supplies through the Crow's Nest Pass into Alberta and south into the States. He was much admired, under two names—"Mr. Pick" and "The Emperor Pick"— but he was just a thug with a keen sense of public relations. His fleet of McLaughlin cars were equipped with cement bumpers for smashing through police barricades, but he gave to the poor at Christmas time, and served on the town council of Blairmore, Alberta, which happened to be along his delivery route. He paid off police and provincial liquor agents as a matter of course and in return was left pretty much alone. In fact, the Attorney General's department in Edmonton was in business with Picariello, selling him empty beer and whiskey bottles for use in his business. In one transaction, in May 1919, he bought 720 dozen bottles from the government for $288.

Picariello was known to carry large amounts of money with him and, one afternoon in August 1920, three other thugs, riding CPR train No. 63 along with Picariello, produced guns and robbed the train just outside Sentinel Station. They were after Mr. Pick's roll, but he managed to hide it under a seat cushion, and the men only collected $400 and some watches before escaping. Justice pursued, however, and before the case was finished, three policemen and one of the robbers had been shot and killed, another robber was hanged, and the third sentenced to seven years in prison. I guess they were fun days; maybe you had to be there.

Picariello's still was raided in 1921, and 213 barrels of contraband booze were seized. He got off with a fine of $20, and all but four of the 213 barrels were later returned to his warehouse — a court found that the booze wasn't really booze, because the alcoholic content was low. However, his immunity lapsed after the government of Alberta, hotly pursued by irate voters, moved to crack down in 1922. Mr. Pick and his son Steve were ambushed by a liquor patrol.

They fled, but Steve was eventually wounded and captured. Piciarello, who had escaped, was outraged when he heard what had happened to his boy. Accompanied by one Florence Lassandro, the twenty-two-year-old wife of one of the mob, he drove to Coleman, Alberta, to confront Steve Lawson, the policeman who had wounded Picariello *fils*. They found Lawson in front of the police barracks at Coleman. A dispute broke out, in the course of which Florence Lassandro shot and killed Lawson as he wrestled with the bootleg king. Picariello and Lassandro were hanged together on May 3, 1923, for murder.

Never mind, boys will be boys, and if we want to kid ourselves that our fathers divided their time between sipping tea and ordering up a single Mountie to quell a horde of Indians, perhaps it doesn't matter much. What does matter, however, is our quaint notion that thuggery is not a problem in modern Canada, because sweet reasonableness is built into our make-up. This twaddle has dangerous consequences; specifically, it allows us to keep gun laws on our books that are more inviting to murderers and thieves than those of most states in that turbulent nation to the south whose shortcomings fill us with such superior disdain. Violence is produced by social problems, by poverty, alienation, overcrowding, insanity, loneliness, and by other violence. The U.S. does not have a copyright on the recipe.

In Canada, the murder rate is increasing more rapidly than the population (from 1.6 per 100,000 population in 1969 to 2.4 in 1974), and more than half our murders are committed with firearms — and that proportion is increasing. There are an estimated six to nine million rifles and shotguns in the country, and God knows how many handguns, submachine guns, and other toys. The law requires registration of handguns, automatic rifles, and sawed-off shotguns, but permits over-the-counter sales of anything that can be classed as a "sporting" weapon, and mail-order sales of rifles, sights, and ammunition.

To show how simple it is to prepare for an assassination, Ontario MLA Morton Shulman, in the spring of 1975, went to a hardware store, bought a rifle, carried it into the legislature under his coat and suddenly produced it in the legislative chamber. He wrought a sensation, but no change in the law. Just the same, we keep insisting that we are gentler than the Americans, and safe from their kind of craziness.

Other people are not so easily fooled. Lulled by heart-warming stories of U.S. students travelling in Europe who borrow Maple Leaves to stick on their haversacks — thus making hitchhiking easier — we see ourselves as loved for our gentleness among foreigners. Not so. Abroad, we have always been seen as a fairly violent bunch; indeed, in wartime, when such things become compliments, we took pride in the toughness of our reputation. In World War I, Lloyd George called the Canadian Corps "storm troopers", and acknowledged that, after the Battle of the Somme in 1916, "they were brought along to head the assault in one great battle after another."

But martial fervour can have its dark side, too. In *Goodbye To All That*, his memoir of World War I, Robert Graves noted: "The troops with the worst reputation for acts of violence against prisoners were the Canadians (and later the Australians)." And several of the old sweats who populate the pages of Barry Broadfoot's *Six War Years* detail Canadian war atrocities that sound much like those of other, lesser breeds. We don't discuss these things in front of strangers, as a rule, but our boys in uniform are just like any other boys.

The one area in which we acknowledge (and take perverse pride in) a reputation for toughness is hockey. Remember the old Penticton V's? Or Team Mayhem, and its visits to Russia? There is a nice irony in the fact that Canada, gentle Canada, has as its national sport a pastime in which violence *outside the rules* is an accepted part of the game. Every hockey team worth its salt has one or two, or three or four, players who have only a nodding acquaintance with the skills of the sport, and none at all with the concept of sportsmanship. Their job is to skate up and down the ice and clobber people on demand. For this they are rewarded with large salaries and public adulation. They are a breed apart — somewhere between Killer Kane and *Pithecanthropus erectus*. We love 'em.

And how, loving them, can we at the same time deny them, pretend that they don't exist? It's done with mirrors, like the disappearing act in a magic show. Like the disappearing act, come to think of it, managed on behalf of that gentle body, Hal Banks.

Banks was the waterfront warlord brought in—with the aid and collusion of the Canadian government and the Canadian labour movement — to clear the Great Lakes' shipping industry of communists. He arrived across the border in 1949, complete with a long prison record that included a fourteen-year sentence to San Quentin (he only served three-and-a-half years). He established a reign of terror on the lakes, a reign marked by the blacklisting of anyone who dared to oppose him, and the beating of opponents and potential rivals. For years, he was well received in Canada; the shipping companies co-operated with him and the government left him to his own devices. In return, Banks always sent his thugs out to help Liberal candidates at election time, and contributed money from union coffers.

There were a few folks, however, who resented his tactics, and were churlish enough to hold his prison record against him. In 1954, a deportation order was obtained on the basis of that record, and went to the desk of the Minister of Immigration, Walter Harris, with the departmental recommendation that it should be carried out forthwith. Harris reversed the department's ruling, and the reign of terror went on. It was not interrupted until inter-union squabbles and a battle with one shipping line brought Great Lakes traffic virtually to a halt in 1962. The federal government then set up an industrial inquiry commission — the Norris Commission — which produced a report documenting years of brutality, intimidation, and corruption. Banks was eventually convicted of perjury and sentenced to five years in jail, but somehow his bail was set at only $25,000, and he simply fled to the U.S., where he remains, unmolested.

In the fall of 1974, new accusations were levelled at Banks' old group, the Seafarers' International Union, alleging that intimidation and blacklisting were once more part of its tactics, that it was being sheltered by federal politicians, that it had played an active role in the last election. The Liberal administration, after an internal investigation whose methods and evidence were never unfolded to the rude public gaze, announced that the charges were unfounded, and that all was well on the waterfront.

What to make of all this? Well, for one thing, that it is sometimes hard to move against crime in this country because of our inborn belief that we are not a people prone to violence. There may be thuggery in Detroit, in Chicago, in New York, but not here.

A fifty-seven-year-old man is sitting on a bench in a downtown park. A stranger approaches and asks the time; he is told. He asks for a cigarette; the man says he has none. The stranger then smashes him in the face, breaking his cheekbone, and walks away. Detroit, 1967? No, Toronto, 1970.

A man decides he is tired of his wife; besides, he has a mistress. So he puts a life insurance policy worth $200,000 on her, then slips a bomb aboard the plane she is about to board. The plane explodes in mid-air, and twenty-three people die. John Dillinger, Chicago? No, Albert Guay, Quebec City, 1949.

In the lonely, picturesque countryside outside a small prairie town, a farmhand takes up a rifle and kills nine members of the family he works for, from a man of forty-seven to a baby of two. No, not Kansas, not *In Cold Blood*, but Shell Lake, Saskatchewan, where no one even locks the doors at night, in 1967. Not far away, at Buffalo Narrows, two years later, a nineteen-year-old Métis labourer hacks seven people to death with an axe.

One Friday evening, six members of a motorcycle gang called "The Atoms" swagger into a beerhall and begin a fight with members of a rival gang, called "The Gypsies". The brawl spills out into the parking lot, where two men, one from each gang, are stabbed. They are taken to hospital and there, a few hours later, members of both gangs turn up with knives, chains, and clubs. The fight starts again and another "Atom" is badly wounded, but the hospital staff manage to barricade the doors and the fight drifts off. Still later, the gangs have at each other again, outside police headquarters; one man has his face shot off at point-blank range, another is killed by a blast in the chest. And once again, no, not in Harlem, but in the bustling little city of Sherbrooke, Quebec, in 1974.

We feel a superior sort of horror when we read about the twisted vengefulness and bitterness evident on both sides in Northern Ireland. But in Windsor, Ontario, Leonard Craig, 23, was beaten and kicked to death in 1973, and William Hulko, leader of the "Satan's Choice" motorcycle club pleaded guilty to a charge of manslaughter. A few days after the charge was laid, Hulko's wife, Cathryn, eighteen, and a sixteen-year-old girlfriend, disappeared. They were found in a ditch five months later; they had been shot six times each in the eyes, mouth, and head.

And so it goes. A Quebec probe into violence in the construction industry during late 1974 and early 1975 turned up case after case of beatings and intimidation. It also discovered such refinements as "loan-sharking" with the interest set as high as 1,000 per cent, where the penalty for non-payment was collected by thugs with boots and clubs. Captain Henri Marchessault of the Montreal police testified that the average loan shark cleared, one million dollars a year. The inquiry chairman commented that corruption seemed as basic to the construction industry as the nail, and the province's Labour Minister remarked that Quebec "could not control" lawlessness in the industry. He spoke truly; the provincial police compiled a list of 551 illegal "incidents" on Quebec construction sites, of which 25 resulted in criminal convictions.

This stuff gave Ontario citizens a moment of quiet superiority, but only a moment; within weeks, details of Ontario construction crime—featuring home-made bombs —were unrolling before a similar commission in that province.

My point is not that Canadian construction workers are any more prone to brutality than their opposite numbers in New York. Rather, as always, my point is that we are brothers to the world, and like the rest of the world, we react violently, oppressively, brutally in the same situations as other people. Mass murderer Richard Blass was made a hero in Montreal in exactly the same way and by exactly the same kind of people who immortalized Bonnie and Clyde. Mugging and purse-snatching are replacing girl-watching among the sports of downtown Vancouver, Toronto, and Montreal for the same reasons that they blossomed in Chicago and Detroit. The difference in our crime rates from U.S. statistics — and we are still substantially below our American cousins in such refinements as rape, robbery, murder, and assorted mayhem on both a total and per-capita basis—reflects not our sweeter nature, but lesser pressures. And we seem intent on closing the gap by throwing up cities as large, as crowded, and as hostile as theirs.

I have no solution to all this; I merely think it would be useful if we could stop kidding ourselves that we can escape the consequences of our present urban development because we are the gentle elect of God.

CHAPTER 8:
TOLERANT US

There is a sense of quiet pride which lies deep within many
Canadians, a feeling which permits us, as we contemplate the
future of our country, to savour those qualities of self-reliance and
tolerance, of moderation and bonhomie which are so abundant
here.

Prime Minister Trudeau, 1970.

For the June 1975 issue of *Maclean's* magazine, I wrote a
little essay about Quebec. In it, I said that I was prepared to
concede on the language issue, that I was tired of fighting
about it, that I thought Quebeckers might very well decide
to set up in business for themselves as a separate state—as
long as they were suitably sneaky about it, and avoided
direct confrontations — and that I wished them well. I
pointed out, what I thought everyone knew, that French
Canadians are no more tolerant than the rest of us on the
language issue, and noted that while I sympathized with
them in their need to defend their language and culture, I
didn't think I was doing them, or me, a bit of good by
batting my brains out trying to speak bad French in the
hope that it would improve national relations. I said that I
proposed to treat Quebec as if it were a nation not my own,
and that I proposed to speak French there only to people
whose English was even worse than my French.

The response to that article was, frankly, horrifying.
From the corporate bowels of Maclean-Hunter there came a
cry of alarm and revulsion, and a bitter attack on me for
daring to raise the language issue. I was stoutly defended
by my superiors, and the din died. But then the letters
began to pour in; some of them were thoughtful and intelli-

gent, whether they agreed with my thesis or rejected it, but most of them were appalling. Out of all that I had written, my readers—most of them—had grasped only the fact that I had commented on the rudeness with which Quebec yahoos, like yahoos everywhere, treat minorities. They read my whimsical—I thought—declaration of a separate peace with Quebec as an attack on French Canadians, and they rose, cheering, to give me the most stunning and misplaced burst of applause of my career. One letter, shorter and pithier than the others, but a fair summary of their tone, read simply: "You say 'Fuck the French', and I say, 'Right on, Man'." After a time, I gave up trying to answer these letters, and simply burned them.

The exercise made me ponder furiously on the futility of literature—though not furiously enough to give up. It also gave me a frightening insight into the amount of intolerance that still snaps at our heels, 108 years after we were plastered together as a single nation.

The notion that we are a tolerant people is buried deep in the bone of every native-born Canadian; we are weaned on descriptions of our adaptability and flexibility; our adult ears droop with the constant dunning of after-dinner speakers affirming that our ability to get along with each other is one of the miracles of the modern world, and an example to other less marvellous nations. In reality, such tolerance as we have shown has been, in large measure, imposed, first by the British, who were our masters and designed the rules, and later by the exigencies of Canadian survival. The only real miracle of Canada's togetherness is that we have not yet torn each other limb from limb, and I am beginning to believe the size of the country is responsible, rather than its sweetness. There has always been plenty of room to dodge.

Certainly our leaders have been tolerant, at least in public; they have worked hard to foster understanding and sow goodwill. In part, that was because you couldn't rule this pasted-together nation without support from its two major groups, and in part, I like to believe, because politicians tend to be more tolerant, informed, and far-sighted people than the rest of us. But this mutual hushing of the underlying bellows of bigotry, the usual exchanges of bilingual compliments in tortured language, have mostly been conducted at the summit. The people have been left out of it, and they are still left out of it.

Racial suspicion and language intolerance are as pronounced today (perhaps more pronounced) as they were in 1867, and neither legislation nor language courses, neither executive fiat nor letters to the editor, has softened the harsh edge of our discontent with each other. Many of us, kindly and intelligent people, believe that the answer is more of the same, more courses, more speeches, more regulations, more adjustments to the fine-tuning of the civil service act, and that all this will somehow, someday, appeal to our finer natures and send our children forth into the world, bilingual and benign. I sincerely wish these people well, but I wonder about their grasp of history.

Consider for a moment where we came from, how we got where we are, where we seem to be going. When Canada came into British hands after the Seven Years' War, the mother country was quick to offer guarantees of language and religious freedom to the defeated French. The Articles of Capitulation in 1760 promised that "the free exercise of the Catholic, Apostolic and Roman religion, shall subsist entire". This gesture had nothing to do with tolerance. The British had pronounced on the subject of tolerance in 1755, with their ham-handed and brutal expulsion of the Acadians from the area around Grand Pré, Nova Scotia, where families were torn asunder, wives and husbands, fathers and sons shipped to remote outposts thousands of miles apart. The British were as ready as any other people to put down subjects of the wrong race, religion, or language, as their history showed. But in 1760 the conquerors believed that the northern half of North America would always be peopled by "the French race", and the practical way to keep them under control was to keep them, in turn, under the wing of the French and Catholic Church.

It was a question of ruling, and ruling without tying up half the British army, and a question of providing a buffer in case those fractious fellows in the thirteen English-speaking colonies to the south, should get out of hand—as they did in 1776. The Quebec Act of 1774, which the Americans were to consider (quite rightly) as a calculated rebuff, reaffirmed the intention of the Articles of Capitulation. It gave Roman Catholics the right to hold office, and priests the right to collect tithes, and it gave Quebec French civil law (with British criminal law thrown in, to placate the unquiet British minority). The act succeeded in calming the early anxieties of the French; it did not persuade them to take up arms against the revolting Yankees, but it did keep them from accepting the invitation to be liberated from British domination and to join in the great American experiment, with its dangerous democratic notions.

After the Revolution came the Loyalists, thousands and thousands of them. In a twenty-five year span we were transformed from a French and European colony into a dual North American state. Two new English provinces — New Brunswick and Upper Canada — sprang into being, and so did serious racial and religious problems. There were also battles within the English and Protestant sector of the country that were to prove crucial. The Constitutional Act of 1791, the act that split Canada into upper and lower berths, set aside an area, equal to one-seventh of all the lands granted to settlers in both provinces, for the support of the Protestant clergy. French Catholics weren't ecstatic about this, but nobody asked them; Lower Canada (Quebec) was managed by an appointed governor and council. English Protestants settled down to squabbling over the Clergy Reserves. The word "Protestant" was equated with "Church of England", and the Anglicans gleefully hogged all the land to themselves. Battles over the Reserves continued until 1854, when they were secularized and the proceeds given to the municipalities. These battles prevented the English from getting together to lambaste the French; internecine strife explained more than good-heartedness about the survival of their rights.

The domination of Montreal by English merchants was fiercely resented by the French, but not half so much as our side resented the Catholic penchant for turning out babies — the *revanche de berceau* by which the French would right the wrongs of the Plains of Abraham. (It has been one of the longest, dumbest exercises of our national life, this constant adversion to the Plains of Abraham; every time a French Canadian makes a rude gesture, an English Canadian somewhere wants to know who won in 1759, anyway; every time a cultural issue pops up, a French Canadian somewhere sighs, "*Je me souviens*".) Between 1783 and 1812, the population of Lower Canada trebled, to 330,000; in 1812, Upper Canada's population was a meagre 90,000. Therefore, when the two provinces were joined together by the Act of Union in 1841, great care was taken to see that Canada West—the old Upper—and Canada East—the old Lower — were given equal power in the joint legislature. Representation by population — sacred phrase — would have given the French control, and we were not to have that.

Indeed, as Radical Jack Durham, whose Report laid down the basis for the union, made clear, the whole idea was to join the two races, wipe out the barriers and assimilate the French:

> There can hardly be conceived a nationality more destitute of all that can invigorate and elevate a people than that which is exhibited by the descendants of the French in Lower Canada, owing to their retaining their

peculiar language and manners. They are a people with no history and no literature.

The way to calm these funny folk was to take away their "peculiar language":

> I expected to find a contest between a government and a people: I found two nations warring in the bosom of a single state: I found a struggle, not of principles, but of races; and I perceived that it would be idle to attempt any amelioration of laws or institutions until we could first succeed in terminating the deadly animosity that now separates the inhabitants of Lower Canada into the hostile divisions of French and English.

Accordingly, English was made the sole language of the joint legislature, and for eight years it remained so. We were going to talk those blaggy Frenchmen into submission. It should have been easy; with the English in charge of Canada West and a strong, officially-favoured minority in Canada East, we could do pretty much as we chose. What we chose, as already noted, was to fight among ourselves. Canada East voted *en bloc* and so did Canada West; the result was deadlock; government business came to a virtual standstill. Now, as the population in English Canada rose —more through immigration than the cradle—to pass that of French Canada, the cry went up for "Rep by Pop". Democracy was in vogue, but of course nothing could be done without the consent of both provinces, and nothing was done.

Confederation, when it came, was as much a ploy to get around the legislative deadlock by drowning the French in a broader union as it was a reaching for nationhood. The *Kingston Daily News* of April 13, 1864, noted: "The Union has been the saviour of the Franco-Canadian nationality in Lower Canada, but Upper Canadians are not prepared to endure the cross any longer." The solution would lie in the

135

formation of "an Anglo-American union, in which Canada and the embryo provinces to the west of us shall gain admission". The *Newmarket Era* was even blunter: "The coalition, backed by the Lower Canada majority [has] forced upon the West laws and institutions obnoxious to the people . . . . Lower Canada is still determined to maintain her power to domineer . . . . [Confederation] would accomplish the removal of the political evils to which Upper Canada is subjected."

And the new nation remained riven by questions of language, religion, and race. We have stopped using "race" to signify the difference between English and French, but it was the normal designation of our forefathers; when they referred to the "racial" question, they did not mean blacks invading an Alabama soda fountain, they meant the ongoing language battle.

The Riel Rebellion of 1885, which began with the attempt to defend western territories against the invading railwaymen, was exacerbated by memories of Riel's execution of Thomas Scott (an Ontarian who was English and an Orangeman) in the 1870 Rebellion. Riel was found guilty of high treason by an English jury; the same jury exonerated his English-speaking colleague, William Jackson, on the plea of insanity, although there was far more evidence of insanity in Riel's case than Jackson's. The verdict split the nation—as so often—into two camps: Quebec and the rest. Wilfrid Laurier, already recognized as the federal Liberal leader in Quebec, contended, "Had I been born on the banks of the Saskatchewan I would myself have shouldered a musket to fight against the neglect of governments and the shameless greed of speculators." In English, Protestant Ontario, the Toronto *News* was screaming, "Strangle Riel with the French flag! That is the only use that rag can have in this country." Sir John A. Macdonald, the public apostle of moderation, voiced his private thoughts quite differently; on the eve of Riel's execution, he wrote,

"He shall hang though every dog in Quebec bark in his favour."

Riel was gone but not forgotten, and religious and language strife when on. Honoré Mercier was swept to power in Quebec mainly on the strength of anti-English feeling provoked by the hanging. In 1887, the Mercier government passed a bill to incorporate the Society of Jesus, the militantly evangelical Catholic society that had previously been banned; soon after, another law was passed to compensate the Jesuits for property that had passed into the hands of the province on Confederation. Ontario was apoplectic, and demanded that the federal government disallow the Quebec legislation. D'Alton McCarthy, a Toronto lawyer and MP for North Simcoe, told a shouting, cheering meeting in Toronto, "Do you realize that if Canada is to be a nation we must stop French aggression? Do you know that, tracing history from the time of Lord Durham, who wanted the country to assimilate, that the French have been becoming more and more French? They are opposed to national unity and are determined not to become British subjects." McCarthy organized an "Equal Rights Association" whose apparent aim was to see that the French had no rights at all; he called on English Canadians to "take in hand our French-Canadian fellow subjects and make them British in sentiment and teach them the English language."

All this went down well outside Quebec. *Saturday Night*, that mouthpiece of British pluck, said it all: "Why beat about the bush? What are we here for? Why did Wolfe take the trouble to fight with Montcalm? Was it not to conquer Canada? Was it not to make the Anglo-Saxon supreme?"

Macdonald refused to disallow Mercier's legislation; such an act would have created more problems than it solved. In time, that crisis solved itself, as so many did under Macdonald's policy of benign neglect, but neither he nor time could straighten out the Manitoba Schools Question.

137

When the province of Manitoba was created in 1870, with a French-speaking majority, its school system was modelled on that of Quebec, with separate, and equally-supported, Protestant and Catholic school systems. As more and more English-speaking settlers poured into Manitoba, the English became predominant, and the cry went up for "national" — that is, public and English — schools. D'Alton McCarthy arrived on the scene from Ontario to help the cause along with inflammatory speeches about the French — "this bastard nationality" — and the Roman Catholic faith—"which now threatens the dismemberment of Canada".

The campaign succeeded, and in 1890, Manitoba passed laws to abolish denominational schools and the use of the French language in teaching. Quebec Catholics, who had been zealous in their defence of provincial rights when the English were screaming for disallowance of Mercier's legislation, now demanded that Ottawa should throw out the Manitoba law. The federal Conservatives, banking on precedent, simply stalled, and when they were defeated in 1896, the problem was dumped in the lap of Wilfrid Laurier, who, exerting his famous "sunny ways" to the full, reached a compromise with Manitoba. Roman Catholics were given limited school support, and it was agreed that, at any school where ten or more children spoke a language other than English, instruction must be given in their mother tongue. This solution created new problems; as immigrants came flooding into the province, they could make the same claim for Ukrainian or Polish or German as the locals could for French. Manitoba threatened to turn into a tower of Babel. In 1916, Laurier's compromise dissolved, and English became the official and only language of instruction in Manitoba schools. It remained that way until, in recent years, French was allowed to creep back into the curriculum; today, language rights are as fiercely debated, and as unresolved, in Manitoba as they were in the 1890s.

In fact, the joined problems of language, religion, and schooling have never been solved anywhere in Canada where there was a strong enough minority to kick up a fuss.

Ontario was riven by the bilingual schools issue throughout the first two decades of this century. There were two curious aspects to this on-going battle. One was that many of the bitterest clashes came between members of the same religious group. Irish Catholics were afraid their schools would be taken over and Frenchified, and French Catholics were afraid they wouldn't. In some areas of eastern Ontario, particularly in Ottawa, the issue was sorted out in pitched battles on the street. (We once had a babysitter in Ottawa who had married a French Canadian. Both were devout Catholics. She described how, in 1917, she used to kiss him goodbye at the door, then hustle off down to the school to join a mob harassing French nuns who were being brought in to teach in Irish schools. Then she would pop around to the church to confess for belting a nun with her purse; then she would dash home to prepare lunch for her husband. She had a French name but an Irish tongue, and when she vilified "them Frogs" on one occasion, a neighbour complained that she hardly expected such language from someone with such a name. She retorted primly, "Kittens can be born in an oven, but that don't make them tea-biscuits.")

The other curious aspect of the language hassles was that, as Professor Marilyn Barber points out in *The Ontario Bilingual Schools Issue*: "The French Canadians of Ontario were not simply responding to attack or to fear of attack; conscious of their increasing strength, they were taking the initiative. Their intention was not to *defend* their rights, but to *extend* their rights [emphasis in original]."

On the one side, there was the shrieking of the Orange newspaper, *The Sentinel*: "It is admirable to deal generously with the conquered race. But is it not fatal to grant them concessions which threaten the stability of our institutions?

... What is intended by this movement [to secure bilingual schools] is to strike at the integrity of the Empire." On the other was the drum-banging of *Le Moniteur*, a French-language weekly published in Hawkesbury, Ontario: "Stand together, put party interests to one side and march ahead for the triumph of our nationality . . . in union there is strength!"

In Quebec, English farmers in the Eastern Townships found that the only schools available were run by Catholics and for Catholics. Most of the farmers were Protestants, and they could either see their children raised in what they considered to be a poisoned atmosphere, or move out. Many moved out, and their plight was extravagantly detailed in a book called *The Tragedy of Quebec*, by Robert Sellar, the Presbyterian editor of the *Huntingdon Gleaner*. In 1907 Sellar wrote: "The text-books are Catholic, the whole atmosphere of the school is Catholic. The farmer cannot in conscience send his little ones to it, and so the French Canadian, who has been wanting his farm, gets it, and a week after he is in possession a priest comes to see the new acquisition of his church."

Having seen what damage could be wrought by bigotry, the English Protestants might have argued for the virtues of tolerant acceptance. They did not. In Ontario, said the *Sentinel*, the French Canadian was welcome only if he would "co-operate in the upbuilding of the Anglo-Saxon community". Fat chance. The *Sentinel* knew the sneaky French would never let go their peculiar language: "It is this refusal to assimilate that makes the French so difficult to get along with."

What was abominable about the French was their Frenchness, for which they refused to take the cure, so the battle dragged on. Bilingualism dominated the Ontario elections of 1905 and 1908, which saw the Conservatives swept to power. In 1970, when William Davis swept to power, the issue was still up to bat, still swinging lustily at any passing head. In 1910, there were pitched battles on the issue in Ottawa and Hawkesbury; in 1972, re-runs were playing at the high-school in Cornwall.

In other provinces, where the minority was not so strong, there were fewer problems. The Catholic menace was beaten back in British Columbia before the lapse of the old century; laws forbidding the teaching of French were in place on the prairies for the first three decades of the new. (One of John Diefenbaker's celebrated early law cases was his successful defence of a Saskatchewan woman charged with the heinous crime of teaching French past Grade One.) The substantial French minority in New Brunswick presented some difficulties, but they were mainly a poor, bruised lot, gratefully accepting the ascendancy of the Anglo-Saxon until well into the 1960s. As soon as they found that they could assert themselves, they did, and the result has been a backlash that in recent years has made Moncton — the heartland of Acadian discontent — a new racial battleground. In the 1974 federal election former Moncton mayor Leonard Jones was elected as an Independent almost solely on the basis of his opposition to bilingualism.

In times of crisis — reputedly those testing times that draw people together — our unhealed racial wounds rub raw again. The French wanted nothing to do with the Boer War, which they regarded as a noxious British Imperialist venture (quite right, too). Asked to contribute money and bodies, they made rude, Anglo-Saxon-sounding noises. When Laurier bowed to his English supporters and sent a Canadian contingent, Henri Bourassa, the fiery Quebec nationalist, resigned from the Liberal party, and shafted his leader with a reference to British traditions: "The principle at stake is that prize axiom of English liberalism: No Taxation Without Representation. And the tax in blood constitutes the heaviest form of public contribution."

At least the French were not conscripted in the Boer War;

when they were, in World Wars I and II, they protested, with words, with riots, with desertions.

Soon after Prime Minister Robert Borden announced his intention to introduce conscription legislation in May 1917, rioting broke out in Montreal and Quebec City. A Montreal mob descended on the offices of the newspaper *La Patrie*, smashing up the joint and shouting rude slogans — the most printable of which was "Down with Conscription". Two Quebec newspapers were attacked, as well. Meetings, disturbances, fistfights, and occasional riots marked the festivities for months until, on August 9, 1917, a group of conspirators dynamited the home of Lord Atholstan, whose newspaper, the Montreal *Star,* stood four-square for conscription (literary criticism, in our fathers' day, took the form of direct action). No one was hurt, but a reaction set in, and a tough line—what we would call a law-and-order line—was taken against the conscription critics after that. Calm was gradually restored. Not all the anti-conscription forces were French — an angry mob of English-speaking farmers marched on Ottawa when promises to exempt farm youths from selective service were broken—but most of them were, and the battlelines were generally drawn on racial grounds. Bourassa, once more, spoke for his people more forcefully than Laurier: "Those who have undertaken to bleed Canada white to uphold the forces of England and France in Europe tell us occasionally that our first line of defence is in Flanders. I say that our first line of defence is at Ottawa."

During World War II, those conscripts in the armed forces who would not volunteer for active service overseas — not all, but most of them Quebeckers — were called "Zombies", and they were spat at, slugged, handed white feathers, and treated to all the other acts of kindness we direct to people simple-minded enough to object to the organized slaughter of war. On the other side, as Barry Broadfoot's *Six War Years* made clear, sailors in the Canadian navy who were trying to keep the St. Lawrence clear of German subs couldn't go ashore in Quebec City except in a bunch. Otherwise they'd get beaten up (one guy had an eye kicked out), spat on, and generally treated like enemy troops.

In 1944, when the nation was seventy-seven years old, Mackenzie King was hailed as the wizard of his age because he kept us from splitting into our component parts on the subject of who our enemy was, and whether he deserved our attention. King had given a pledge not to enforce conscription, but he tore that up and put the matter to a vote. Quebec voted overwhelmingly against conscription, but lost, because the rest of Canada voted overwhelmingly in favour. Then, when attempts were made to move the Zombies out of their camp at Terrace, B.C., they mutinied, took over the camp, and turned their cannon (they were artillery-men) on the trains lined up to carry them off to war. (There was no fault to be found with the courage of the Zombies; apparently, it was sense of direction that was wanting.) A bloody battle was averted by the sneaky decision to give everybody leave, and the mutineers downed arms and went home. When they returned to camp, they were rounded up and sent off to fight. This time, they went.

Terrace is the most famous of these "incidents" but there were many others during the war, all hushed up by the censors — who also hushed up the fact that some Zombies were prodded aboard the ships at gunpoint, or lashed up the gangplank with bullwhips.

It seems to me that if two groups of people cannot decide whether they would rather fight somebody else or each other, they lack something in the way of brotherly love. I am suggesting that, far from showing tolerant acceptance of each other, Canada's *peuples fondateurs* have always swung between outright hostility and bare civility. Had French language rights not been written into Section 133 of the British North America Act, I am willing to bet they would not have survived for two decades. It is surely significant that, with all the applesauce dished out about a century of love during Canada's centennial in 1967, no one saw fit to point out that, in no province except Quebec was there a complete tax-supported school system in both languages.

Was this because French Canadians are more tolerant? No, because they were weaker; until the late 1960s, it was the English who called the shots in Quebec. The Royal Commission on Bilingualism and Biculturalism set up by Prime Minister Lester Pearson reported that the English held power — both political and economic — out of all proportion to their numbers. They kept their rights because they had the strength to protect them. And, as soon as that strength began to fade with the transfer of power to the French majority, those rights came under attack.

French Canadians saw clearly that if immigrants to the province continued to be absorbed into the English language group—as over ninety per cent of them were doing in the 1960s—they would soon be a minority in their own province. The *revanche de berceau* had given way to the safety of the pill, so that was out. What to do? In the Montreal suburb of St. Leonard, the council attempted the gradual elimination of English in the schools; that led to street protests, legislative demonstrations, and riots. New legislation was passed, strengthening the French language, but still guaranteeing the rights of parents to choose English for their children. It was not enough and, in 1974, the National Assembly passed Bill 22, a law directing Quebec immigrants firmly into the French system and making the province, in Premier Robert Bourassa's words, "an officially francophone state".

I have no quarrel with Bill 22—were I a French Canadian, I'd have been up in Quebec City protesting that its provisions were not stringent enough, and making rude gestures at the appalled Anglos—but it should be recognized for what it is, a frankly discriminatory piece of legislation. It turns its back on 200 years of enforced language equality in Quebec and puts that province on a footing with every other Canadian province (except, just recently, New Brunswick). That is to say, in Quebec, as elsewhere, tolerance and equality are on everyone's lips, but the school system, and language matters generally, are firmly in the hands of the majority.

The only difference between earlier racial conflicts and the Bill 22 battle—which continues as I write this in the fall of 1975—is that the group singled out for discrimination, Quebec Anglophones and what Montrealers call "the Allophones", are well-entrenched, well-heeled, and able to fight back. Legal and political battles, marches and counter-marches, brought refinements and new interpretations of the legislation, which was already full of more twists than a snake-farm.

In embattled St. Leonard, a largely Italian suburb of Montreal, children swarmed to take advantage of a regulation that promised English schooling for anyone who could pass an English comprehension test, only to run afoul of another regulation setting quotas for the overall English school population in the area. In all, 187 children who passed the test that entitled them to enrollment in an English school were shunted off to French schools; their parents raised hell in two official languages and Italian. Jerome Choquette, then the Education Minister, tried to take a stand on common sense; he said that the children of persons whose mother tongue was English should be enrolled in English schools, and all others in French (the rough rule, in reverse, in other provinces). But the Quebec cabinet, which had been tacking back and forth since Bill 22 first passed, balked at this, and Choquette resigned. Meanwhile, Anglo-Quebeckers are drifting into a seige mentality, but nothing is being solved.

Canadian history is not trickling down to a triumph of

harmony; it is turning into a Mexican standoff. We have not been able to get along without French Canada, nor French Canada without us. When it finally dawns on Quebec that the rules are now changed, that they can, indeed, go their own way as long as the break is not so abrupt as to rouse our martial fervour, you won't see their tails for dust.

The great French-English debate, which our leaders have announced with clocklike regularity over the past century as being just about to come to an end, is about to be joined again. We will not be helped, in the coming festivities, if we cling to the notion that, at bottom, we are full of the juice of human kindliness as we look across the language barrier. However we sort out our future relations, it will be helpful to recognize that our past relations have normally been rocky, that the tolerance and bonhomie so readily spotted by some of our political prophets have been rare and precious indeed, and should not figure too largely in our expectations. We will be better served, in the negotiations to come, if we forget about quiet pride in our tolerance and concentrate on the fact that the average French Canadian—just as in Lord Durham's day—would not take all the rest of this broad land wrapped up in a pink ribbon in exchange for his "peculiar language and manners".

CHAPTER 9:

OUR COPS ARE COPS

What is more indicative of the health and progress of a country than the style of its laws, the manner in which they are observed and — this is where we come in — the manner in which they are enforced?

L.H. Nicholson, Commissioner,
RCMP, 1953.

One night during the winter of 1953, I was sitting in the press room of police headquarters on College Street in Toronto. It was a quiet night and, about 2 a.m., I turned down the police radio, which had carried nothing but routine reports for half an hour, put up my feet, leaned back, and started to snooze. I could not have been dozing for more than a few minutes when I was brought bolt upright by the sound of a man screaming. It was high-pitched, a scream of agony, drawn out, then ending suddenly in a gasp. There was silence for a moment, then angry voices, a terrible, dull, thudding sound, like something striking flesh, and another scream. The sounds appeared to come from upstairs, where the police conducted interrogations. I scrambled out of my seat and ran down the hall to the duty office, where a sergeant and a constable were working over the night information sheets.

"What the hell's going on?" I blurted.

The sergeant, a middle-aged, friendly type, looked up. "Nothing," he said. "It's a quiet night. Go back to sleep."

"Quiet be damned, somebody's getting the hell beaten out of him!"

The sergeant looked up again. "Nothing to worry about, kid," he said. Just then there was another cry, then a series of racking sobs. For some reason that sound, a grown man's crying, upset and frightened me more than the screams. "Sergeant," I said, "for Christ's sake, do something!"

"I don't hear a thing, kid," the sergeant said. "Do you hear anything, Constable?"

The constable said he didn't hear anything. I went back to the press room and, eventually, the sounds stopped. I guess the guy confessed.

I have always had a high regard for Toronto police, for Canadian police in general. Certainly there are occasional maniacs on the force—one cop on the morality squad used to show me his illegal blackjack, and tell me what he did to prostitutes with it; I believed him, too. But usually these sadists are found out, as that one was, and thrown off the force. There are crooks, too, like the gang that operated in North York during the 1950s; they were a ring of police thieves, and every time one of their number discovered a break-and-enter during his routine patrols, the gang would converge on the spot and clear out everything of value the original thieves had left behind, before reporting the break-in. They obviously felt that anything worth doing was worth doing well. They were caught, too. But in the day-to-day operations of their department, most of the police I know—in Toronto, in Dartmouth, Regina, in RCMP outposts scattered across the north — are decent, hard-working men who try to do a reasonable job under difficult conditions.

But they are cops, and they carry into their work a set of preconceptions that have nothing to do with the regulations laid down in official orders. For instance, people who wear nice clothes, drive big cars, and carry themselves with confidence should be treated with deference, while those with long hair and scruffy clothes may be pushed around with impunity. For instance, that Indians, blacks, and foreigners are trouble-makers. (On many forces, normal police lingo for long-haired boys is "pukes"; blacks are "spear-chuckers"; Indians are Indians, the name itself is considered insult enough.) And, for instance, that the general run of mankind is beneath contempt.

There is something about police work that gets in under the hide and rasps the soul like sandpaper. Year after year of studying the aberrations of others, of chasing and catching crooks only to see them get off on a technicality, of facing the indifference and even hostility of the general populace — that does something, after a while, to most cops. I once spent some time patrolling with two officers in the area near Harbord Collegiate in downtown Toronto, a near-ghetto of blacks and immigrants. One officer wore a uniform, the other did not; the uniformed cop was often shouted at, sometimes spat after, as we walked through crowded areas. That gets to you.

I know very few cops who have been in the business more than ten or fifteen years who have not become either burningly bitter or slyly cynical. They believe that every man's hand is set against them, that most people hate each other, that, but for the restraints of officialdom, the rest of us would turn and rend each other — and, based on our experience with police strikes in Montreal and Dartmouth, they may be right. They believe that the world contains no innocents, only uncaught crooks. There are exceptions, of course, but they are rare. I know what is meant by the phrase "cop mentality"; it exists, and it worries me.

Elsewhere in this book you will find references to the use of police as strike-breakers, as political snoops, as the provocateurs of riots. Those actions come, I believe, from the conscious manipulation of the police by the political process. We object when the process goes too far, when the riot gets out of hand, or the wrong people get beaten up in a strike, but mostly we approve. "Canadians are not a cruel people," says Alan Borovoy, general counsel for the Canadian Civil Liberties Association. "We don't ban parades,

149

we re-route them." The police may be improperly used—they often are—but they act with the tacit consent of the populace.

What I am talking about as the cop mentality, however, is something else again. When our police are brutal, when they abuse ordinary individuals, when they set aside time-honoured rights, then we are offended. It is the thesis of this book that Canadians don't mind a little oppression, on the theory that it is always someone else who is likely to be oppressed—some freaky Frenchman or Jehovah's Witness or Indian—but we do resent the cop mentality. When the Toronto newspapers launched a series of articles in the fall of 1974 alleging police mistreatment of ordinary citizens, the city worked itself into a froth. A commission was appointed, and it discovered, indeed, some instances of police brutality; much more often, however, it found that the charges were unproveable, highly exaggerated, or downright false. The quick intensity of the reaction to the furore was interesting; it shows that we draw a clean line between, say, swooping on Quebeckers in the middle of the night on political charges—which is apparently acceptable—and cursing out a middle-aged Calgary man who has been drinking and driving—which is not.

During the Toronto investigation, a number of citizens sprouted lapel badges that said "Our Cops Are Tops"; in most cases, this didn't mean that the wearers approved of police beating suspects, it was a rejection of the notion that they did, or could, or would. (In Barry Broadfoot's *Six War Years*, a number of Canadian veterans of World War II noted that when they returned home and calmly mentioned that Canadian soldiers, like other soldiers, had shot prisoners when they became a nuisance to guard, they met instant rejection. Their listeners simply would not, could not, believe that our boys would do such things.) Similarly, we expect a lot of our police, and when they go berserk we are shocked and offended. Our expectations, as I see them, cover four main points: we expect the police to obey the law themselves; we expect them to treat people with a measure of equality; we expect them not to use unnecessary force, even if provoked; and we expect them to accept the underlying assumption of our system of justice, that an accused is innocent until proven guilty.

We expect our police to be square, aware, and fair. These are high, but fair, expectations for modern, well-trained police. How do they measure up? No one knows for sure. Our police forces, led by the RCMP, are incredibly secretive, incredibly sensitive to criticism. (I once had a long, drawn-out battle with the RCMP headquarters in Regina over an article which they had seen before publication, and which contained the word "cop". They thought it was an offensive word, and I did not.) In almost every instance of alleged police misbehaviour, the investigation is carried out by the police department itself, often by comrades of the officers named. This saves the bother of calling in strangers, who might not understand. In the overwhelming majority of cases, the charges are found to be groundless, but it does not follow that the investigations were properly conducted. Three recent cases, all involving Indians and the RCMP in Saskatchewan, underline the point.

In 1972, an RCMP corporal beat up an Indian in a small Saskatchewan town. The Indian filed a grievance, the officer was put on trial and pleaded guilty. Although the Indian was flown from his hometown down to Prince Albert for the trial, he was never asked to give evidence. Instead, he sat in a hotel room while character witnesses favourable to the accused were called. The secret hearing ended with a $50 fine. Hell, you wouldn't want to call the Indian to the stand in a case like that; he's bound to be a sorehead.

In the summer of 1974, an Indian complained that he had been kicked in the mouth by a Mountie, hard enough to knock him unconscious and break a tooth. He filed a grievance and an RCMP officer turned up to investigate, but the Indian backed off, and later explained, "We went into the officer's room. He was in uniform. He told us that he would take a statement from us. All of us refused to make a statement. I did not trust the police to make an investigation." Eventually, the Métis Society persuaded the witness to co-operate, and a hearing was held. The RCMP was found blameless by the RCMP. Sort of navel gazing, on horseback.

In June 1974, an Indian who resisted arrest was subdued, then taken to the police detachment garage and there, he maintains, he was beaten up by two officers and his arm broken. He refused to press charges: "I do not want to lay a complaint against the RCMP because they might get back at me."

Alan Borovoy of the Civil Liberties Association, who collected these cases, argues that "The indispensable condition of public confidence is independent investigation." We have no such independent investigation into police behaviour in Canada, so we don't really know how widespread the problem is. But even a cursory glance at recent cases will show that there are frequent, serious lapses from the conduct we expect. (This is one area where I intend to confine myself to recent history; our standards in this line have changed so radically in recent years that I see little point in raking over the ashes of the past. Anyone who wants to do that will find an excellent source in Lorne and Caroline Brown's book, *An Unauthorized History of the RCMP*.)

Take, for example, the expectation that the police will obey the law themselves.

In Charlottetown, P.E.I., an undercover RCMP agent persuaded four youths to procure LSD and marijuana for him. Then he arrested the youngsters and charged them with trafficking. In court, it was contended that the officer had broken fourteen various laws in the course of his work.

In Ottawa, an informer arranged with police that he

would stage a break-in, and persuaded a friend of his to drive the get-away car while he and another man pretended to force their way into a house that was, in fact, open. Then the car driver was charged with breaking and entering, and sent to jail. His two "buddies", of course, got off scot-free. The conviction was eventually quashed, not because of the conduct of the police, but because you can't break and enter an open house. Before that verdict was reached, the man had spent more than four years in jail. It must have been a hell of a comfort to know he was innocent.

Such cases raise a fundamental question: Are police entitled to lure people into crimes that might not otherwise be committed? Believe it or not, Canadian law is vague on the subject. Some police regard entrapment as anathema. Police Chief Roger Smith of Dartmouth once told me, "Our job is to prevent crime, not promote it." Others feel quite differently. The deputy chief of a western Ontario city, who shyly declined to allow himself to be identified, told me, "We have to use whatever tools we have; if that includes entrapment, okay. Just so we get the bastards." This is known as creative corruption.

Entrapment is used as a matter of course against drug pushers, petty thieves, burglars, and bootleggers; it also works against ordinary people with no criminal bent.

Gordon Shipley, 22, a student at Carleton University in Ottawa in 1969, lived at the YMCA, where he met and made friends with an older man, known to him as Al Thompson, but who was in fact Constable Lawrence Lowes of the RCMP. Lowes was posing as a shop clerk while searching for drug traffickers. The men became close friends, but Shipley didn't really know much about the drug scene — Lowes later described him as "rather naive", and when it became clear, in Lowe's words, that "Mr. Shipley was taking too much time for what it amounted to", he began to apply pressure. He said he wasn't making enough money as a clerk to live on; he thought he might sell drugs, and could Shipley get some for him at the university? Shipley said, no, he didn't know anything about drugs. Lowes kept pressing, so Shipley asked around and discovered that, yes, indeed, there were people selling the stuff on campus. Still, he didn't produce any; in fact, he refused point-blank to get involved. But Lowes had borrowed some money from Shipley, and the student wanted it back. Lowes said he would pay, but only on one condition—Shipley had to get him some drugs. Finally, through a girl at the university, the student procured $30 worth of hashish. The joke was on him; he was promptly arrested and charged with trafficking in drugs — a penitentiary offence.

The case was not allowed to come to court; Shipley's lawyer had it quashed on a pre-trial motion. In a way, that is too bad, because the court might have pronounced on the issue of entrapment. As it is, this dubious technique is still surrounded by hazy law — and it is still widely used.

It is also common for police to violate the law to obtain statements from accused persons, not only by beating them, but by lying to them, tricking them, bribing them, and holding out improper inducements. And what do our courts say about this? They think it's just fine.

John Wray was charged with holding up a service station in Peterborough, Ontario, in 1968, and shooting the attendant, who died. He was charged with murder, but the police really had very little to go on. So Wray was held incommunicado for a period of eighteen hours and grilled; he was also lied to, and threatened. Finally, he gave the police a statement; it was not a confession, but it did tell the police where they could pick up the rifle that had been used in the killing. That statement was used in the trial, and helped to convict Wray of murder. But the defence appealed, and the Ontario Appeal Court held that "the confession or statement by the accused was procured by trickery, duress and improper inducements, and was clearly inadmissable". The Crown appealed, in turn, to the

154

Supreme Court of Canada. In a split decision, our highest court decided that it didn't matter how the evidence was obtained; once the police had it, they could produce it in court. Mr. Justice Emmett Hall, who dissented from the majority in that decision, told me he regarded it as "a monstrous perversion. . . . It says that the police can do anything, break the law in any way to get a statement and it's quite all right."

The new Right To Privacy Act contains a clause that specifically excludes evidence obtained by an illegal wiretap — illegal wiretaps have been part of the ordinary police tool-chest for years — but the new law has yet to be tested in court. Walter Tarnapolsky, author of *The Canadian Bill of Rights,* writes that the new act "seems to indicate some trend amongst our legislators to start limiting the rule in *Regina* v. *Wray*", but at the moment our police appear to have carte blanche to act illegally in the name of the law.

An interrogation manual that turned up in a cottage in P.E.I. after two RCMP officers had been staying there throws a bizarre light on police attitudes in this line. The booklet, a kind of do-it-yourself third degree kit, was written by Chief Inspector A.R. Roberts of the Calgary city police, and adopted by the federal force. It suggests that in any interrogation, "we are going to do everything that is legal and right" to obtain information, and if that doesn't work, why, the wraps are off:

> There is a point which is reached in every interrogation when you still may not have that statement and you know if you go any further in the specific technique that you are employing that your statement will be ruled inadmissable. . . . I suggest that, at this point, the Marquis of Queensbury rules go out the window and the interrogator must open up his bag of tricks and go for . . . any evidence which may be placed in court, regardless of the method employed to secure that evidence.

In short, the police should obey the law unless that clumsy approach doesn't work, and then they should chuck it and get on with the job. If the Marquis of Queensbury can't hack it, call in old Duke Knuckles. What is alarming about this suggestion is that it appears, in the Wray case, to have obtained the blessings of our highest court.

Immigration cases provide another area for widespread harassment and illegal activity on the part of Canadian police forces. During the furore over American draft-dodgers in Canada, the RCMP had a special six-man bureau in its headquarters in Ottawa whose task was to co-operate with U.S. officials in keeping track of, and harassing, draft-dodgers. There was not a shadow of justification in Canadian law or policy for this, but it happened nonetheless. In some instances, draft-dodgers who had obtained jobs were fired after a call from the RCMP, who just wanted the boss to know he was harbouring a fugitive.

On January 25, 1970, three deserters from the U.S. army, who had passed Canadian immigration procedures and were legal residents of British Columbia, were simply kidnapped by RCMP officers and turned over to U.S. authorities. They were picked up at a highway restaurant and taken, first to RCMP headquarters in Chilliwack, then to the border crossing between Huntingdon, B.C., and Sumas, Washington. There, they were delivered to American immigration officers. One of the deserters, John Kreeger, managed to escape and run back across the border, but the other two were slapped into a military stockade. Kreeger's flight drew press attention and eventually a public inquiry, which had no difficulty finding that both the police and immigration officials had acted illegally.

In short, the expectation that the police will themselves obey the laws they are sworn to uphold has no firm foundation in fact. Nor is there much evidence that the police attempt to apply the law equally.

When Henry Doyle, 19, a student at St. Thomas University in Fredericton, New Brunswick, drove to his girl friend's one evening early in 1970, he had one rear taillight out on his car, although he didn't know it. As he pulled up to the girl's house in Nashwaaksis, an RCMP patrol car pulled up behind him, a policeman got out, came over, and asked for his driver's licence and registration. Doyle produced them, then reached for a hanky. The officer accused him of trying to "hide something" and said he was going to search him. Then (according to an affidavit Doyle swore out for the late—and lamented—New Brunswick magazine, *The Mysterious East*) Doyle objected that he couldn't be searched unless he was under arrest, but the officer said he was going to do it anyway, and that he was charging the student with obstruction. Finally, he put handcuffs on the boy, pushed him over the hood of the car and searched him. He found nothing, and at once became conciliatory. When Doyle asked why he had been searched, the cop replied, "Well, I was searching for anything I could get on you." The incident ended with the Mountie saying, "Listen, Harry, I don't want you to go away with sore feelings. I just want you to know that I have every right to do what I did, and you should forget about it."

If you want an insight into the operation of Canada's police system, simply picture that scene with a banker, doctor, or society matron in the role of the driver whose car was missing a taillight. The cop would be missing a badge.

Perhaps we shouldn't criticize the police for simply reflecting the inequity that is built into our society and our judicial process; I think we are entitled, however, to ask what they are up to in incidents like the Fred Quilt case.

Quilt was a Chilcotin Indian who had a drinking problem, right up until Sunday, November 28, 1971, which was the day he was fatally injured. That day, Quilt, his wife, Christine, his sister-in-law, and his twenty-year-old son had apparently been drinking vanilla extract, and they fell asleep in the family's pickup truck on the gravel road that links Bella Coola, B.C., with the Interior. A public nurse who passed the truck informed the RCMP at Alexis Creek, and a police tow truck was sent out, with two officers. What happened after they arrived at the scene is a matter for debate. Christine Quilt claims that her husband was pulled from the truck, then jumped on by an RCMP officer; the police version is that he was pulled out of the truck and held upright, but fell down on the gravel road. Then the Quilts were driven home to the Stone reserve. At some point after he left the truck, and for some reason, Quilt's smaller intestine was severed; he was soon in agony, but, although he was visited at the reserve by a doctor and two nurses over the next forty-eight hours, he was not moved to hospital until Tuesday, November 30. He died within two hours of his arrival at the hospital.

An inquest was called at Williams Lake for January 13, 1973, with an all-white jury under the direction of Coroner S.S. Leith, a former RCMP officer. The jury, one of whose members was an RCMP auxiliary, heard, mainly, the evidence of whites. All the Indians who went to the inquest—including the Quilt family—went at their own expense; all the whites were subpoenaed, and their expenses paid. At this inquest, Christine Quilt testified that she had seen Constable Darryl Bakewell jump up and down on her husband, screaming, "Get up, you son of a bitch, get up!" The jury did not believe her, and returned a verdict that, while Quilt's death was "unnatural and accidental, we attach no blame to any person in connection with the death."

This verdict set off a protest in the Vancouver Indian community, and signs blossomed there that read JOIN THE RCMP AND KILL AN INDIAN. Harry Rankin, a controversial Vancouver lawyer and alderman, took up the case, and managed to win a second inquest in July, at Kamloops. Conflicting medical evidence, and the confusion, evasions, and language problems of the Indian witnesses made the case another easy victory for the RCMP, although, this time, the jury did at least pin down the fact that: "The injury was sustained between the time Quilt was removed from the Quilts' vehicle and assisted to the police vehicle on the Chilcotin Road on November 28th."

Rankin, a tough and unorthodox lawyer, made some tough and unorthodox statements to the press while the case was unwinding. Among other things, he said: "The police force is an arm of the state and if they were told by the people higher up to lay off this business, it would deal with seventy-five to ninety per cent of that right there. But they don't care if the police act up. They just don't want the police to get caught acting up." He also said, "The Fred Quilt case is not an isolated instance of police violence. It is a symbol that has brought Indians together to fight for something better."

For these statements, Rankin was called before the Law Society of British Columbia, but defended himself successfully on the ground that his remarks were made in support of the rights of his clients. I went to see Rankin in 1975 to ask him about the Quilt case; I wondered if he thought his vindication before the law society was a partial victory, and if the fuss over the inquest would make any difference in the treatment of Indians. He replied, "You can't have a victory where nothing changes, and as far as Indian treatment by the RCMP is concerned, not one goddam thing has changed."

The underlying concern in the Quilt case raises another of our expectations about the police—that they will not act with unnecessary violence. Let us look, briefly, at four recent, widely-scattered incidents.

One sunny morning in February 1970, Walter Robert Redel, 40, director of the Lands Branch in the B.C. Department of Lands and Forests, went for a stroll in Quebec City. He was there to help plan a conference of resource ministers, and had taken advantage of a lull to see Quebec, a city he had never visited before. He rode the elevator outside the Chateau Laurier down to Lower Town, walked around for a while, and headed back towards the hotel. As he was walking, an unmarked car pulled up beside him, and two men leapt out, brandishing handguns. They shouted that they were police, and told him to get in the car, but Redel suspected that they were holdup men, and resisted. They were police, however, and proceeded to prove it by beating him unconscious with their guns; then they picked him up and bundled him into the car. Come to Quebec and see the stars.

When Redel came to, he was sitting in the car with his hands manacled behind him. He saw a radio-telephone and concluded that his assailants were not gangsters after all, so he asked them why they hadn't simply identified themselves properly. One policeman told him he should not have resisted arrest, and flashed his badge. At the police station, Redel produced his hotel key, government identification papers, B.C. driver's licence, and business cards. They were ignored; then he was stripped and thrust, naked, into a police cell, without being charged, and without any chance to telephone for help. He was interrogated, and held for several more hours until the cops were satisfied that he had done nothing wrong. Then he was given his clothes and told to leave. The police explained that they had mistaken him for a suspect in a conspiracy to rob a local bank. Redel went to a Quebec hospital, where he received several stitches for cuts over his left eye and below his nose. He also suffered the fracture of a small bone behind his left eye.

The Redel case produced a public uproar and, eventually, an apology from the Quebec Provincial Police, whose plainclothesmen had administered the beating. (What can I say, dear, after I say I'm sorry?) Most of the fuss was over the fact that Redel was an innocent visitor to a city "where hospitality is spoken". But surely there is a more important question: Is it normal police procedure to club down anyone who shows signs of hesitating to enter an unmarked car? How often is the kind of treatment meted out to Redel inflicted on people who are too young, too poor, or too unconnected to kick up a fuss?

The question of how much force must be applied to arrest someone who is — rightly or wrongly — considered to be dangerous is a delicate one, but the tendency appears to be to use force first and judgment later. One evening in August 1972, the police in Ste. Thérèse, Quebec, set out to arrest André Vassard, 16, whom they believed to be selling marijuana to other youths in the town square near the police station. As they approached the boy, he ran, and two police officers chased after him; one of them fired a warning shot in the air, but the boy kept running. Then Constable André Goulet, who had also drawn his gun, apparently stumbled; the weapon went off and Vassard went down, dead, with a bullet in the head. (Police are always having accidents with their guns in the presence of youths who appear to be resisting arrest; in Toronto, in 1969, Portuguese immigrant Angelo Nobrega was shot and killed by accident after a police chase that began when the cops saw three youths begin talking among themselves after they spotted the police car. Naturally, they gave chase, cornered the kids, pulled them out of their car, and then the accident happened.) Even accepting the police version—more than much of the town was willing to do—what the hell were the police doing pulling their guns on an unarmed kid? Were they in fear of their lives? Did they think he was going to blow smoke at them?

Enough of Quebec, let's look at another case out West, the case Lorne and Caroline Brown call The Muskego Affair in their *Unauthorized History of the RCMP*. Michael Muskego was one of four juveniles who escaped from the Saskatchewan Boys School in Regina on October 10, 1970. He was an Indian, from the Onion Lake Reserve. He was fifteen. The boys stole a car in Regina, and drove it out of town, where the motor seized, so they abandoned it. They took a farmer's car, short-circuited the ignition system, and set off again. The farmer reported the theft and an RCMP officer spotted the missing car on the highway near Chamberlain; he turned on his warning light and gave chase.

Muskego, at the wheel of the stolen car, refused to pull over; he told the other boys that he had been arrested before, and beaten up, and that wasn't going to happen again. He tried to outrun the police car, and, at breakneck speed, dodged around two hastily-erected police roadblocks, at Davidson and Kenaston. He was reported going through the tiny town of Bladworth at 100 miles an hour. A third roadblock was set up just south of Saskatoon, with a hole in the middle just wide enough for a car to pass through. Muskego drove through that hole, and, as he did so, RCMP Constable John Ayton Bezzola, an expert marksman, fired a .308 rifle into the car from a distance of twelve to fifteen feet. The bullet went through the side of the car near the front door, and struck Muskego in the heart. The car went out of control and flipped end over end. Muskego was dead when the police swarmed over to the wreck, but, miraculously, none of the other boys was seriously injured.

In first reports of the incident, no mention was made of the gunshot; instead, a roundup of police reports over the weekend mentioned, "an unidentified fifteen-year-old boy killed in the crash of a stolen car near Saskatoon". Then the Saskatoon detachment issued a story that the shot had been fired because the police believed the car to be driven by one Wilfred Stanely Robertson, who was wanted in connection with the shooting of two RCMP officers in the McDowall district of Saskatchewan. That story lasted two days; then Assistant Commissioner J.L. Vachon issued a statement in Regina saying: "At no time was it felt that the vehicle driven by Michael John Muskego might in fact contain Robertson, nor was it the reason a shot was fired at the vehicle." The final police version was that the shot was fired because it was necessary to stop the speeding car before it got into Saskatoon and wreaked havoc in the early-morning traffic.

That being so, why didn't the police simply block off the entire road, instead of leaving the slot through which Muskego drove to his death? That being so, why didn't Constable Bezzola use a shotgun—which he had on hand—to take out a tire, which is what he said he was aiming at when he shot Muskego? Those questions were not asked at the coroner's inquest, which was presided over, predictably, by a retired RCMP officer, and in which, predictably, an RCMP sergeant helped the coroner to prepare his questions and which, predictably, concluded that "In considering all the circumstances the police action was at all times properly exercised and good judgment used. . . . We, the jury, attach no blame to any of the authorities involved."

Attaching no blame is one of the things we do best in police cases, but every once in a while it goes the other way. In February 1975, an Alberta provincial court judge dismissed charges of impaired driving and assault with intent to resist arrest against one Kenneth Kingsmith, and reprimanded the police for the kind of conduct that "destroyed the confidence the public should have in police authority". The case was a climax of sorts in a long string of charges against the Calgary police that had Police Chief Brian Sawyer worried and upset. "You have to ask yourself 'What the hell is going on?'" he said, and, "Do the police feel that only by beating up on people can justice be done?"

Fair questions. In the months preceding the Kingsmith case, one constable pleaded guilty to assaulting a prisoner, two were found guilty of assault causing bodily harm during a tavern arrest, and another admitted firing a flare gun at two youths he spotted "fooling around" with an imitation rifle in a pickup truck when he came strolling by, off duty. "Fooling around" is not yet a capital crime, but the word is slow getting to Alberta.

The Kingsmith case was straightforward. Kingsmith and his wife were stopped for speeding on their way home from a party. The two police who stopped them were wearing blue jeans and driving an unmarked car. They took Kingsmith into their car for questioning, swore at him, and when he swore back, one of them slapped him. He got out of the car to call his wife as a witness and "that's the last I remember. When I came to, I was getting bashed against the car."

He was taken to the police station and locked up overnight, then charged with ability impaired, and with biting one of the police on the finger during the scuffle. The court found that Kingsmith had not, in fact, been impaired, and was not guilty of assault.

In virtually all of these cases, the assumption of the police from the beginning has been that anyone they lighted on was guilty of something. Sometimes, all too often, this assumption can lead to a horrifying miscarriage of justice.

One day in June 1967, while Howard Gowan, 47, was working alone in the pasture of his farm near Wymark, Saskatchewan, two RCMP officers arrived in a patrol car and asked him to get in for a "talk". Gowan had made a bit of a nuisance of himself with the force; he claimed he had been receiving obscene phone calls, and that the police would do nothing about them. He had also filed formal complaints because he didn't think the RCMP had pressed the investigation of two incidents of cow-stealing with sufficient vigour. An officer had told him to "quit bringing in complaints", but now here they were at the farm, obviously ready to set things right. Gowan gladly got into the car. But the police didn't want to talk about obscene phone calls or missing cows; instead, they drove Gowan straight to Swift Current Mental Health Clinic. There he was questioned by

164

a psychiatrist, then taken to RCMP cells, where he was locked up.

He had been charged with a violation of Section 20 of the Saskatchewan Mental Health Act. This law, which is still on the books, says that a peace officer can arrest anyone who is suspected of being retarded or mentally imbalanced and is creating a disturbance in a public place. Later, Gowan was to ask, "How can they say I was creating a disturbance in a public place when I was alone in my own pasture?" It seems a valid question.

No warrant is required for an arrest under this law — all you need is a suspicion and a warm body; Gowan was never aware he was being charged. He telephoned his wife, Madeline, from RCMP headquarters, but couldn't tell her much, because he didn't know why he was being held. When he tried to call a lawyer, the request was refused.

Gowan was taken from his cell and driven to the Saskatchewan Hospital at Weyburn, where he was admitted for psychiatric treatment. He was hospitalized from June 22 to July 28, 1967, during which time he received electric shock treatments and drug therapy. His wife, who was allowed to visit him when she finally found out where he was (not from the police; she was informed by staff of the mental health clinic), later said, "He was really good when he went in . . . but he was nothing but skin and bones and didn't even know he had a family when they got through with the shock treatments."

Medical science having done its bit, Gowan was turned loose after thirty-six days of confinement. He launched another complaint against the RCMP, and eventually his wife — not Gowan himself — received a letter of apology from E.L. Martin, then commanding officer of the Swift Current branch. Martin's letter expressed "sincerest regrets" over the incident, and acknowledged that someone in the force, not identified, "strictly speaking acted outside the authority provided in the Saskatchewan Mental Health Act". Just the same, she wasn't to get too upset, because, "our member, acting as he did on professional advice, had in mind only the welfare of your husband, yourself and family and the general public." That was nice.

Gowan's story was reported by Ann Walker in the Regina *Leader-Post* in 1975, and finally investigated by Saskatchewan's ombudsman, Ernie Boychuk. He told me in January 1976 that he wasn't allowed to discuss the case; he did say, however, that Gowan complained that he had been improperly picked up and improperly held, and "There is no question that he has some valid points." Whether anything will ever be done to redress a grievance now nine years old remains to be seen.

In sum, from the evidence available it is clear that none of our high expectations of the police—that they will obey the law, that they will treat citizens equally, that they will shun violence, that they will follow the presumption of innocence — can be counted on in practice.

Our cops may be better than those of, say, New York or Detroit or Chicago, but they are still cops, and they still need much more control, much more discipline, and much more public investigation than they are now getting.

CHAPTER 10:

WATER ME NO GATES

Canada's history is as dull as ditchwater, and her politics is full of it.

Maurice Hutton, 1935.

One day during the last throes of the presidency of Richard Nixon, someone at the *Toronto Star* pasted a headline on the staff bulletin board. It read: WATERGATE COULD NEVER HAPPEN HERE, and underneath was a thoughtful scrawl: "And if it did, nobody would report it."

The burden of this chapter is to examine whether Canadian political morality is on a higher plane than in the U.S., or whether we just don't blab so much. As far as I know, we have never gathered together all the elements of that noisesome sequence of events called Watergate—and by Watergate I mean not only the political espionage involved in the burglary of the Watergate Hotel, but the long series of bribes and payoffs that went before it, the lies and evasions that followed it, and the attempts to smother the truth and silence the critics that were characteristic of the Nixon presidency. I don't think we have had all those elements packaged into the same neat time-span achieved by Nixon, but I do think they have played a major role, a continuing role, in the way the Canadian political system works.

When a federally-appointed official goes to jail for conspiracy, fraud, and forgery in a kickback scheme, as Kenneth Elliott, the Hamilton Harbour Commissioner, did in July 1975, I worry about corruption. When twelve officials of dredging companies go on trial on charges of rigging bids to get profitable federal government contracts, as they did in the fall of 1975, I worry some more. When a provincial cabinet minister pleads guilty—as former New Brunswick Tourism Minister Charlie Van Horne did, also in 1975—to using his office to line his pockets, I wonder whither we are drifting.

When the RCMP security section is turned loose on reporters who have been critical of the provincial government—as it was in Alberta during 1973—I wonder if we have all that much to learn from the FBI. When a commission of inquiry finds that a government has tolerated widespread corruption, political payoffs, and conflict of interest —as the Cliche Commission found in Quebec in 1975—and the provincial premier says, specifically on the subject of conflicts of interest — "It's only puritans from outside Quebec who worry about things like that"—noxious parallels spring to my mind. When the federal government stalls and evades on charges that the Seafarers' International Union is involved in improper activities, and has received government protection, and when that same government emerges from a privately-conducted internal investigation to announce that everything is jake, as happened, again, in 1975, visions of cover-up dance in my wee little head.

Finally, when a federal government enacts election-expenses disclosure legislation which conceals more than it discloses, and when that government adopts regulations that allow it to conceal virtually anything a cabinet minister decides may be prejudicial to the national interest, and when, time after time—on environmental issues, on the Mackenzie Valley Pipeline, on housing matters, on airport expansion — the government blocks publication of publicly-funded studies that contain embarrassingly critical comments, why then I wonder who the hell we are to cock a snoot at the Americans. They have a Freedom of Information Act and an Election Expenses Act that at least ring bells when things go wrong; hell, *they* had to tell *us* that our Mounties open other people's mail.

Our prime minister is not a crook; he does not sanction

illegal activities, dirty political tricks, or the organized inter-
ference with the judicial process that became the hallmarks
of the Nixon era. So far, so good; but that is a long way from
saying that our politics are clean, or ever have been.

We have had fifteen prime ministers since Confederation. One of these, Sir Charles Tupper, held office so briefly
that he scarcely counts; one, Arthur Meighen, served
twenty months spread over two terms, and had no opportunity to get into the swing of things; one, R.B. Bennett, did
survive a five-year term with clean skirts, but then, he had
the Depression to occupy him; and one, Pierre Elliott
Trudeau, is still in office with the verdict still out on his
administration as I write this. The other eleven men headed
governments that were, *in every case,* involved in major
scandals, kickbacks, or cover-ups. Every blessed one. I will
put that up against the Americans every time, for consis-
tency, if not splendour. As the *Saturday Review* remarked
way back in 1891, "Canada's . . . opportunities and means
are not so great as those wielded by the lobbyists and
log-rollers of New York, but the most has been made of
them."

Sir John A. Macdonald needs no introduction to students
of corruption; his was the one faux pas that brought down a
government — the Pacific Scandal. That mess broke open
when a group of Americans, who thought they had the
Canadian Pacific Railway contracts sewed up, deduced that
Macdonald was about to go back on his word, and dump
them. So they arranged for a raid on the Montreal offices of
John J. Abbott, a prominent Tory, and the CPR solicitor,
who had served as bagman for the party's railway connection. Incriminating documents were stolen from Abbott
and sold to the Liberals. Included was Macdonald's famous
telegram of August 26, 1872, to Abbott, begging another
election payoff: "Immediate. Private. I must have another
ten thousand — will be the last time of calling. Do not fail
me. Answer today." Abbott did answer, too: "Draw on me

for ten thousand dollars." There was also a letter from Georges-Etienne Cartier, Macdonald's Quebec lieutenant, asking for $20,000 to be sent to the party's central committee. There were also letters showing payoffs to Cartier, to Sir Francis Hincks, the Minister of Finance, and Hector Langevin, Minister of Public Works.

Liberal MP Seth Huntingdon had raised a considerable stink about CPR election payoffs before, to no avail, but disclosure of the Abbott correspondence created a furore and led to the appointment of a Royal Commission. It found no impropriety—that is the way of Royal Commissions — but publication of its testimony showed that CPR president Sir Hugh Allan had poured at least $343,000 into the Conservative coffers for the 1872 election. The Governor General of the day, Lord Dufferin, neatly summarized the Commission evidence in private correspondence: "A greater amount of lying and baseness could not well be crammed into a smaller compass." Macdonald defended himself with lies, evasions, and denials, but he was defeated in the House of Commons, and handed over power to the Liberal leader, Alexander Mackenzie.

Mackenzie has gone into our history books as an upright stonemason, not strong in the head, perhaps, but honest. Yet "Honest Sandy" Mackenzie was enmeshed in the same kind of kickbacks — on a smaller scale — that had brought down the Tory chief. Mackenzie established a system of tenders on government contracts, and he took over the Department of Public Works himself. Ostensibly, the idea was to rule out graft and patronage but, as Pierre Berton pointed out in *The National Dream*, "In practice it turned the department into a broker's office."

Mackenzie had barely dusted off his chair when a new firm called Sifton, Glass and Company came knocking at the door. It was owned by John Wright Sifton of Petrolia, Ontario, the prime minister's friend and fellow Liberal, and David Glass, a London, Ontario, lawyer. Glass, a Conservative, had been the first of his party to switch sides during the Pacific Scandal; Mackenzie owed him. In 1874, Sifton and Glass put in a bid for a contract to build telegraph lines along the CPR right of way west to Fort Garry, Manitoba. They got the contract, despite the fact that there were three lower bids, after Mackenzie intervened to set aside the tendering rules he himself had designed. Once they had the job, they renegotiated the contract for more money; they got it, too. The line they built was a mess, so skimpily done that most of it had to be rebuilt at public expense. But they pocketed a sizeable profit; Mackenzie pocketed his morals.

Then there was the matter of Charles Mackenzie, the prime minister's brother. He was the silent partner in the firm of Cooper and Fairman, which mysteriously received contracts from the Department of Public Works despite the fact that other companies put in lower bids. Then there was Joseph Whitehead, a Liberal MP who walked off with two contracts with the aid of Mackenzie and Senator Donald McDonald, a prominent Liberal who also happened to be Whitehead's brother-in-law. In one contract, the price was fattened by $930,000 worth of unauthorized "extras"; in the other, Whitehead got the job without tenders being called.

Murmurings public and private led to the establishment of a Royal Commission into the financing of the CPR; it produced three volumes of evidence detailing corrupt practices. But by that time, nobody cared, for Macdonald was back in office again.

In his new incarnation, Macdonald promptly plunged into the McGreevy Affair, which takes its name from Thomas McGreevy, a contractor and Conservative MP for Quebec West. McGreevy was the brother-in-law of Hector Langevin, with whom he shared quarters in Ottawa during parliamentary sessions. Langevin, who had been disgraced in the Pacific Scandal, was polished up a little and given back the Public Works portfolio in 1878. He was thus in a

171

position to steer work into the hands of the dredging firm of Larkin, Connolly and Company, which cherished as one of its partners Robert McGreevy, brother of Thomas. Robert obtained his position there, in fact, because he promised to steer fat contracts to Larkin, Connolly with his brother's help. So he did, and in return, Larkin, Conolly kicked back a percentage of every contract into the Conservative election fund.

All went well until the McGreevy brothers got into a personal quarrel so bitter that Robert went to Ottawa to rat on Thomas. Macdonald was warned of a brewing scandal, so he called in Langevin and Thomas McGreevy; they denied any impropriety, and that appeared to be that. But Robert McGreevy was still mad, and took his story to J. Israel Tarte, editor of the newspaper *Le Canadien*, and on April 30, 1890, *Le Canadien* broke word of a new scandal.

It had now become accepted form to use Royal Commissions, but on this occasion a parliamentary committee was put to work instead. In due course, it showed that Larkin, Connolly and Company had received $3,138,234 worth of government contracts through the McGreevy connection —and this, we must remember, was 100 years ago, when a dollar really was a dollar—that it had cleared a fat $905,468 profit on these and kicked back $171,407 in payoffs. These payoffs included contributions to the Tory party, diamonds, and other expensive gifts for Public Works employees, and donations to a newspaper run in Quebec by Langevin's son-in-law.

Some of the members of the committee found Hector Langevin to be corrupt, but they were out-voted, and he was officially found to be merely "negligent". He resigned and is now honoured with his own building, the Langevin Block, in Ottawa.

Things did not go so well for Thomas McGreevy, who was thrown into jail. There had to be a scapegoat, and he was elected. Sir Richard Cartwright, Mackenzie's finance minister, later wrote, "Millions of corruptly gotten money, to be expended for yet more corrupt purposes, passed through his hands, and yet for all that I believe Mr. McGreevy was by far the most honest man of the lot." Cartwright believed that McGreevy was kept from telling all he knew by pressure from Tory cabinet ministers: "There were few days during the time he spent in jail on which Mr. McGreevy, if so disposed, could not have held a Cabinet Council in the corridor."

McGreevy was thrown out of the House of Commons on September 29, 1891; less than six months later, on April 6, 1892, MP James Edgar rose to lay a new scandal at the feet of Sir John Abbott.

Abbott was the same chap who had been the railway lawyer and bribe-distributor in the Pacific Scandal; now, elevated to prime minister for his good offices, he was to hear that others could work the same racket. Edgar said that Sir Adolphe Caron, a cabinet member (he was at different times Minister of Militia and Postmaster-General), had steered over a million dollars in federal subsidies to the Quebec and St. John Railway, of which he was part owner, and that much of this money was kicked back to election funds for Caron and other Tories. He had also helped another company, the Temiscouta Railway, make off with $649,200 in subsidies, and much of this, too, went for election bribes.

Edgar wanted a Royal Commission to look into his charges, but Mackenzie Bowell, Caron's cabinet colleague, cut him off at the pass. Bowell moved a substitute motion— which passed— setting up an inquiry only into the raising of the subsidies, and leaving out the payoffs. By the time that commission had reported, Abbott had been succeeded by Sir John Thompson as Prime Minister. Once more, the commission evidence was devastating, but the report flaccid, and Thompson simply refused to act. Caron remained in the cabinet until the Conservatives were defeated in 1896.

By that time, every prime minister had been involved in

scandal or cover-up except Sir Charles Tupper, who only held the job for nine weeks. (To make up for this deficiency, Tupper's son Stewart and Macdonald's son Hugh got caught up in a crooked government land transaction.)

The Liberal victory brought Wilfrid Laurier to power, and it must be said of him that he conducted his scandals on a decent scale. The first broke while he was still in opposition; it was yet another railway scandal, involving the Baie des Chaleurs line in Quebec. Payoffs of $100,000 went to Laurier's Quebec organizers, and $10,000 into his own campaign. He handled this by looking noble as all get-out and deploring muckracking.

Using those tactics, Laurier was able to survive a whole complex of scandals that broke under his feet during 1906, 1907, and 1908. None of these was major, but all followed the same pattern. When the steamer *Arctic* was being fitted out for a northern expedition, a contract for supplies was given out without tenders, and there were huge overpayments to Liberals. When the Northern Atlantic Trading Company billed the government $5 a head for bringing in immigrants, it was shown that it had done nothing to earn it; but payment was made, anyway, to the prominent Liberals who owned the company. Huge blocks of choice Saskatchewan land were sold to the government backers for $1 an acre, and they quickly resold to immigrants for $8. A patronage system through which government purchases, crown lands, and public franchises were directed to worthy party sources in return for kickbacks to the election fund came to light. Laurier blocked investigation by taking a line Nixon was to echo nearly seventy years later: "I disdain to discuss these issues. My soul is turned toward greater events and questions, and it is the future of the country I lay before you." Another minister of Public Works, Charles Hyman, was forced to resign, but Laurier escaped unscathed into our history books and our $5 bills. No wonder he smiled so much.

Robert Borden, who succeeded Laurier, also took the

high ground when scandal broke, but that may have been because he really didn't know what the hell was going on. He couldn't control Sam Hughes, his Minister of Militia in World War I. Under Hughes' brisk but erratic leadership, Canadian manufacturers made millions out of Canada's war effort, selling the army boots that dissolved on contact with mud, lousy food, bum ammunition, and the Ross rifle. Hughes has made it into our histories because of the Ross, a gun that looked beautiful, fired single shots with admirable accuracy on the shooting range, but wouldn't work worth a damn in combat. After a suitable number of Canadian troops had died kicking the jammed bolts of their rifles, 342,000 Ross rifles were scrapped in 1916.

But Hughes deserves mention as well for the kickback system he organized around army procurement. He set up a group called the Shell Committee, staffed by his friends and political supporters, and proceeded to let most armament contracts through this group. The Shell Committee in turn helped to finance a New York firm that suddenly went into the munitions business and cleaned up huge profits on government contracts from Ottawa. Attempts to pry into the practices of the Shell Committee were stonewalled by Borden (national security, of course) until a group of opposition MPs hired a lawyer and a private detective to conduct their own inquiry. The private eye broke into the New York apartment of one of the Shell Committee and emerged with enough evidence to force the calling of — guess what? — a Royal Commission. This commission, in the routine way, cleared Hughes of any wrong-doing, but it did note that he had awarded contracts to his friends, relations, and constituents and that Honorary Colonel J. Wesley Allison (Hughes made all the paunchy businessmen who comprised the Shell Committee into Honorary Colonels), a particularly close friend of Hughes (who called him "the biggest and best man in Canada, and the cleanest, too"), was guilty of deception, if not fraud.

Hughes survived the scandal, and when Borden finally

fired him it was because the Militia Minister, in one of his frequent rages, wrote a personally abusive letter to the Prime Minister.

Borden was followed into office by Meighen, whose two brief bursts of power, in 1920 and 1926, were unmarked by major blemish. Then there was Mackenzie King, whose two big scandals — head and shoulders above a dozen lesser messes — were the Customs Scandal and the Beauharnois Scandal.

Shortly after the 1925 election, which King survived, but only with a minority government, a parliamentary committee brought in a report detailing massive corruption in the Customs Department. Bribes, payoffs, and kickbacks had become commonplace in the financing of a smuggling trade between Canada and the U.S. What is more, the committee was able to show that King knew of the scandal and had refused to act to clean it up. The Tories levelled a vote of censure based on the committee report. King, who depended on twenty-four Progressives to keep the Liberals in power, nearly lost control of the House on June 25, 1926, but was able to stall a vote until adjournment. He then went to Governor General Lord Byng and asked for dissolution and a new election. Byng refused, contending that Meighen had the right to try to govern. When Meighen in turn lost a vote of confidence after three months of office, King was able to turn the subsequent election into a battle on the constitutional issue of Byng's refusal to grant a dissolution. He won on that high ground, and the Customs Scandal disappeared without a trace.

King was not so fortunate with the Beauharnois affair, owing to the unhappy circumstance that the investigation was not conducted by the ruling party, but by a successor government, which is harder to muzzle. After the Bennett Conservatives came to power in 1930, a House of Commons committee discovered that, just before the election, a promoter for the Beauharnois Power Corporation, which was interested in developing a hydro project on the St. Lawrence River, had given the Liberal party between $600,000 and $700,000 (another $100,000 had gone to the Tories, as the corporation coppered its bet). The money had been given to Senator Andrew Haydon, a friend and advisor of King's—as well as treasurer of the Liberal party—and to Senator Donat Raymond, trustee for the Quebec wing of the party. The payoff could not be denied, so King did the next best thing, he denied knowing about it: "All the time that I have been leader of the party I have never asked a single individual to make a contribution to a political campaign. I have had no knowledge of what the campaign funds were." This was a pretty good line (it still is; Nixon's talk of over-zealous underlings followed the same general script). But, unfortunately for King, he had gone on a Bermuda holiday with the chairman of Beauharnois, and his hotel bill — which had been charged directly to the company — bobbed up in evidence. Whatever else, King was proveably accepting gifts from a company that stood to gain enormously as a result of government favours; he told the House of Commons that he was walking in "the valley of humiliation".

But he didn't offer to resign, or anything silly like that, nor, once he got back into power, would he permit any changes in the election laws that kept the payoff system limbered up. All he did was to arrange things so that it was harder than ever to get information out of government, and when the scandals of his later years broke—they included the famous horses on the payroll of the army—none was ever directly traceable to King. However, there was never any question that King cheerfully abused power on behalf of his party; he once announced that "not one five-cent piece" of federal money would go to any Tory provincial government.

Louis St. Laurent, who succeeded King, was a much more admirable man, but it was his fate to become mired in the crudest abuse of power this side of Watergate — the Great Pipeline Debate.

The Trans-Canada pipeline was to bring gas from the Canadian West to eastern markets; it was to be built almost entirely by Americans, who would get all the profits, although more than eighty per cent of the money was put up by the Canadian taxpayer. C.D. Howe, the Boston-born Minister of Trade and Commerce, introduced legislation setting up the deal to the House of Commons on May 8, 1956. He demanded that the bill should clear all stages by June 5, so that money could be turned over to the pipeline company in time for a July construction start (it later turned out that the contracts had, in fact, been signed before the legislation was even tabled). Debate on six of the seven clauses of the bill consisted, at the resolution stage, of 207 words from the lips of C.D. Howe. The Trade Minister's arrogance was already a by-word; but on the pipeline bill he went too far, and the outraged opposition parties managed to force seventy recorded votes, all of which they lost, but each of which used up precious parliamentary time. René Beaudoin, the House of Commons Speaker, abandoned the historic impartiality of his role, and savaged the rules of Parliament to help the government meet Howe's artificial timetable.

On May 24, when Parliament moved into committee to study the bill clause by clause, Howe moved closure at the end of each clause, contrary to the rules of the House. He was supported by Beaudoin. On May 31, St. Laurent, who had been sitting on the sidelines, finally got into the debate, but only to make another closure motion to get the bill out of committee again. The government was still on time.

But then Colin Cameron of the CCF got up on a question of privilege, alleging that a letter in that day's newspaper had constituted an affront to the Speaker (so it had; it accosted him directly for his role in the parliamentary farce). Beaudoin obligingly helped Cameron to draw up a motion, the nice fellow, and ruled that it was debatable. The CCF was ecstatic; they could now drag out debate on the Cameron motion long enough to derail the Liberal's pipeline timetable. That night, after the House adjourned, and while opposition MPs were home sweating out nice long speeches for the morrow, a group of top Liberals went calling on Beaudoin to bring home to him what he had done.

The next day, as soon as the House met, he announced that he had decided the Cameron motion was not in order after all. But he had already accepted the motion, so he moved to return the House to the time before he had made his first ruling, so that he could legally reverse it. That was a Speaker's motion, and not debatable, and while the opposition howled, with MPs raging out of their seats to shake their fists at the Speaker, the Liberal majority rammed it through. The bill went through on time, and Trans-Canada got its cheque on June 7.

St. Laurent's scandal was not a matter of dollars but of arrogance, and it helped to bring about the party's defeat at the hands of John Diefenbaker. In turn, Diefenbaker's great scandal involved sex — that is to say, Gerda Munsinger. What is intriguing about the Munsinger Affair is that it remained buried for five-and-a-half years.

On December 7, 1960, the Commissioner of the RCMP reported to E.D. Fulton, then Minister of Justice, that the Associate Minister of Defence, Pierre Sevigny, had an illicit sexual relationship with one Gerda Munsinger, a German-born prostitute then living in Montreal. Munsinger had been arrested by German border police in 1949 on charges of minor espionage activities, so she was not allowed to follow her American husband, Michael Munsinger, to the U.S. Instead, she came to Canada and worked as a party girl. She met Sevigny in 1958 and they got along just fine. She also got along just fine with George Hees, Diefenbaker's Trade Minister, and the RCMP was worried that she represented a security risk. Fulton reported to Diefenbaker, who called in Sevigny and told him to end his relationship with Gerda. Two months later, Sevigny reported that the woman had gone back to West Germany, and that was that. He was not disciplined, nor asked to resign; indeed, his own boss, Defence Minister Douglas Harkness, was not told of the affair, and it might never have come to light except for a parliamentary battle in March 1966.

By that time, Diefenbaker had been defeated by Lester Pearson, and Pearson was under attack for his refusal to order an inquiry into the case of a postal worker, George Victor Spencer, who had been dismissed from government service without a hearing, on security grounds. In the heat of that debate, Liberal Justice Minister Lucien Cardin, who had obviously been going through old files, shouted out that the Tories vere not free of scandal, and blurted out the name of Gerda Munsinger (he gave it first as "Monsigneur", which confused everybody for a few days). A judicial inquiry under Mr. Justice Wishart Spence finally rolled out the details of the Munsinger case after she was tracked down in West Germany (she had been reported dead, and that confused everybody, too). For weeks the Munsinger affair titillated us all, but it carried some grave concerns, not the least of which was how extraordinarily easy it is to cover up major peccadillos by major figures in this country.

By the time the Munsinger Affair was concluded, we had already been through the major scandal of the Pearson régime, the series of events now grouped in history under the heading of the Dorion Inquiry, after Chief Justice Frederic Dorion, who conducted the official inquiry.

It was shown that our old acquaintance, Montreal drug-pusher Lucien Rivard, had Liberal-party friends who had offered a bribe to the executive assistant of a federal cabinet minister; the object was to arrange Rivard's release on bail. It was shown that Guy Rouleau, Pearson's parliamentary secretary, and chairman of the Liberal caucus, had made representations on Rivard's behalf, and that Rouleau, as a favour to Rivard, had written to the National Parole Board to arrange the transfer of one of the drug-pusher's pals from the penitentiary in Vancouver to Montreal. It was shown that the Minister of Justice, Guy Favreau, took it on himself to stop the RCMP investigation of Guy Rouleau. Then there were some peripheral matters, such as allegations that two cabinet ministers had received special favours from firms doing business with the government (there was little to these charges) and that a third cabinet member, Yvon Dupuis, was improperly involved in the acquisition of a racetrack franchise in Quebec.

The Dorion Inquiry was a raucous mess; it showed that the Pearson government was marked by incredible moral laxity and that favours could be, and were, purchased in Ottawa. It came on the heels of the Norris Commission, set up to probe into the doings of Hal Banks and his group of jolly tars, described in Chapter 7. It left those of us who lived through it and covered it determined never to take a lofty tone with other nations rocked by scandal, and some of us even remember that determination.

I have confined myself to scandals at the federal level (regretfully by-passing the McBride and Sommers hoo-dahs in B.C., Municipal Affairs Minister Alf Hooke's troubles in Alberta, Churchill Forest Products in Manitoba, the Highways and Hydro Scandals in Ontario, the Glace Bay heavy water plant muck-up in Nova Scotia, the Van Horne trial in New Brunswick, the frozen-food plant ripoff that led to the defeat of P.E.I. Premier Walter Shaw, the Vald-manis Affair in Newfoundland, and scandals rich, ripe, and beyond number in Quebec), but I cannot leave the subject without reference to one provincial matter that seems to have been excised from our memories and re-cords, although it carries some haunting parallels to some aspects of Watergate. I am referring to what E.B. Jolliffe, the provincial leader of the CCF, described as "Colonel Drew's

Ontario Gestapo". It is significant, I think, that the only major treatment of this remarkable affair appears in Gerald L. Caplan's good but little-known book, *The Dilemma of Canadian Socialism: The CCF in Ontario*.

The major elements of the story are unchallenged, although there is much disagreement about their implications. Shortly after the Drew government assumed office in Ontario in August 1943, a political police office was established on the second floor of an old police garage on Surrey Place, just off Queen's Park in downtown Toronto. Ontario Provincial Police Captain William J. Osborne-Dempster was put in charge, provided with funds never authorized by the legislature, and set to work as a political spy, using the code name D-208. He signed his reports to Deputy Commissioner McCready of the OPP, "Yours to Command, D-208". What the reports contained, mostly, were snippets —many of them quite false—linking anyone critical of the government to communism. Files were kept on such varied provincial personages as Jolliffe, B.K. Sandwell, editor of *Saturday Night*, CCF MPP William Dennison (later mayor of Toronto), Liberal MPP David Croll, former Premier Mitch Hepburn, and R.C. Wallace, Principal of Queen's University. The "Special Branch", as Dempster's organization was called, did not appear in the Public Accounts of Ontario, nor were Dempster's name and salary listed, as required by provincial law.

Although Dempster's ostensible task was to keep track of communists, his Branch spent most of its efforts in a smear campaign against the CCF, which was then the official opposition in Ontario. Files were opened on every CCF parliamentarian, and the papers were combed for any complaints against the capitalist system, free enterprise, or international finance. Anyone who made such complaints came under suspicion.

Three copies of each report went to higher-ups in the OPP, and were distributed to designated cabinet ministers (although Attorney General Leslie Blackwell denied any knowledge of Dempster's activities, he did admit to having seen forty-one D-208 Reports; he said he didn't pay much attention to them, because they seemed to be about "Communist activities". Why wasn't the Attorney General interested in communist activities? Communism was illegal at that time).

In addition, copies went to two peculiar propagandists, Gladstone Murray and M.A. Sanderson. Murray, who had been General Manager of the CBC until a House of Commons Committee asked him to resign in 1943 for failing to account for money he had received, was employed by the Canadian Chamber of Commerce to head an anti-socialist campaign. He received enthusiastic support from the heads of such companies as Imperial Oil, Noranda Mines, International Nickel, and Massey-Harris, and he used the police-gathered material for propaganda pamphlets. Sanderson, whose first name was Montague, but who revelled in the nickname "Buggsy", was the manager of the Reliable Exterminator Company, but spent a lot of his energy and money combatting the wicked socialists, partly for glory, and partly because the publicity helped business. He used Dempster's reports (and paid Dempster for what he later claimed was part-time work for the extermination company) as the basis for a huge and crude ad directed at CCF candidates running in Toronto municipal elections on January 1, 1944. The ad, headed "THIS IS THE SLATE TO RUB OUT NEW YEAR'S DAY", contained the flat assertion that the CCFers were all communists. (They sued for libel, and a "special jury" consisting entirely of businessmen heard the case; it found the ad to be wrong and libellous, and then awarded the CCFers one dollar each in damages. That was a year later, of course; in the meantime, they all lost in the election.)

Working under Dempster was Constable Alvin Rowe, who stuck at it for several months, and then decided that the activities of the Special Branch were improper, and should be exposed. He went to Agnes Macphail, a prominent CCF MPP, and she in turn went to Jolliffe.

On May 24, 1945, with a provincial election campaign under way, Jolliffe went on the radio to charge that there was a secret political police force in the province, that Premier George Drew knew about it and sanctioned it, and that it was being used against the legitimate opposition, including the CCF and Liberals. The Ontario public simply would not believe Jolliffe, although he reeled out figures, dates, incidents, and facts, and although he produced evidence that the police had infiltrated unions, rifled their files, taken their documents, and prepared blacklists of troublemakers—all in violation of the law. Jolliffe did win from Drew the promise that he would set up a — yes — a Royal Commission once the election was over, and that's all. The "Gestapo" charge — Jolliffe's loaded term for the Special Branch — probably did the CCF more harm than good; in any event, the party lost heavily in the 1945 election.

In due course, Mr. Justice A.M. LeBel, formerly a prominent Liberal lawyer, was named to the Commission, but he was given an extremely narrow frame of reference. He was not to range over the activities of the Special Branch, merely to decide whether Drew was personally responsible for the setting-up of "a secret political police organization, for the purpose of collecting, by secret spying, material to be used in an attempt to keep him in power."

Although no less than thirteen witnesses connected Drew indirectly with the Dempster operation, there was no proven direct link between the Premier and Dempster (the only evidence in this line was testimony that they both dined at the Albany and Empire clubs — Dempster moved well — and shook hands). LeBel concluded that Jolliffe's original charge, therefore, was not substantiated, and applied a smooth coat of whitewash to the whole operation.

He made some findings that have to be regarded as bizarre; for instance, that Dempster's real work was to investigate communism, although he did not submit a single report on communists. He also found that while Dempster's reports were frequently misleading and false, they were not intentionally so, and he said it was "incredible" that "big business" — in the persons of Buggsy Sanderson and Gladstone Murray — would be "in the market for the purchase of palpable falsehoods". The Attorney General was mildly rebuked for not paying more attention to the D-208 reports, and Buggsy Sanderson was rebuked for paying Dempster thirty dollars a week; it was illegal for Dempster to receive the money, and Lebel found the relationship "improper", but that's all.

The affair had a curious dénouement. Alvin Rowe, the chief witness against the government, died in a plane crash not long after the commission hearings. Today, the transcript of the hearings appears to have vanished; there is no trace of it in the provincial library or archives, nor in the Attorney General's office, nor in the Premier's office. One of the few men who worked with that transcript before it disappeared was E.C. Guillet, former provincial archivist. He prepared a manuscript, which has never been published, that supports most of Jolliffe's charges. It is called, "Political Gestapo".

You'll be glad to know that Ontario has no Special Branch any more. It does, however, have a peculiar outfit called a Security Division, which appears to be responsible to no one, and whose funding is not publicly accountable. What does it do? Damned if I know.

CHAPTER 11:

JUST US

It is hereby recognized and declared that in Canada there have existed and shall continue to exist without discrimination by reason of race, national origin, colour, religion or sex, the following human rights and fundamental freedoms, namely,
(a) the right of the individual to life, liberty, security of the person and enjoyment of property, and the right not to be deprived thereof except by due process of law;
(b) the right of the individual to equality before the law . . .

Canadian Bill of Rights, 1960.

At 4:15 p.m., December 27, 1967, Emile Roussy, 37, Prisoner 8309, lay on his bunk in cell 3821 at LeClerc Institution, just outside Montreal. He was waiting for the dinner call; he wasn't thinking about anything much, just lying there waiting at the tag end of another day in jail. Suddenly, a guard shouted, "Hey, Roussy! Get up! Gosselin wants to see you."

Roussy sat bolt upright, then swung his lean form out of the bunk and stood up slowly. He had this inane feeling that if he moved too fast, he would shatter the spell. He kept thinking, "This is it, my God, this has got to be it!"

Roussy had spent five years, one month, and twenty-two days in prison for bank robbery; 1,878 days, and hardly a day went by that he didn't protest, to guards, to other inmates, to anyone who would listen, that he was innocent; 1,877 nights, and hardly a night went by that he didn't lie on his bunk and stare at the ceiling and fight off the panicky feeling that he would never be believed. He walked to the steel-slab door, with its peephole window; it was standing ajar, for LeClerc is a medium-security institution, and prisoners are locked up only at night. He swung the door open, blinked at the brighter light in the cell-block corridor, and stepped out, nervously brushing his brown prison uniform with its sewn-on number.

In the spare and functional administration office, Assistant Warden Laurent Gosselin looked up as Prisoner 8309 entered. "Roussy," he asked, "is there any charge against you except this bank holdup?"

"No."

"Well, I think you've been acquitted."

Roussy sat down on a metal office chair. "Don't make a joke," he cautioned, "This is not a thing to joke about."

"It's no joke; you're to call your lawyer."

A few minutes later, Montreal lawyer Bruno Pateras made it official; the Quebec Appeal Court had quashed the conviction against Roussy; he was free to go. Hanging on to the phone, Roussy tried to think of something appropriate to say. Finally, it came. "Okay," he said. He hung up the phone and began to laugh.

The next day, he received a cheque for $376—his prison pay. He also got a new suit, shoes, socks, underwear, shirt, tie, and overcoat. The guards all wished him luck, so did Assistant Warden Gosselin and Warden Patrick Desgros-seilliers. The prison psychologist, Odette Charron, said, "We're sorry"; everybody else just said, "Good luck".

We're sorry, of course, meant sorry for five years out of his life by mistake, sorry for the long days and empty nights, for the steady dissolution of his broken family, for the times when he vomited after every meal for days on end because of tension. Sorry, too, I hope, for the fact that the high-sounding phrases of the Bill of Rights have nothing to do with common practice. Roussy was not given equal treatment before the courts; he was convicted, when all was said and done, for being Emile Roussy.

He was not a savoury character. He was born and brought up in Hull, Quebec, and had his first scrape with the police when he was fourteen — a charge of assaulting another boy. He quit school at fifteen, in grade eight, and went to work for a bakery for seven dollars a week. Over the next four years he held a number of jobs, none of them very good; then he met Cecile Lebel, courted her, got her pregnant, and married her. That was in 1949; she was eighteen, Roussy nineteen.

"We weren't very grown up," said Roussy. "There were a lot of fights — mostly about money." In 1950, he quit his job as a plasterer and joined the army, because a pal did. He served three years, came out not much better off, and went to work as a beer waiter, then a house painter. He was making about sixty dollars a week, not much for a family that by now included five kids, not much for a pretty wife who liked nice things. The fights with Cecile got worse, and Roussy took to drinking, which didn't help.

One night in October 1966, sitting in a beerhall, Roussy was grousing about his wife and his finances to two other men, one an ex-con he had met playing pool, the other a stranger. These two men knew where you could get some money in a hurry; there was a storeowner in East Templeton, not far from Hull, who always kept $10,000 — they were sure it was $10,000 — in cash around his house. Why not take that? So they drove down, broke in while the storeowner was watching TV with his wife and eighteen-year-old daughter, tied them up and ransacked the place. "The father seemed pretty upset, but the daughter just kept watching TV," Roussy recalled. They searched the house and found the stash — ten dollars. They went home.

When Roussy told Cecile what he had done, she was furious; she called him "voleur" — robber — which was accurate, if undiplomatic, and a few days later she stormed out. The marriage was over. Roussy called the Children's Aid; he couldn't look after his four boys and one girl; he knew he was headed for jail. And so he was. On December 13, 1956, he was picked up and received an eight-year sentence for armed robbery, assault, and breaking and entering. Cecile came to the trial, and visited him a few times in jail, then disappeared; the children went into a foster home.

In St. Vincent de Paul Penitentiary, Roussy worked as a painter, minded his own business and got out, with time off for good behaviour, in April 1961. (The Queen visited Quebec twice while he was in jail; each time, all prisoners were given one month off for each year of their sentences. For Roussy, this meant sixteen months' remission. Quebec's jails are full of ardent monarchists.) With sixty-five dollars in prison pay, Roussy went back to Hull, visited his kids, then moved in with his elder brother, Hormidas, and Hormidas' common-law wife, Thérèse, a large, square, formidable redhead who told me cheerfully, "Every dick in Hull knows me, because I've been playing cards for thirty years. . . . They keep trying to hang a charge on me, keeping a bawdy house, but it was only a game of cards. That's the way it is with these bastards. Excuse the language."

Roussy worked as a painter until October 1962, when he was laid off. On November 5, he drove to visit some friends, drank a little beer and called in at the unemployment insurance office for a line on another job. When he got to his car outside the government building about 2 p.m., two detectives arrested him at gunpoint.

About ninety minutes earlier that day, two masked men had burst into the Champlain Street branch of the Provincial Bank of Canada in Hull. One of them, carrying a revolver, stood by the front door and said, in English, "Don't move." The other vaulted the counter and scooped $2,316 out of an open cash drawer, dumping it into an IGA shopping bag. Then he moved to where cashier Réal Parent was checking a deposit from the Rotary Club—proceeds from an Oyster Fiesta—and grabbed four white bags containing $5,600. Both men fled. Cashier Parent seized a revolver

189

from his drawer and dashed after them, out into the street; he fired five shots at their car as it pulled away, and apparently hit the car door with one ricochet.

About this time — the exact moment was never clear — Mr. and Mrs. Paul St-Louis were eating lunch in their kitchen, about four blocks from the bank, when they noticed two men walking quickly across the street. Either one or both of the men were carrying a white sack, or sacks. They got into a car and drove off. Mrs. St-Louis thought their behaviour was strange, and wrote down their car licence. Soon after, St-Louis went out, down to the Caisse Populaire, where he heard about the holdup at the Provincial Bank. He rushed back to tell his wife, and noticed an empty car parked on the street next to their place. Inside, he found two masks, a coat, and, scattered on the seat and floor, seven one dollar bills and one twenty. There was a bullet mark on one door of the car. St-Louis knew he must have seen the bank robbers changing getaway cars; he called the police and gave them the licence number his wife had written down. It was Ontario licence C-93571, registered to one Emile Roussy.

Within minutes after this number was broadcast on the police radio, two detectives cruising downtown Hull spotted the wanted car in a parking lot outside the unemployment insurance office; they waited until Roussy came out, and arrested him. At his trial in March 1963, the case against Roussy was entirely circumstantial. No one could identify the bank robbers; no weapons or money bags were ever found on Roussy or in his car; and the police were never able to recover any of the loot. Not that they didn't try. "They came to my place four, five times," Roussy's sister-in-law Thérèse said indignantly. "The dumb cops. They know I ain't no thief. I told them, 'If I had a forty-five revolver, I'd shoot you bastards'—excuse the language. And one beef stew says to me, 'We like you, Thérèse, you speak plain.'"

The chief evidence against Roussy was the licence number. Then, there was testimony that another man, Jean-Louis Gélinas, 28, had stayed with Roussy the night before the robbery, and then suddenly blossomed into the expansive owner of $2,200, although he had been on welfare. Gélinas had left his fingerprints in Roussy's car, and had sent $500 to a lawyer, Marcel Bourget, of Hull, for Roussy's defence. If Gélinas was involved in the robbery, and Roussy's car was involved in the robbery, could Roussy be far behind? Roussy produced two witnesses — both taxi-drivers who knew him — who swore that he had been in the hotel beverage room at the time of the robbery, but District Judge Avila Labelle discounted this evidence on the technical ground that it had not been raised at the preliminary hearing.

What really convicted Roussy, however, was his record. If a man would commit robbery once . . . . He was sentenced to ten years in jail on March 18, 1963, and returned to St. Vincent de Paul. This time, however, instead of the calm acceptance he had shown in 1956, he at once began a frantic scramble to prove his innocence. (Later, Bruno Pateras, the lawyer who finally won the case, told me that what impressed him about Roussy was the fanaticism of his campaign; it just didn't seem logical that a man who knew in his heart that he was guilty would fight so hard.) Roussy asked his original lawyer, Bourget, to file an appeal, but there was no money for that. Then he tried another lawyer in Montreal who turned him down. Then he wrote the Legal Aid Society in Hull, only to find that there was no such group. Then he wrote to the Society in Montreal, but they said they couldn't take his case—after all, he lived in Hull. He wrote to the judge at his trial, to the Quebec Minister of Justice (then Claude Wagner), to the president of the Quebec Bar Association, to everybody he could think of, all to no avail.

By mid-1964, Roussy was getting discouraged; then he

heard that federal Justice Minister Guy Favreau would be visiting the jail. Because he was a painter, and a model prisoner, Roussy was able to make sure he was out in the yard, painting, when Favreau came by. He ran over and asked the minister to see if he could get him a copy of the Criminal Code. Favreau told a guard, "See that he gets what he wants."

Roussy got his lawbook early in 1965, and began to study it. He got some inkling, for the first time, of how the legal system works, and wrote a letter to Quebec Chief Justice Lucien Tremblay. His Lordship replied within three days, telling Roussy he would need a transcript of the original trial. It took over a year for Roussy to scrape up the $600 for a transcript, by writing begging letters to friends and relatives, and using his own prison trust fund. He studied the evidence carefully and prepared a 200-page argument, all written in longhand, which he sent off to Chief Justice Tremblay. Once again, the reply was swift; the chief justice persuaded the Montreal Legal Aid Society that it could, after all, find a lawyer for Roussy.

Bruno Pateras, who received Roussy's brief in March 1967, knew at once that he could win the case and, after one more set-back — the entire Roussy file disappeared from the Hull courthouse and reappeared, just as mysteriously as it had vanished, five months later—an appeal was heard on October 11, 1967. Roussy was finally cleared and released on December 27.

By the time he got back to Hull, his children were split up and living in towns spread from St. Catharines, Ontario, to St. Avelin, Quebec. Only Lise, 17, was still in Hull. She had been in eleven foster homes, and wanted no more of them. "Whenever anything disappears," she told me, "they say I stole it, because my father is a crook."

I haven't seen Roussy since 1968, when he was back working as a painter, and living with Lise. I have no idea what happened to him, or to Lise, or any of his other children. For all I know, he may be back in trouble with the law. The one thing I do know is that the justice he received had nothing to do with the equality promised in Canada's Bill of Rights.

On October 20, 1972, Harold Ballard, president of Maple Leaf Gardens in Toronto, and a governor of the National Hockey League, was sentenced to three years in penitentiary on charges of fraud and theft involving $205,000 in Garden funds. Ballard did not, in fact, serve his time in Kingston, but in a cottage-type prison in Muskoka, with its own swimming pool and mini-golf course, and, in his words, "terrific" food. Other charges, of evading income tax on $134,000, were dropped. Ballard's trial lasted from May 23 to July 14, and he was represented by J. J. Robinette, one of this country's most eminent lawyers. The difference between Ballard and Roussy—besides the minor technicality that Roussy was not guilty, while Ballard was—lay in the fact that the former was a poor man with a record, and the latter a rich man with none. I have no objection to the long, scrupulous trial that led to Ballard's conviction, nor to the fact that he received decent treatment both before and after. I simply ask—could what happened to Roussy have happened to Ballard?

A few days after Ballard's last court appearance, a woman was haled into the same Toronto courthouse where he had been convicted. A neighbour had charged her with public mischief after a quarrel. She was slapped into custody on a remand for mental examination, without ever being allowed to utter a word on her own behalf. Could that have happened to Ballard? (She was later released, and the case against her dismissed.)

In April 1972, while the lawyers were winding up the Ballard trial, Peter Redman, an Indian from Shoal Lake, Ontario, was charged with stealing a thirty-nine cent piece of bologna. He was held in jail for nineteen days awaiting trial, then the charge was withdrawn. Could that have happened to Ballard?

In September of that same year, while Ballard was waiting for his sentence, an Indian was convicted of juvenile delinquency in Sioux Narrows, Ontario. The Indian was six years of age. Could that have happened to any offspring of Ballard's?

In 1971, the Civil Liberties Association conducted a penetrating study of the operations of the provincial criminal courts in five cities — Halifax, Montreal, Toronto, Winnipeg, and Vancouver. These are the courts in which over ninety per cent of criminal cases are tried; their clients are, mostly, poor people, or people with records. The kind of justice they receive has nothing to do with anything laid down in the Bill of Rights, or any other law.

For example, the assumption — reinforced in the Bill of Rights — is that every accused is innocent until found guilty. That being the case, you would expect police to proceed, as often as possible, by way of summons, rather than simply collaring a suspect and throwing him in the can. Harold Ballard's case went by way of summons; 72.8 per cent of the cases the civil liberties group studied began with an arrest. Why? Presumably, because the accused were so dangerous to the public weal that they could not be allowed loose. Yet, in 221 cases where bail was set, 87.7 per cent of the accused posted the bail and went free until trial. The act of putting up money turned them from dangerous to non-dangerous persons. No, it couldn't be that. The civil libertarians were never able to solve the mystery of all those arrests, but it did come up with a hint; if a police officer proceeds by way of summons, he has to do all the book-work himself; if he simply arrests the suspect and bangs him into custody, the paperwork falls on the staff in the station.

Once arrested, more than seventy-five per cent of the accused spent twelve hours or more in custody before they were either released on bail or brought before a court; one out of every five suspects suffered pre-trial confinement of anywhere from one week to three months. And all, of course, were presumed to be innocent.

194

The notion that every accused is entitled to make a phone call was dealt a body blow by the study; thirty per cent of those who asked for this privilege were denied it (in Winnipeg, the figure was 42.2 per cent). One woman, arrested on a charge of assaulting a policeman at a political demonstration in Toronto, asked to call her husband; the request was repeatedly refused over a four-hour period. Finally, she lied, and said she had children at home, and had to make a phone call to arrange for their dinner; then she was allowed to use the phone. She had no children, but used the call to get in touch with a lawyer, who got her released four hours later. At the subsequent trial, she was found not guilty.

In fact, it was difficult for most of the accused to get in touch with a lawyer until they had been in custody for some time; only nine per cent had legal counsel within four hours of arrest; sixty-nine per cent waited longer than twenty-four hours, and forty-two per cent longer than three days.

Again, the notion that prisoners are advised that they may remain silent has a lot to do with American TV police series, and nothing to do with Canadian reality; three out of five prisoners said they received no such caution; one out of every four said they had been hurt by the police during interviews, although the overwhelming majority of these said they would file no complaint because "nobody would believe me".

In short, for most Canadians charged with criminal offences—the unrich, the unlettered, the un-well-connected —there is no presumption of innocence.

Nor, once they arrived in court, was there much in the way of a trial. Jammed courts, impatient judges, and what appears to be a streak of bone-laziness saw to that. The average daily court session monitored in the study lasted 140 minutes; the average daily court adjournment—for the day—took place at 1:45 p.m. The average amount of time it took to dispose of a charge was eleven minutes, and to dispose of an accused (some faced multiple charges), seventeen minutes. Even serious cases went hurtling through the judicial process, because most of the accused pleaded guilty, and little time was wasted on such matters as extenuating circumstances or character references. Among those who pleaded guilty and were sent to jail for two years or more, seventy-seven per cent had court hearings of less than twenty minutes, and thirty-seven per cent less than ten minutes. The Civil Liberties Association concluded that our criminal courts are marked by "Widespread punishment without proper proof of guilt, and widespread departure from the letter and spirit of the due-process safeguards. Right through the criminal process, the protection of the accused invariably is subordinated to other considerations."

It is the "convenience of administration", in the phrase of one court study, as much as anything else, that explains the widespread abuse of our mental health laws. (One Saskatchewan case is detailed in Chapter 9.) All that is required to bung someone into detention—if he is unrich or unwary — is an accusation that he is unbalanced. We don't like crazies. A study released in 1972 covering 787 people who were remanded in custody for psychiatric examination in Toronto indicated that all you have to do to make a magistrate reach for his gavel is to hint that the accused is unbalanced: "Minor offences, such as vagrancy, malicious mischief [and] wilful damage were used by the courts to remand twenty-three men and six women to one hospital alone." Charges against 80 of the 787 people incarcerated were later dropped, and "about seventy people remanded for between thirty and sixty days were found not to be in need of, or unsuitable for, treatment." To cap it all off, in most cases when a psychiatric finding *was* made, and treatment reccommended, it was simply ignored by the court who had shoved the accused away.

We have constructed a legal system that advertises equality and dispenses inequity; it works moderately well for the well-to-do and poorly for the poor. It is surely significant that nearly all of the spectacular cases of injustice in our recent history have involved people from the lower or lower-middle classes.

Remember Wilbert Coffin? He was a prospector, ne'er-do-well, and sometime drunk was who was tried, convicted, and hanged in 1956 for the murder of three Pennsylvania hunters in the Gaspé region of Quebec.

Coffin had met the three men in the bush, and helped them repair their truck; later, he came upon their abandoned vehicle and pilfered some items from it. When the trio were reported missing, a widespread search was instituted. Coffin had gone away to Montreal to visit his mistress, and up to Val d'Or to talk to a potential investor in his prospecting business, but he was back in the Gaspé when the search began, and he told the police about his meeting with the hunters — though not about his theft.

The search discovered the bear-mangled bodies of the men scattered over a wide area; they had been shot. At once, back in Pennsylvania, a cry went up for vengeance; the Pennsylvania Federation of Sportsmen's clubs posted a reward, and agitated for action from the Quebec government. Tourism was a big business, and the province, anxious to preserve its reputation as a fine place for people to come and shoot things, moved swiftly. Coffin was taken into custody as a material witness on August 10, 1953; he was held for weeks without recourse to a lawyer, interrogated almost constantly, had a spy planted in his cell to pick up an offguard confession — there was none — and was brought to trial in August 1954. The case against him consisted of the evidence that he had met the men, the fact that he had pilfered items from their truck, and the fact that he paid off some debts after their disappearance. Finally, there was evidence that Coffin had been seen with what might have been a rifle in his truck.

Coffin's defence was that he had seen the hunters with

two other men, who were driving a jeep with Pennsylvania licence plates (the inference being that these strangers, who were never actively sought by the police, might have done the killing); that he had left the area before the hunters disappeared; that he had been drinking when he pilfered the goods from their truck, and that he denied, flatly and repeatedly, having anything to do with their deaths. This defence was never put forward; Coffin's lawyer, a bizarre and publicity-prone gentleman who announced at one point that he had lined up 180 witnesses, called no evidence whatever.

This blunder had a double effect: In the first place, it convinced the jury of Coffin's guilt. One of the jurors told Jacques Hebert, author of *J'Accuse les Assassins de Wilbert Coffin*, "When Maher stood up to tell us he had no defence to offer, we decided that Coffin was guilty. A man who does not defend himself must be guilty." In the second place, the lack of a defence undercut all future attempts to upset the guilty verdict; there was no recorded legal evidence on which to base an appeal.

In fact, the most crucial piece of evidence in the entire case was apparently deliberately suppressed. The police had found a note on the windshield of the hunters' vehicle, dated June 13, 1953, in which one hunter let his companions know that he had returned to the truck that day. Coffin was able to prove that he was in Montreal by June 13, which made it highly unlikely that he was the killer. But it didn't matter, because the note was never produced in court. *Toronto Star* reporter Jean Beliveau found out about it after the trial, and wrote a story underlining its significance; still the note did not appear; it had vanished, along with everything else in the Coffin files, from court custody.

Coffin received no real defence until he escaped from the jail in Quebec City in September 1954, leaving a note to say that he had gone to try to prove his innocence. He went to lawyer Maher's office — explaining to a cab driver who he was and why he was going—but Maher told him to go back to jail, so he did that. The case became a cause célèbre, and Toronto lawyer Arthur Maloney arrived to help Coffin, but it was too late.

Premier Maurice Duplessis took strong exception to attempts to reopen the Coffin file, and blamed "outside agitators". He kept constant pressure on the courts, and seemed to be personally offended by Coffin's attempts to assert his innocence. Then, when it became clear that, because of the original defence error, no new trial would be granted, Coffin asked the Premier for a personal favour. Could he be allowed to marry his mistress in jail before he was hanged, and thus legitimize their son? Duplessis turned him down flat. "We cannot permit these two people to meet," he said, "That would be contrary to public interest and the proper administration of justice."

Coffin was hanged on February 10, 1956. His last words were, "I am not guilty, and may God have mercy on my soul."

The newspaper *L'Action Catholique* was glad the sentence had not been commuted: "It was important that things should come out this way. The victim being an American tourist, the authorities could not, without serious reasons, commute the death sentence to life imprisonment. It could have had regrettable effects on our touristic publicity."

Remember Stephen Truscott? He was arrested, at the age of fourteen, after twelve-year-old Lynne Harper was found raped and murdered in June 1959, near the small town of Clinton in southwestern Ontario. Truscott's father was a Warrant Officer in the Air Force; Lynne's father was a Flying Officer. The case against Truscott was built almost entirely on the fact that he had been seen giving Lynne a ride on the handlebars of his bike, and that the town had worked itself into a near frenzy in its thirst for revenge. After Isabel LeBourdais' book, *The Trial of Stephen Truscott*, raised serious doubts about his original conviction, a legal battle developed that ended with the Supreme Court of Canada taking the unusual step of, in effect, rehearing the case. But all that had gone before proved, once more, to be crucial. Mr. Justice Emmett Hall, who wrote the lone dissent from the court's finding that all had been in order, told me, "Whatever the facts were; whoever killed Lynne Harper, one thing is clear—Stephen Truscott did not ever receive a fair trial." He also suggested that the real barrier Truscott faced was that to overturn the earlier verdict would have been to admit incredible sloppiness in the lower courts, and a shocking miscarriage of justice.

The Truscott case has an interesting postscript. A 1975 movie clearly based on the case was the subject of a letter to the newspaper from a nice grandmother from Vancouver who objected to the film because "the story chosen is one of the saddest in Canadian history — something we'd all like to forget". Precisely.

Remember Julian Roux? He was a smalltime thief who was convicted in 1963 of the murder of seventy-five-year-old Henri Denault in Victoriaville, Quebec. Roux and another man broke into Denault's house on the night of March 17, 1963. The next morning, around 5 a.m., the house caught fire and burned down, with Denault inside. Roux was charged with having set the fire, and convicted of murder. He spent nine years in jail before he was able to prove that he had been in Asbestos, thirty miles away, when the fire was set.

Remember Harold Shatford? He was sentenced to fifteen years in jail in April 1971, for a robbery he did not commit. Police in Toronto put Shatford, a man with a long criminal record, into a lineup after a department store cashier told them that the man who robbed her was well-dressed and good-looking. Shatford was the only well-dressed, good-looking man in the lineup, and he was promptly identified, tried, and convicted. Later, another man (also a handsome rogue) admitted that he, and not Shatford, had been the robber.

Emile Roussy was not a particularly winsome character; neither was Wilbert Coffin, nor Stephen Truscott, nor Julian Roux, nor Harold Shatford. In the ordinary course of events, more respectable citizens would probably have escaped conviction. Canadian legal safeguards work mainly for those in the mainstream of society, as three quick instances of injustice on a lesser scale will show:

In April 1971, Refrod Francotte, 48, spent eleven days in a Toronto jail on a charge of stealing a dime from a newsstand. Bail had been set at $20, but he didn't have the money, so Judge Hugh Foster refused to allow him out to await trial. Foster said, "The important thing is to register a conviction as soon as possible, if the man is guilty. If the man doesn't turn up for another six months, the witnesses will have forgotten what he looks like.... If there is no friend in Toronto who would trust him for twenty dollars, why should the court trust him?"

In December 1970, Robert Lemieux appeared in court to argue for reduced sentences for his clients, members of the Front de Libération du Québec. Lemieux himself had been charged with seditious conspiracy, and sent to jail without bail, for his role in aiding the FLQ. When he appeared in court to argue for his clients, his hands were handcuffed; all the time he made his futile argument, he gestured with manacled hands.

In April 1972, Saul Izreig, a naturalized Canadian citizen, and a Moslem, appeared before Toronto Justice of the Peace Lorne Taylor on a charge of having driven through a red light. Taylor doubted if Izreig and his two witnesses—also Moslems—could take the oath, but was finally convinced that they could. He dismissed their testimony with a pithy phrase, "Moslems be damned", and added, "If this is the kind of Canadian imports we're getting, let's forget it.... I just don't believe you and your people."

These are instances where single people have been selected for injustice, but there are two laws in Quebec that make the entire provincial population liable to mistreatment — the Coroner's Act and the Fire Marshall's Act. Under these notorious laws, suspects may be, and often are, held in custody, pronounced guilty by public authorities long before a charge is laid, required to testify against themselves, and deprived of all the safeguards available in other provinces. The Acts have been the subject of controversy for years, and have been used, time and again, in violation of the Bill of Rights and customary practice. Mr. Justice Emmett Hall points out, "All anyone has to do to break down that kind of law is to get a case before the Supreme Court of Canada, which would be bound to hold the thing invalid. You have to ask yourself why the government of Canada has never followed such a course of action."

Due process of law is a very fine shrine, and it is nice to know that there is a piece of parchment somewhere that says we are equal before the courts; but for a great many Canadians, the fine-flowing phrases of the Bill of Rights are not worth the paper they are written on.

CHAPTER 12:

WE LOVE OUR NIGGERS

And why is all this done? I will tell you: it is because you are the subjects of the Queen as I am. She cares as much for any one of you as she does for one of her white subjects.

Alexander Morris,
Address to Indians, at the signing
of the Treaties at Forts Carlton
and Pitt, 1876.

Inuvik is in the Mackenzie Delta, just south of the Arctic Ocean, and there was a wind blowing across the town that seemed to come straight from the North Pole, picking up ice pellets as it came. I was standing with my back to the wind, so the Northern Affairs official, poor sod, had to face into it to talk to me. Beside us was the Utilidor, about four-by-four feet square, raised on cement blocks and covered with galvanized tin—and ice, of course. The Utilidor carried heat and electricity and water to the apartments and houses of Inuvik, and carried away the sewage. It ran smack through the middle of the Indian village, but not into any of the Indian homes.

A few minutes earlier, I had been in a shack—tar paper on the outside, raw wood on the inside. It was about twelve feet square, divided into two rooms; there was no electricity, no water, no light, no plumbing, and not much heat, despite a roaring metal stove. An Indian woman, nursing her baby, sat by the stove with her parka pulled up around the two of them, not for modesty, but for warmth; it was about forty degrees below zero outside (this was in the pre-Celsius era) and only a few degrees above freezing inside. That shack was within six feet of the Utilidor, which snaked past it bearing heat and comfort to the white folks beyond, and I had hauled the Northern Affairs official out to explain what was going on.

He got it into his head that I thought the arrangement of warmth and light and water for the whites and cold and dark and pneumonia for the Indians carried racial overtones, and he wanted to set me straight. "We don't put up with any racist crap," he said, and I said that was nice. No, the thing was that it cost about $120 a month to service a home on the Utilidor, and nobody made a nickel in profit. Well, of course, the Indians couldn't afford that. Now, the deal was slightly different if you happened to be a federal civil servant; in that case, you got to live in one of the subsidized housing units. On the average, you paid $100 a month for a three-bedroom apartment, with the Utilidor service thrown in. And how many whites were on the Utilidor? Well, all of them. And how many Indians? Well, none. But it wasn't a matter of race; it was just government regulations.

That conversation took place ten years ago, and I hope and expect that conditions have changed in Inuvik since then. But not the attitude; the attitude is and always has been the same. We are not racists. Americans are racists. South Africans are racists. But we, thank God, regard all people as equal, and if those who get shafted happen to wear tawny or yellow or black or red skins, that isn't racism, just government regulations.

Sometimes, of course, it is hard to explain to people; sometimes they get the wrong idea entirely. When I left Inuvik, I went to Frobisher Bay, in the eastern Arctic, and discovered that the RCMP there had gone out and shot most of the Eskimos' huskies, on the grounds — perfectly true, too — that they were a damn nuisance to the whites in the settlement. At that time, the Eskimos still did some hunting, and the snowmobile hadn't taken over completely; for some people, the huskies were, literally, their livelihood. Unfortunately, the Eskimos misinterpreted the shooting; one of them told a visiting anthropologist, "First, I thought of killing the policemen. But I don't mind now. Maybe afterwards there won't be so many dogs since the police are shooting them. Maybe the police will kill Eskimos then, just like the dogs."

There, you see? Perfectly ridiculous. That Eskimo thought the dogs were being shot for racial reasons, when there isn't a racial bullet in the whole RCMP arsenal. It was all a matter of regulations. Frobisher at that time was on the same Utilidor system as Inuvik, with a twist; that is, the Eskimo village was entirely separate from the whites, so the Utilidor didn't have to go through the shacks to serve the white folk. Just the same, it was misunderstood and, from time to time, pitched battles took place between young whites and Eskimos along the Utilidor, and they were sometimes bloody.

When I suggested to a northern service officer that these pitched battles reminded me of Watts, the racial battleground of Los Angeles, he was genuinely grieved. He said, "We are here to help these people, can't you see that?" And I said that was exactly how our Victorian grandfathers described it when they massacred the natives of Tasmania so they could teach their kids about the Bible, and the northern service officer said he despaired of making me understand.

Well, I admit it, I'm slow; when I look back along the corridors of Canadian history, I see a series of vignettes, all of them open to misunderstanding: the wanton slaughter of the Beothuck Indians of Newfoundland; the brisk slave trade in the colonies; the destruction of the Indians, always for their own good, with such neat tricks as seeding smallpox germs in blankets given to them; the exploitation, humiliation, and slaughter of Orientals brought in to work on the CPR, the *Komagata Maru* incident (described in Chapter 3); the incarceration of Japanese — but not German — Canadians during World War II, and so on. To an uncritical mind like mine, a mind incapable of drawing fine distinctions, it looks as if there is, after all, a hint of racism in our make-up.

When Jack Johnson, the black boxer, married a white girl, *Saturday Night* magazine suggested in a forthright editorial that this "impudent nigger", this "black baboon" should be lynched. His action, the editorial pointed out, besides "breaking the law and outraging the ideals of decent society", endangered the lives of thousands of "pure and innocent white women in districts where Negroes are in a majority". The girl, needless to say, was a "pervert" and a "gangrene". In an editorial like that, written in 1912, unsubtle persons will think they detect a hint of prejudice.

Saturday Night was not blazing any trails, it was simply reflecting widely-held Canadian views. Thirteen years later, in 1925, it turned its attention once more to the subject of marriage between the races. The federal government had, in its wisdom, prepared a document describing the difficulties and dangers of interracial marriage. *Saturday Night* approved of the document, but thought the government should go much further. Canada had the advantage of the U.S., because laws relating to marriage and divorce were under federal authority here, and not there: "Nevertheless, the U.S.A. has progressed farther than Canada towards the total prohibition of these most undesirable unions." Interracial marriage should forthwith be prohibited by law, said *Saturday Night*.

We were not narrow-minded in our approach; blacks and Indians were not the only sub-human species to feel the sting of our displeasure; as we have already seen, Orientals were not only excluded, bullied, deprived of the vote, and beaten up, they were subjected to every kind of humiliation our busy lawmakers could dream up when they went to seek employment. And this is not ancient history; I am not

206

speaking now of the Vancouver race riots of 1887 and 1907, but of comparatively recent days. During the 1935 federal election, the Liberal party ran a strident ad in the *Vancouver Sun* to warn that "A Vote for any CCF candidate is a vote to give the CHINAMAN and the JAPANESE the Same Voting Right that you have! A Vote for a Liberal Candidate is a VOTE AGAINST ORIENTAL ENFRANCHISEMENT." This went down well; the Liberals came out of the election with more B.C. votes — and seats — than any other party.

The last restrictions on Chinese-Canadian voting rights were not lifted until 1947, and on Japanese until 1949. By that time, American racial problems were beginning to occupy our attention and fire our sense of superiority. We began to take a firm stand, internationally, against any form of racism. Indeed, when John Diefenbaker was prime minister, he cloaked himself and this nation in the mantle of righteousness when he went to Commonwealth conferences as guardian of the world's conscience on racial issues. I bet a nickel that Diefenbaker forgot to tell his applauding audiences that, in 1939, the Supreme Court of Canada upheld a tavern owner's right to refuse a customer beer on the grounds that he was a black, or that Nova Scotia had legally segregated schools until 1963 (in fact, Ontario didn't close its last black-only school until 1965, two years after Diefenbaker left office).

When we tell other nations about our heritage of tolerance, I wonder if we tell them about Peter and Fred Kelly, who began to work on behalf of fellow Indians in Kenora, Ontario, in the mid-1960s, and were jumped by a group of whites and beaten. I wonder if we tell them what happens to government workers who get involved with native problems. When William Grant, the Indian agent for the Yukon, found that he had too much money for welfare, and none for badly-needed houses, he cut through red tape to use welfare funds for housing. So he was fired and charged with conversion by fraud. The judge who heard the case convicted Grant, but praised him for what he had done, and imposed a minimum fine of $10 on each of ten charges. The government promptly appealed for a harsher sentence, and got the fines raised to $500 each. When Gerry Gamble, a community development officer in Cornwall, Ontario, helped Indians in the area to organize, the government fired him for "failure to form positive relations with officials". When Anton Karch, another community development officer, helped Indians in Cowichan, B.C., stage a protest parade, he was transferred to remote Fort St. James, and quit. When Mrs. Jean Goodwill, an Indian, and co-editor of the Indian Affairs Branch publication *Indian News*, supported a native protest in Alberta, she was fired.

I am giving you here only a few of the cases I investigated in 1968, when our reputation for tolerance and fair play was firmly established in the court of world opinion. I am still receiving material suggesting that things haven't changed much (when, in 1975, a lady in Kenora, Ontario, wrote a book called *Bended Elbow*, complaining that the local Indians were drunken, shiftless ne'er-do-wells, it sold 3,000 copies under the counter at the Kenora bus station, making it a strong candidate for local best-seller of all time), but journalism is a faddish business, and I haven't done any stories in this line recently. All I ask is, if we have a reputation for fairness, where does it come from?

Part of the answer, I suggest, is that we are such a regional country that it can never be said of us that Canada (modern Canada, that is) is against blacks, or Indians, or Chinese; there is a lot of prejudice against blacks in Toronto, but not much in Vancouver; Indians are despised in Calgary and Saskatoon, but have no problems in Halifax; Chinese Canadians seldom suffer in Montreal, but have a hell of a time on the west coast. And so it goes. We have learned to adjust our bigotry to the minority to be served; there is a certain amount of tradition in the practice, as anyone can tell you who has ever visited Dresden, Ontario.

Dresden, a comfortable town in the southwestern corner of the province, has few Orientals, and no prejudice against them. It does, however, have a number of blacks and a traditional reputation as Canada's Jim Crow centre. The town's main tourist attraction is the grave of Uncle Tom, of *Uncle Tom's Cabin* fame. (His real name was Reverend Josiah Henson, and one of his descendants, "Tex" Henson, a paratrooper and wartime hero, left Dresden when a local restaurant refused to serve him a cup of coffee.) The town grew up, under the name "Dawn Settlement", as the terminus of the Underground Railway before the American Civil War, but its black population always found itself facing conditions astonishingly similar to those that prevailed way down along the old plantation.

In 1949, Sidney Katz, then writing for *Maclean's* magazine, ambled along to the town when he learned that, in Dresden, blacks could not be served in a restaurant, get a haircut, visit two of the town's three poolhalls, join a service club, or hold a decent job. Katz ran into restaurant owner Morley McKay, who told him that he used to keep two prints of Uncle Tom over his soda fountain, but had to take them down because "The niggers became too cocky. They used to come in and say 'You show pictures of Uncle Tom, but you won't serve us.'" This line maddened McKay: "Do you know that for three days afterward I get raging mad every time I see a Negro? Maybe it's like an animal who's had a smell of blood." Maybe.

Despite the fuss raised by articles like Katz's, Dresden stuck to its principles. That same year the town voted 517–108 — a fairly high turnout for a total population of 2,305, including 350 blacks — to continue the by-laws authorizing discrimination in stores. Even after the province stepped in with a Fair Accommodation Practices Act in 1954, two restaurant owners refused service to black customers. They were charged and convicted, but the cases were quashed on appeal. Another case, in 1955, was more

209

successful, and the overt discrimination in Dresden disappeared, by outside fiat.

As in Ontario, so in the Maritimes; there is a substantial percentage of blacks, and few Orientals; there is racial tension between whites and blacks, but not between whites and other races. Nova Scotia, which has most of the blacks, has most of the problems. Indeed, that province has the distinction of a lawcase, from 1947, that might well have blown all the way up the eastern seaboard from South Carolina or Georgia.

A black woman entered a movie house in the mining town of New Glasgow, and asked for an orchestra seat. The theatre had a rule, however, that blacks could sit only in the balcony; perhaps to make up for this, it charged ten cents more for orchestra seats. The woman offered to pay the extra dime, but this was refused. At that, the pushy hussy bought a balcony ticket and went and sat in the orchestra, right among the white folks. She was forcibly ejected, and then arrested. It seemed that out of the extra dime collected for orchestra seats, one cent went to the province by way of tax; she had avoided that tax when the theatre refused her dime, so she was prosecuted (on a charge of tax evasion), convicted, and fined twenty dollars, plus six dollars in costs. When she appealed, the Nova Scotia Supreme Court upheld the conviction.

They have the blacks pretty well in hand in New Glasgow these days, but just up the line at Antigonish, the problem of uppity dark folks remains. In 1972, a series of stabbings, assaults, and gang fights broke out after dances held at the local parish centre. When Lyndon Watkins went there to investigate the trouble for the *Globe and Mail*, he ran into a lawyer who provided him with one of my favourite quotes of all time:

> The attitude is this — and I grew up in a small Nova
> Scotia town which has 500 blacks, so I think I under-

stand it. The people say "We love our niggers. This is a happy town, as long as they don't get into fights and stick knives into white people."

All of these incidents, as I say, cloud my mind, and make me see racism where, I am assured by volley after volley of editorials, speeches, pamphlets, stories, and books, it does not exist. When Paul Smithers, a black, kicks a white boy and causes his death in Mississauga, Ontario, after a hockey game in which racial insults were exchanged, and the concerned authorities rush out to tell us that the issue is one of hockey violence, not racism, I am willing to listen and try to believe. When, in February 1975, Jamaican-born Bromley Armstrong, appointed to Ontario's Human Rights Commission, has his office stoned by white nationalists, my faith is tested. (They tied an imitation ticket to Africa on one stone, and a note addressed to "The Nigger Rights Commissioner" to another.) When Paki-bashing becomes a kind of neighbourhood sport in Vancouver—as it did in the spring of 1975 — I come close to downright disillusion. (I don't mean to imply that only Pakistanis get bashed in Vancouver; almost anyone who looks as if he might come from Asia or the East Indies is eligible. One day early in 1975, Bijay Singh, an East Indian, returned to his home in the Killarney Park area to find a mob of white youths standing around smashing all the windows with stones. When he tried to interfere, they chucked rocks at him instead, then beat the hell out of him. He was unable to work for two weeks. He took the hint and moved out; his was the fourth East Indian family to flee racial violence in the same neighbourhood over a three-month period.) And when my Toronto mailbox overflows with the outpourings of the Western Guard, advising me that "Every Friday evening—" blacks come pouring over the border from the U.S. intent on defiling white purity—"Like sharks at the smell of blood, the maddening rush is on for the coveted target—white meat", why then, I am willing to say flatly, out loud, that bigotry is not foreign to my native land.

But never mind; as long as the policies of the nation are directed against racism, progress can be made; as long as our institutions themselves are dedicated to equality, occasional incidents, however regrettable, may be written off as the workings of a few loonies. As long as our legal structure stands four-square with Indian agent Alexander Morris, and assures our minorities that "The Queen cares as much for any one of you as she does for one of her white subjects", why then, we are getting someplace. Is it so?

I ask you to consider the cases of two of the Queen's Indian subjects, and how they came to be murdered, one in Saskatchewan, and one in British Columbia, and what was done about their deaths, and I ask you to ponder the question: What would have happened in these cases had the victims been white and the accused Indian?

Allen Thomas was a Saulteaux, from a reserve near Jackfish Lake, about twenty miles north of North Battleford, Saskatchewan. He was slender and handsome, with an eagle nose, broad cheekbones, and dark eyes. He was twenty when he was killed, in 1963. That spring, Thomas, with some relatives and friends, was camping on the fairgrounds just outside the small town of Glaslyn, twenty-three miles north of the reserve, in the lovely, wooded, rolling country that occupies so much of Saskatchewan. The Indians worked on farms nearby, weeding, planting, clearing brush, doing any odd jobs that came along. They hadn't much else to do, anyway; since the days when the Saulteaux (a branch of the Ojibwas) were a proud, fierce band, hunting had pretty well been wiped out, and jobs are not easily come by for people who are poor, uneducated, badly fed, sometimes dirty, and often drunk. By the white man's standard, and with the white man's help, the Indians of northern Saskatchewan are mostly a miserable lot, and when they get "uppity", as happens from time to time, trouble follows swiftly.

The townspeople began to complain that the Indians living in tents on the Glaslyn fairgrounds were uppity, or if not uppity, at least a damn nuisance. They had the permission of the town council to camp where they were camped, but that didn't make it right in the eyes of many of the area's citizens.

On the night of May 11, 1963, a bunch of the boys came into town, and joined a group of townspeople in a beerhall discussion of this and that, and the subject of Indians came up (not for the first time). One of the few moderately coherent accounts of what happened is contained in the statement one Jerry Dale Hobbs gave to the RCMP on May 19.

"I came into Glaslyn about 10 o'clock p.m. on Saturday May 11, went to Dart's store and we shopped there for half an hour . . . could be a little longer than that, too. Then we went to Read's drug store, Tracy and I and my brother and from there . . . we went to the beer parlor, went in and sat down with Jackie Woods, Alfred Lobe, George Batary; Billy Batary was there, too.

"We had three glasses of beer and it was closing time. We sat there and talked about farming and almost everything 'til about 20 minutes after 11. Then we said, Alfred said 'Let's go to Jack's for a beer. Wayne Dick is home and we'll have a beer with him.' Jack said, 'Sure, come on up to the house', so I went with Alfred. . . . Then all the rest came too."

William John Mackie, the "Jack" of this passage, lived near the fairgrounds, and although Jerry Dale Hobbs is vague on this point, the group of men who gathered at his place seemed to have a pretty fair idea that something was up. While they were milling around the trucks outside Mackie's, an Indian came on the scene. He may have wondered why a group of white men were foregathering at midnight not far from the campground, but he got little satisfaction. Here's what Hobbs recalled happening next:

"In the meantime there we got out of the truck we were standing there talking and an Indian come up to us he says 'What the hell you doing?' Alfred said something to him, I don't know just what it was and he walked up to Alfred right close and Alfred slapped him and he fell down on his backside. I said to the Indian 'Come on, get up, don't lay there.' I picked up his cap and put it on his head and I helped him up. I pointed him west and I said 'You better go.' Then we went into the house nothing more was said there was a bottle of beer opened for each of us. We were sitting in the house for a while and then somebody said 'Are we going?' I didn't know what they meant."

It is curious that Hobbs didn't know what they meant, because Mrs. Viola Mackie, who came home from work about midnight, later recalled that the men were sitting around talking about going to the encampment "to have some fun with the Indians", and she warned them: "Leave them Indians alone."

Anyway, Hobbs soon found out. "So everybody went outside — they said 'We're going to drive down to the Indian tents.' So Alfred and Howard took their trucks and we drove in a bunch in each truck. I was in front with Alfred and Jack in Alfred's truck.

"So we drove down past them and we came up to some houses and we stopped. And there was a bunch jumped out; there was a horse with a long piece of rope and hobbles on. Somebody took them off. I don't know who it was. Then we got back in the truck and drove back to Jack's and we went back in the house again and we sat there for a while talking, joking."

The Indian encampment contained about twelve people in three tents; the first part of the evening's entertainment consisted in two truckloads of whites driving past the tents and then turning loose a hobbled horse. This called for celebration back at the house.

"Then we were all in the living room there and there was a bunch talking of scaring the Indians. I don't know who said that." (Hobbs never knew who did anything specific.) And there was a bunch went outside. They said, 'Let's go down and scare them. Maybe pull down their tents.' So there was a bunch strung out it was dark out there so I said to Danny Williemeit, 'We might as well go along and see what they're going to do.' So we started out.... They were quite a bunch ahead of us. We walked down the road towards the first Indian tent. I guess it was Max Bear's, I didn't know that at the time. When we got there we were all mixed up—some were up ahead some were dropping back — when I got there the tent was down."

Max Bear, his wife, his seventy-nine-year-old mother, and his five-year-old boy were in the tent when it was pulled down. Bear later said that he asked Hobbs, whom he knew, why they and all their clothing and personal belongings were being kicked around by the whites and he was told — quite wrongly — that the Indians were not allowed to camp where they were. Bear's wife claimed that he was hit in the eye by Hobbs.

After that, it got pretty confusing. Some of the Indians, including Allen Thomas, were up at the town water tower, drinking beer. When they came driving back into the camp, they found two tents down and white men milling around; they were attacked at once, and dove into the bush to hide. Paul Moccasin, one of the Indians, said he lost sight of Allen Thomas in the flight. Moccasin was found in the bush by the white men, beaten and kicked, and got away again.

In another car, two other Indians, Billie Gopher and Clarence Martel, arrived to find the Gopher tent down and everything scattered. Gopher said he jumped out of the car, ran up to Alfred Lobe and hit him. Lobe ran away and Gopher ran after, until he saw another carload of white men arriving. He ran back to his car, piled in, and drove to the RCMP station for help.

During the mêlée, Allen Thomas, who was drunk enough or brave enough to put up a fight, was knocked down and beaten to death.

His cousin, Annie Thomas, later testified that she saw men running around with sticks and hitting a man on the ground.

"After this I can see somebody laying on the ground and somebody standing over this person....And after that I can hear somebody making noise, moaning, making a pitiful sound....And then I got scared and I just, I just ran, I just ran away."

With all the Indians scattering there was no one to see what actually happened to Thomas except the white raiders. Here is Hobbs' account of what was going on:

"Then there was some fellows went up towards Bill Gopher's tent. When I come out and Danny and Billy Batary and Tracy, this tent Bill Gopher's was tore down. So we ran around the tents to a gully we laid down there. I was afraid there might be some shooting. I didn't want to get shot . . . I heard something pop — thud — it sounded like somebody got hit. Tracy said 'Somebody sure got hit or something.' We got up.

"There was a bunch of us got up we walked up this way towards in between the tents. Then I seen Howard Mc-Connell get hit he was bent over. Then I seen an Indian get onto his back was hanging onto him. He wiggled around— got him off his back and threw him down—that's all I seen him do. I'm sure he never beat him.

"There was an Indian he wasn't too burly of a fellow. He had a long stick looked like a tent pole or something like that. He was swinging it around. Then he was the one that hit Howard I figure anyway."

Hobbs saw Billy Gopher's car and saw the Indian drive off to town, so when headlights were seen returning, the

216

white raiders faded into the bush. The men gathered once more at Mackie's and there, George Batary, who hadn't gone on the raid, recalled Alfred Lobe saying "We fixed up one Indian."

When the police arrived, Thomas was found mortally wounded, with a fractured skull; he was dead on arrival at hospital.

Nine white men were arrested and charged with non-capital murder. They were held briefly, then released on bail. The group comprised six farmers and three townsmen, including Alfred Lobe. The Crown chose to proceed against all of them at once, which might have saved money, but prevented calling any one of them as a witness against the others. The coroner's inquest into Thomas' death broke down when the lawyers for the accused argued they could not be called to testify, since the evidence of each would become incriminatory of others. In effect, they would be required to testify against themselves, contrary to our jurisprudence. The defence argument was carried all the way up to the Supreme Court of Canada, which supported it. By that time, nearly two years had passed. Eventually, a preliminary inquiry was held and after it was over, charges against six of the accused were dismissed for lack of evidence, while three—Alfred Lobe, 48, Howard McConnell, 41, and Donald Michnik, 22, went to trial.

It was a walkover; all of the Indian witnesses had been too busy running, or fighting, or going for help, to see what happened to Thomas, and none of the whites could remember a thing. The three accused were again charged jointly, and they could not be examined about each other as long as they all stayed out of the witness box, which they did. Mrs. Viola Mackie remembered telling the whites to leave the Indians alone, but she couldn't recall anything else. George Batary remembered Lobe talking about fixing up one Indian, but nothing further. Mrs. Nellie Williemeit was at the Mackie place that night, and heard the men talking, but just couldn't recall what was said. Wayne Dick, who was on the raid and had been charged, then released, found his memory had gone, too. John Mackie was able to remember that the men were in "an average happy mood" when they came back to the house, but couldn't for the life of him recollect why it was they kept running up to the Indian encampment. And, of course, Jerry Hobbs, whose recollections were already selective a week after the killing, when he made his statement to the police, had gone pretty well fuzzy on the whole thing by the time of the trial.

The Crown moved to have many of the white men declared hostile witnesses, so they could be cross-examined, but their memories refused to come back. By and large, the defence counsel simply lay low; no defence witnesses were called, and few of the Crown's were cross-examined (except the Indians, of course).

There was no direct evidence linking any of the accused to Thomas' death, and an all-male, all-white jury brought in a verdict of not guilty on May 13, 1966.

Mr. Justice Walter Tucker, who conducted the trial, said, "I hope that nothing like this ever happens in this part of the province again", and stressed that he didn't want the verdict to be taken as "approval of racial prejudice in any way".

The Saskatchewan press carried modest accounts of the doings at Glaslyn, and full and righteous reports on the civil rights marches taking place in the American south during the time the case wound its way through the courts. No parallel was ever drawn with events closer to home. Indeed, if there is a lesson in Thomas' death, it is that Indians shouldn't camp near whites. You never know where boyish hi-jinks will lead.

Rose Mary Roper's slaying, on the other hand, was not so much a matter of hi-jinks as of mystery. She got into a car with three white men, and they admitted that she was roughed up some before she was left, lightly clad, in freezing weather, by a garbage dump. But when her battered, nude body was found there the next day it certainly was a surprise to all concerned.

Rose was a pretty girl; she was 18, but looked younger, slight and well-formed, with large, dark eyes and straight black hair cut in bangs across her forehead. But she was an Indian and it is a matter of recorded fact that she drank beer, and dropped out of school, and was not a virgin.

On the evening of April 8, 1967, Rose Roper was in the beer parlour at 150 Mile House, on the Cariboo Trail in B.C., not far from her home. She was there with some Indian friends, but, at some point, got talking to three white youths, Alfred William Kohnke, Stephen Arthur Croft, and Robert Leslie Wilson, who were later charged with her death. All were in their early twenties, all from the Williams Lake area, just down the road. Rose had gone to school with Kohnke, and when she found the youths were on their way to a dance at Lac La Hache, she asked for (or was offered, the evidence is not clear) a ride to her aunt's place there. The white youths went outside and tossed a coin — they were later to say it was to decide who should go back in and ask if Rose was coming with them. In any event, she did go, and Alfred Kohnke and Rose got into the back seat of Bob Wilson's Fairlane, Wilson and Croft got in the front, and they started off.

But they didn't go to Lac La Hache; they drove that way, then headed off the main road onto a trail that goes by an area used locally as a garbage dump. What happened after that, only the three whites really know. The Crown case was that the three formed a plot to take Rose into the bush and rape her (and that the coin flipping was connected with that intent); that she objected, and was killed in a struggle, either while being hauled out of the car or on the ground outside. She died of a broken neck, but had head injuries, extensive bruises, and a cut under her chin. Her clothes were scattered all over the area; buttons were ripped off her blouse; and her back was covered with moss and grass, although she was found lying face down. One of the accused had hand injuries and another had scratches and abrasions; they said these came from a car accident later that night.

The statements and testimony of the accused contained gaps, contradictions, and some flat lies. In general, their story was that they took Rose up the road to have sexual intercourse with her, and that she was willing. But it turned out that she was menstruating — or at least they thought she was menstruating — so they became cross with her, and she with them. She threw some beer around the car, so Bob Wilson slapped her. Then she was either kicked out of the car or, alternatively, dragged out and left, drunk and screaming, beside the trail. That's the gist of their story, but it underwent a kind of evolution between the original telling and the version the three gave in court when they were charged with manslaughter.

Here is what Alfred Kohnke said happened at the dump, as he told it in his original statement to police:

"I was still in the front seat with Bob [Wilson] and Steve [Croft] was in the back seat making time with Rose. She didn't appear to be coming across so the three of us, Bob, Steve and myself started taking all her clothes off. We took off all her clothes and left them in the back seat. Steve couldn't get an erection so he changed places and sat in the front seat with me and Bob. Steve told me to go in the back seat but I didn't feel like it so I told Bob to go back which he did. Bob thought she had the rags on [i.e., was menstruating] so didn't have intercourse with her. Steve told her to get dressed. She put on her jeans, I think they were on backwards. Rose then asked for another beer, which I gave her, and she poured it all over the back seat. Bob got mad and called her a bitch and slapped her across the face and told her to get out. Steve opened the door and as she was getting out he gave her a push. She stumbled out of the car onto the road.

" . . . I put Rose's panties on the aerial of Bob's car and we took off and drove to Lac La Hache where we went to the dance. Bob or Steve then put Rose's panties on another car at the dance hall."

Just a boyish prank, really, with no harm intended, a few beers, a little gang-bang gone awry, then off to the dance.

Wilson told the same story as Kohnke with some variations, according to evidence given by RCMP Col. Michael Voynovich at the trial. This is from the transcript of his testimony: WITNESS: Wilson said "She took off some clothes and I helped her take some more off. I was feeling her up. She had panties and a brassiere on and she said "Let's pretend" and I said, "Hell, pretend, I didn't come here to pretend." And then he went on further and stated to the fellows in the front seat, "Hey, she has got the rags on, if you don't believe me, take a feel." And Mr. Croft said, "Yes, I had a feel, she had a tube up her privates." And she started screaming, she had a bottle of beer in her hand.

The girl began to throw beer around the car, and Wilson got "a little angry" and slapped her a few times, so she called him "a dirty white bastard". He told her to get out of the car, and, as she left, Stephen Croft kicked her "on the ass end".

There were some problems with these two versions, including the fact that they contained at least one lie. At the trial, Croft, who was the leading witness for the defence, brought out a revised edition. In this version, the three boys undressed the girl, with her consent, then, discovering that she apparently was menstruating, demanded to know why she didn't tell them that before they started out. She only mumbled in reply. The beer-throwing and slapping remained as in the earlier story, but now, suddenly, Rose wasn't ordered out of the car, and she wasn't kicked. Instead, she had slumped onto the floor and Croft, who was standing outside in this version, reached through the open door, grabbed her by the legs, and hauled her out onto the ground.

Croft was asked, in cross-examination, why he had told a different story earlier, and replied, "I guess I figured the more serious of the two, pushing and pulling and said that to help myself." Kohnke explained further that the story had been adjusted after they learned the girl had died of a broken neck. Admitting that they had dragged the girl out of the car sounded dangerous, so they simply lied.

Wilson also lied on a crucial issue. In his first story, Rose started calling him "a dirty white bastard" as soon as he asked her why she hadn't said she was having her period. But that made no sense because she wasn't, in fact, having her period. In court, Wilson said the name calling had started after he hit her.

Two days after the killing, Kohnke and Croft went to the RCMP office to report being in a car accident; they were shown a picture of Rose and asked if they had ever seen her. They lied and said "No". Later, they consulted with Wilson, and all three returned to the RCMP with their first version of the evening's events.

The defence used two tactics to deal with all the lies on the record. Defence counsel told the court to disregard all the earlier flounderings as "unreliable" and to accept only the court version. Then eight character witnesses were brought in to say that the three youths were of good character, and didn't lie.

Kohnke also offered some remarkable explanations for other oddities in the testimony. Rose's blouse was ripped around the buttonholes, and two buttons were found on the ground next to a beer bottle. If she was a willing partner in the removal of her clothes, how did that happen, and how, if her blouse came off inside the car, did the buttons get outside? Kohnke said that maybe the buttons came off inside and were laid on top of the blouse and then maybe, when they "set out" Rose's clothes after she was hauled out of the car, the buttons stayed on top of the blouse and got outside that way. But how did she manage to get grass and moss on her back—grass and moss like that from a mound above a small embankment near where the car was parked? "I imagine she would have walked up and laid down, maybe."

We are still left with two puzzles. The doctor who performed the autopsy on Rose discovered that she was not, in fact, menstruating, but he did find a wad of paper in the lumen, the entrance to the vagina. He speculated that it was either put there to serve as a crude contraceptive, or that somebody else put it there.

If Rose was a willing partner, why didn't she simply tell Wilson, or Croft—or anyone—that there was no problem? The entire projected romantic dalliance was wrecked because, apparently, the whites thought Rose was in no fit state for games. But she was. If their version is correct, Rose either didn't know that her period was over, or was so drunk that she had lost the gift of speech — except for swearing and mumbling.

The other major puzzle, of course, is: Who killed Rose? The youths say they left her, mad and drunk, and either mostly clothed or mostly naked, sitting beside the trail, about half a mile from the highway. It was below freezing and late at night, so nobody would call them gallant, but there it is.

However, somehow, Rose was killed, stripped naked, her body bruised, her back rubbed in moss and grass, and her clothes scattered over a 300-foot area. Did someone come along after the white youths left, see Rose, take an instant dislike to her, kill her, strip her, roll her around some, and then wander off, never to be seen again?

Of course, that was not the issue before the jury that heard the case. Defence lawyer H. Lee Skipp summed the thing up in a nutshell: "Now, the theory of the defence in this case is that this girl met her death through what is essentially an accident with no intention, whatsoever, for this thing to have happened to her." At another point, the

223

defence made the argument that when the whites flew Rose's panties from their aerial, it showed they hadn't done anything really wrong, or they wouldn't have paraded the evidence.

The accused youths didn't have to account for Rose's death, they simply had to throw doubt on the case against themselves, and a white jury accepted enough of their swerving stories to bring in an interesting verdict: Croft and Wilson were found guilty of assault on the girl, and Kohnke wasn't guilty of anything.

Mr. Justice T.A. Dohm, after congratulating the jury for being "most conscientious", fined the two guilty men $200 each for assault.

But some people won't leave things like that alone, and local Indians (and some whites too) persisted in arguing that the case had been a gross miscarriage of justice. When Robert Bonner, then Attorney General of B.C., arrived in Williams Lake, he was handed a petition calling for a review of the case. There had been no appeal by the Crown, but after pressure mounted, an appeal was launched. The Crown claimed that the judge had misdirected the jury, and that a properly charged jury could not have failed to convict on the original manslaughter charge.

The judge's address to the jury had indeed been long, rambling, and confused, so confused that at one point His Lordship mixed up the rights of the Crown and accused, and solemnly told the jurors, "To sum it up, the Crown [sic] states that they are entitled to the benefit of any doubt on any of these points, and that is so."

Then there was this summation of what the judge said the Crown was setting out as the possible verdicts against Croft: "If you are not satisfied that there was a common unlawful purpose, that the accused Croft should be convicted because of the assault on her, dragging her out of the car, and they say this could have broken her neck—that is for you to say — you may find that very difficult to be satisfied on just when she did get that broken neck — the doctor said it could have been a blow or fall—they say in the alternative, if you are not satisfied on that that Croft should be convicted for assault causing bodily harm and in the further alternative that he should be convicted for common assault if you are not satisfied that he did cause actual bodily harm."

What jury could make sense out of that? And how, without a clear statement of the law, could a jury arrive at a reasonable verdict?

On February 26, 1968, Mr. Justice H.A. Maclean of the B.C. Appeal Court threw out the appeal. Read as a whole, he said, the judge's charge did not amount to a misdirection, and besides, the Crown had misquoted the judge in its notice of appeal.

So that, at last, was that.

Neither the Thomas killing nor the Roper killing have ever attracted much attention. The media seem curiously uninterested in stories—however full of the popular ingredients of violence and sex — that go so flatly against our traditional view of ourselves, that seem to imply that Indians can expect the same sort of justice as blacks used to get in Alabama.

And that is why I am telling these stories now, for the first time. They make me wonder if the Queen really knows what the hell goes on among all her equal subjects.

CHAPTER 13:
STRIKE ME PINK

And because of the lesser frequency of strikes and the relative
absence of violence and illegality in labour disputes, there has
been far less use in Canada of police and punitive methods
generally.

Encyclopedia Canadiana,
article on Strikes, 1972 edition.

It must have been a weird scene—eighty cars strung out in
a long line, bumping along a bush road after midnight,
some of them with their lights on, the men jammed inside
shouting and waving, calling encouragement, some bumping along silently, lights out, the men inside silent and
grim, hoping somehow to get out of this without trouble.
They were headed for the Val Rita Co-operative, at Risor
Siding, on the Spruce Falls Pulp and Paper Company Railway, outside the northern Ontario town of Kapuskasing.
They were going to pull down the stockpile of logs there,
going to talk persuasively to members of the co-op, and try
to persuade them to stop dealing with the Spruce Falls
Company. After all, there was a strike on.

The strike had begun on January 14, 1963, when members of the Lumber and Sawmill Workers Union walked off
the job to support a demand that their contract be linked to
contracts of other pulpwood cutters in the region. They
wanted area-wide bargaining for greater strength, and the
company wouldn't give it to them. The provincial government, as often happens, stalled the appointment of a conciliation board, so the men went out before the required
legalities had been met. It was an illegal strike, technically,
but legality always becomes a minor point on either side in

labour disputes. The pulpwood cutters tried to close down the Kapuskasing plant, by setting up picket lines, but the inside labourers paid no attention. So the strikers decided to cut off the source of supply. Spruce Falls got most of its logs from a thousand workers who were lodged in eight camps spread around the area; these were the men on strike, but the withdrawal of their labour did not dry up the company's supply. There was a secondary source, settlers in the area who combined farming or hunting or odd-job work with log-cutting in the bush, on independent contracts, at cordwood rates. They were not part of the union, and the strike was nothing but good news for them.

The strikers began a series of lightning raids on these individual settlers, knocking down and scattering their stockpiles of logs, ambushing their trucks on blocked bush roads, then dumping their loads (and sometimes their trucks), and beating up settlers who persisted in dealing with the company. The union leaders did not approve of the violence, but they were apparently unable to stop it.

Word got around that a huge stockpile of logs was being prepared at Risor Siding by a group of about one hundred settlers who had organized themselves into the Val Rita Co-operative (named for a tiny town nearby), to deal more effectively with the company. A number of the strikers decided that they were not going to sit around while that stockpile went chugging off to Kapuskasing, they were bloody well going to stop it. On the evening of February 11, there was a meeting of the pulpwood cutters, and the union executive, which — along with everybody else for miles around—had heard the rumours of the proposed vigilante action, warned the workers to stay away from Risor Siding. The response of many of the strikers was brief and unprintable.

And that is how there came to be a cavalcade winding through the bush in the post-midnight gloom of a bitter cold night in northern Ontario. Of course, the union leaders weren't the only ones who had been tipped off; twenty or more members of the co-op were stationed inside a cabin in the middle of the lumber yard, some of them carrying guns; ten Ontario provincial policemen were on hand with cars, lights, bullhorns, and weapons. About 12:40 a.m., the eighty-car cavalcade came bumping into the clearing, and pulled up. Car doors banged open; 400 men tumbled out to mill around, and they quickly spotted the cops. But the strikers had come to do a job, and, after a moment's hesitation, they began to pour in a dark, noisy mob, towards the chained yard gate and the stockpiled logs.

They had not reached the gate when a small knot of OPP officers emerged under the yard lights, and there was a small conference. The police told the strikers that this was private property, and that they should all go home; the strikers demurred. There was another pause while the raiders withdrew and held a caucus of their own. Were they going to go ahead, with all those cops around, or should they go home? They were, by Jesus, going to do what they had come here for.

Suddenly, there was a rush for the gate, and most of the men poured through the hastily-smashed chain and began to attack the gigantic logpile. Some other, wiser, heads simply drifted quietly away. The police, given a choice between firing into the mob blindly or doing nothing, very wisely drew back. Then the cabin door burst open; if the cops weren't going to do anything, the settlers would. A score of men burst out into the yard, most of them carrying rifles, and they began to fire indiscriminately into the logpile, at anything that moved, strikers and police alike. Two strikers were killed instantly, another was mortally wounded and died later, nine others received lesser wounds. The shooting stopped as rapidly as it began; the settlers threw down their guns, so when the bewildered police advanced on them, it was hard to tell who had been shooting and who had not.

228

Eventually, nineteen members of the co-op were charged with non-capital murder, but nothing could be proved against any of them, and the charges were dismissed. Three men were convicted of illegal possession of weapons and fined $100 each. Charges of rioting and unlawful assembly were laid against the strikers, and 223 of them were fined a total of $27,600. The strike was quickly settled by compulsory arbitration, and, before long, the Val Rita co-op members became employees of Spruce Falls, and joined the Lumber and Sawmill Workers Union, where they presumably paid dues and began to discuss the next strike.

What intrigued me about the battle of Risor Siding when I first read about it in Stuart Jamieson's brilliant study, *Times of Trouble: Labour Unrest and Industrial Conflict in Canada*, was that I had never heard of it before. It had slipped, somehow, into the general mélange of violence, intimidation, brutality, and illegality that marks so many strikes. Except for the deaths of three men, it might have gone unrecorded entirely; after all, it follows the pattern of many major Canadian labour disputes in two essentials — the breach of law and the appeal to violence as a creative technique.

We are not a calm and reasonable people in labour matters, we only think we are; we do not have a history of peace and moderation in these things, we only think we have. Jamieson, the labour historian, thinks there has been "a sort of 'conspiracy of silence' about the whole subject of labour unrest and industrial conflict, particularly of the more violent kind, in this country". We like to see ourselves as distinct from those brawling, bullying Americans, and with the help of our established historians, we have built up our self-image, Jamieson says, as "a country of relatively moderate, peaceful, stable and law-abiding people with a strong penchant for compromise". But, in fact, "There is also a strong element of uncompromising rigidity and violence in the Canadian national character. . . .

Canada during this century has been a country having a record of labour unrest and industrial conflict, with illegal and violent overtones, second only to the United States, and far greater than that of most European countries."

Who, us? Yes, us.

As in so many other matters, the difference between Canadians and lesser breeds is not that we don't do the wicked things that others do, but that we don't blab about them; we are not the kind to kill and tell. In fact, since Jamieson's study was released in 1968, we have surged ahead strongly; in 1974, the latest year for which statistics are available, Canada racked up a loss of 9.3 million working days because of strikes, a solid gain from the 5.3 million working-days lost the year before, a record that put us ahead of those pussy-footing Yankees, according to one group of statisticians, and second only to Italy in national working-time lost because of labour strife. (According to another group of statisticians, our 1974 record was not quite so bad; it depends on how you measure these things.)

Nobody knows how many heads have been bashed, how many hands crushed, how many men have been crippled, how many have been beaten to death, or shot, or stabbed, or brought to some other inglorious end in this country's labour battles. Marc Zwelling, in his book, *The Strikebreakers*, which argues that most of the blame must be laid at the feet of management, rattles off a list of killings: a union organizer gunned down in 1903 while picketing the CPR yards in Vancouver; three men killed in a sawmill strike at Buckingham, Quebec, in 1906; a coal miners' organizer slain — possibly by a provincial policeman — in British Columbia in 1918; two organizers murdered at Onion Lake, Ontario, in 1929; three coal miners shot by the RCMP in Estevan, Saskatchewan, in 1931... and so it goes. If you add in the Risor Siding slayings, and then begin to think about the men killed *by* strikers (rather than simply the strikers slain) — such as the detective beaten to death in

Regina in 1935 (see Chapter 2) and the Mountie killed during the Newfoundland loggers' strike in 1959 — you begin to get an impressive body-count before you even approach the less spectacular displays of violence, the mere beatings, pumellings, fire-settings, car-smashings, truck-rollings, and plant-wreckings that seem to accompany any prolonged labour dispute in this peaceable kingdom.

In all this long catalogue of bashing, thumping, axing, burning, shooting, marching, and counter-marching, I want to touch briefly on a handful of strikes that have taken place during this century and, by ranging across the years as well as across the nation, see if we can discern any pattern to labour violence.

Let us begin, then, on the west coast, with James Dunsmuir. Perhaps to know Dunsmuir was to love him; after all, he became Premier of British Columbia in 1900, and was very decently boosted upstairs as Lieutenant Governor in 1906. But he always struck me as one of the most bloody-minded graspers whose greed ever propelled him to affluence and honour in our history. He became rich in the time-honoured fashion, by inheriting a bundle from his father and using the leverage it gave him to grab everything else worth grabbing. The real break came when a group headed by Robert Dunsmuir, the father, managed to secure a contract for building a seventy-eight mile long railway from Victoria to Wellington, where the elder Dunsmuir owned a colliery. The deal was a shady one, worked through federal Minister of Railways John Henry Pope, a friend and political ally of the Dunsmuirs. Thrown into the scheme were provincial subsidies of 1,900,000 acres of land and $750,000 in cash. No tenders were ever called, and the railway-building contracts were not even advertised before they were handed to Dunsmuir *père et fils*. When questions were raised in the B.C. legislature, the government simply brushed them aside.

The Dunsmuir group had been given the most valuable

coal lands in B.C., lands worth hundreds of millions of dollars. They wrung the last cent out of them by bringing in Chinese indentured labour to exploit, by refusing to pay any attention to the most rudimentary safety regulations, by keeping their men at work in intolerable conditions at miniscule pay, and resolutely crushing all attempts to unionize. James Dunsmuir not only fired men who belonged to a union, he discharged at once three employees who dared to work against him in the provincial election of 1900.

While the Dunsmuirs grew richer, their workers grew poorer; in 1901, the company made all its miners at the Extension works move to Ladysmith, at their own expense; in 1902, the company cut wages by ten per cent; in 1903, the men enlisted the help of the Western Federation of Miners, a U.S. body, to organize the mines, and went on strike for bargaining rights. The strike was quickly broken, with the aid of scabs and professional strikebreakers, and a Royal Commission on Industrial Disputes, which was formed to consider wide-ranging labour unrest in the province, looked into the dispute.

The secretary of this commission was William Lyon Mackenzie King, then Deputy Minister of Labour, and the report he helped to shape was a beaut. Although the testimony showed that the men in the Dunsmuir mines were overworked, underpaid, fired for trivial reasons, and generally brutalized, the commission found that the strike was all the fault of the American unions—"Not trade unionists, but foreign socialistic agitators of the most bigoted and ignorant type" — who led our boys astray. By torturing logic, the commission was able to argue that the company's brutal actions during the strike were the union's fault; everybody knew that James Dunsmuir immediately fired his workers if they joined a union, and locked them out; therefore, the Western Federation of Miners, as soon as it came on the scene, set the stage for all the trouble that followed.

The commission report did nothing to ease labour unrest, but it did help to convince the miners they had nothing to lose by radical action. The Western Federation of Miners withdrew, but the United Mine Workers proposed a plan to organize all coal miners on Vancouver Island, and another wage cut helped their efforts along. But King stepped back in to promote a company union; that solved the immediate problem, but left a festering wound.

Then, in 1911—after James Dunsmuir, who started it all, had gone on to higher things and left his mines in the hands of Canadian Collieries Limited—the United Mine Workers tried again. Predictably, the union leaders were fired again, and, after brooding over that for a time, 3,000 miners walked out of the two Canadian Collieries Mines in 1912. The company denounced the strike as the work of "foreign agitators", and went on working the mines with scab labour. The picketing dragged on, but coal production was not much affected, and the union decided on a wider effort.

On May 1, 1914, a strike was called at every mine on Vancouver Island, setting off a widespread outbreak of violence that lasted three months. In Cumberland, B.C., provincial police were brought in to protect strikebreakers, after a number of them were beaten up and their homes wrecked. At Ladysmith, a crowd of miners stoned a hotel where scabs were quartered, and ran them out of town. At South Wellington, the company "bull pen"—where strikebreakers were kept—was attacked, and the men were driven out. At Nanaimo, twenty-three special police arrived on the ferry to help the company, but they were surrounded by a welcoming committee of strikers, and persuaded to re-board the ferry and go on back to Vancouver. At Extension, a number of miners were shot in an attack on the company bull-pen, and a full-scale riot erupted. The mine buildings were burned down, along with the houses of scabs; non-union workers and the mine manager were driven into the woods and invited to fend for themselves.

Vancouver Island was in a state of violent anarchy. On August 13, 1914, soldiers from the 72nd Militia Regiment (called "Bowser's Seventy-Two", for the Provincial Attorney General) arrived on the island, and the strike was put down. More than 250 strikers were arrested, and many of them were held for months without trial. The miners won some minor concessions — they were allowed to belong to the mine-workers' union, but the union was not recognized as their bargaining agent — and blacklisting of organizers continued. Gradually, the union withered away, and conditions in the B.C. mines did not improve until much later.

The temptation to lay any unhappiness in the work force on outside agitators has always been a powerful one, and we have nearly always succumbed. The 1919 edition of the *Canadian Annual Review*, when it set out to discover what had gone wrong in the Winnipeg General Strike of that year, divided workers into two clear classes:

(1) The moderate, thoughtful, industrious working man, and

(2) The idle or shiftless workman, the scheming or unscrupulous or often very clever leader.

This neat division simplified the philosophic approach to strikes for the *Review*; moderate, thoughtful, and industrious-type workers do not get into strikes, or, if they do, they call them off pretty quickly, while those other lazy buggers are the seeding ground for "Communists, Anarchists, Bolshevists, I.W.W.s, O.B.U.s, and all the variety of Red Socialists, who, in 1919, were helping to keep the world in miserable unrest".

The Winnipeg General Strike was a battle of mythology and reality. The nation's leaders, aided and abetted by our deepest thinkers and economists, managed to convince themselves that union attempts to gain decent working conditions were nothing less than a Bolshevik plot to overthrow Canada's economic system and plunge us into godless communism, red anarchy, and an end to the virtue of our virgins.

The times were certainly ripe; unemployment was high, prices were soaring, wages were low, and the air was permeated with a restless idealism inspired not only by the recent finish of the war to end all wars, but by the success of the Russian Revolution in 1917. During the war, workers had seen their wages frozen by law, while profits soared; after the conflict, while profits continued stronger, wages were cut. Meanwhile, the demobilized soldiers who poured into the work force had weakened the bargaining position of labour.

There were a number of workers foolish enough to conclude that this arrangement was somehow unfair, and that the way to a better tomorrow lay through the portals of the One Big Union movement, which held that all workers should come together in general strikes to wrest control of the economy away from the wicked bosses. The One Big Union movement did not go very far — most Canadian working men share the conservatism of their bosses, they want pay raises, not pamphlets and promises — besides, even the militant union leaders were divided on the issue of craft versus industrial unions (that is, whether workers should be organized by trades across a number of plants, or vertically, with all members of the plant in a single union, whatever their work). Just the same, the rhetoric of the OBU leaders, and of the equally militant Industrial Workers of the World, the union of Bill Haywood and Joe Hill, provided the propaganda for a thesis that Canadian society was about to be turned on its head, with the wrong guys on top. And that is why a strike in the building and metal trades unions of Winnipeg blossomed into something that looked like a do-it-yourself world war.

Workers in the Winnipeg building trades discovered in 1919 that, while their living costs had gone up by seventy-five per cent since 1913, their wages had risen only thirteen per cent over the same period. They wanted a substantial raise, and they wanted it now. But even had their employers wanted to grant it—not a usual condition—they could not. Construction had been frozen by wartime priorities for a period of four years, and was only beginning to recover; unlike many other industries, which had grown fat with the surfeit of wartime gains, they were unable to meet the clamour for wage gains. That, at least, was their argument; the union, alas, did not believe it, and a building strike was called for May 1, 1919.

At the same time, workers in the metal trades, whose repeated attempts to win union recognition had been blocked by the use of professional strikebreakers, damage suits, and ex-parte injunctions (and whose employers were well able to afford a raise) had been having a rough time. They had been through three bitter strikes, and lost them all. They called a fourth strike for May 2, the day after the builders went out. As it happened, city policemen, street-railway employees, and telephone operators were also locked in contract disputes at the same time. These public service employees had learned, through a series of strikes in 1916, '17, and '18, that if they acted in concert they could win, while separately they were easily defeated.

With this background, it was not surprising that, at a meeting of the Winnipeg Trades Council on May 6, a general strike was proposed, to settle all these disputes at once, and victoriously. A resolution was passed to poll every union member in the city on the issue of whether to call a general strike, and that was done. When the ballots were counted on May 13, over 11,000 Winnipeg workers had endorsed a general strike, and only 500 were opposed; it was a verdict far beyond the dreams of those who had proposed the resolution. Accordingly, a general strike was called for 11 a.m., Thursday, May 15. The strike call was a spectacular success; at the appointed time, 22,000 workers in 94 unions downed their tools, picked up their lunch-buckets, and walked out. David Bercuson, in an article for Irving Abella's book, *On Strike*, describes what happened: "Firemen left their stations, telephones were shut down, the city's electrical workers left turbines and transmission equipment unattended; telegraphers and others responsible for keeping a modern city in touch with the world refused to work. At the waterworks, a skeleton staff remained behind at the request of the Trades Council to provide a meagre thirty pounds pressure, sufficient for single-storey buildings. Commercial establishments of every sort, from moving-picture houses to restaurants, were closed."

And, he might have added, down at city hall, up at the legislative assembly, and back in Ottawa, the folks were having fits. This was it: revolution was at hand, the Bolsheviks had landed; we were in for the return of Chaos and One Night. The press, which can usually be counted on to keep the applesauce coming, laid it on in generous dollops, led by a specially founded anti-strike paper, the Winnipeg *Citizen*, which commented:

> For nearly a month, all eyes in Canada have been turned upon Winnipeg. For nearly a month the citizens of Winnipeg have been fighting whole-heartedly and with a very generous measure of success, against a determined attempt to establish Bolshevism and the rule of the Soviet here and then to expand it all over this Dominion.

All the chaps who had downed their tools to paralyse the city — and now went back to work in essential trades, baking bread and delivering milk under the sanction of the strike committee — these people had been "tricked and betrayed into striking" by "the machinations of a number of confessed Bolshevists in the Winnipeg Labour Temple".

A Citizens' Committee of One Thousand sprang up to put the Bolshies in their place and take over the abandoned jobs. Soon there were signs up vying with the strikers' slogans calling for union solidarity and the triumph of the working-class; these new signs said "We Stand By Our Elected Government" and "Down With Bolshevism" and "Deport the Undesireable Aliens" and other uplifting sentiments.

The federal government was soon actively involved. One of the key members of the Citizens' Committee was a senior partner in the law firm that handled the affairs of Arthur Meighen, Minister of the Interior, and there was never any doubt where Meighen's sympathies lay. He arrived in town on May 22, a week after the strike began, with Senator Gideon Robertson, federal Minister of Labour. They took their cue from the Citizens' Committee and immediately began to denounce the foreign plotters who had suborned our virtuous—but apparently dim-witted—workers from the true path. The postal workers who had gone out were given an ultimatum; keep the mails moving or be fired. Some came back (postal workers were softer in those days than in ours), and those who didn't were replaced. The mails began to move again.

The ultimatum was used time and again against individual groups of strikers; they could go back to work, or lose their jobs. They often went back. The striking police were handed a pledge to sign, repudiating the Winnipeg Trades Council (always called "The St. James St. Soviet"), which had called the strike, and when they refused, 240 of them were fired—almost the entire force. Their places were taken by "special police" recruited from among anti-strike war veterans and students, who were paid six dollars a day —more than the regular police. These specials were full of anti-revolutionary zeal, but had no notion of police work, and quickly lost control of the city. Brawls, beatings, and wild demonstrations became normal behaviour as the strike wound on through June. The prophecies of anarchy were being fulfilled, but by the action of the strikebreakers more than the strikers.

On June 6, the federal government rammed through an amendment to the Immigration Act permitting the government to deport any "enemy alien" (we were not at war with anyone, so the term was a little imprecise) in the strike. On June 17, six Anglo-Saxon strike leaders, and a group of "enemy aliens" were picked up under this law and rushed straight to Stony Mountain Penitentiary. Meighen wanted them all tossed out of the country forthwith, but cooler heads prevailed (some of the arrested men were Canadian citizens, such as A. A. Heaps, a trade unionist and later an MP). At the same time, a series of lightning raids were conducted on labour centres, and their staffs were hassled and their files scattered.

These dim-witted moves simply made it more difficult for the strike leaders to keep control of their followers; the remains of union discipline and self-control vanished under the ministrations of the Citizens' Committee and the Specials. On Friday, June 20, the strike leaders were released on bail, but by that time, their followers had already decided in their absence to hold a giant protest parade on Saturday, June 21, a day destined to go into history as Bloody Saturday.

That morning, Mayor Gray of Winnipeg warned the strikers that they would be arrested if they tried to hold their demonstration. His warning was ignored. That afternoon, just before 2:30 p.m., protesters began to mass on Main Street, near the City Hall. A streetcar containing two men came down the street, and, because the streetcar workers were on strike, the crowd took that as a deliberate provocation, and attacked it. While that was going on, the Royal Northwest Mounted Police arrived, fifty-four men on horses and another thirty-six in trucks. They charged twice through the crowd, and were met by a hail of flying stones and bottles; one Mountie, thrown from his horse, was pounced on by the mob, who began to beat him.

The Mounties wheeled and made a third charge, to rescue their fallen comrade. This time, they fired their revolvers into the crowd. One man was killed instantly, and several others were wounded. The police were later to claim that they fired only in response to gunshots from the crowd, but there were none, as a subsequent investigation showed. When the police pistols began to go off, the crowd went into a panic, and hundreds began to run down side streets, where they were met by cordons of six-dollar-a-day Specials, armed with guns and clubs. A series of running brawls broke out, in which many strikers and some policemen were badly beaten. The militia were called in, and within minutes a mixed group of cavalry and machine-gunners, riding trucks provided by the Citizens' Committee, commanded the fast-emptying streets.

The Winnipeg General Strike was over, although it was not formally called off until four days later. Eight strike leaders were put on trial under Section 98 of the Criminal Code, which was hastily jammed into law for the occasion (a description of its peculiar provisions, which place the burden of proof on the accused, is found in Chapter 4). The eight were charged with "conspiring to bring into hatred and contempt the governments of the Dominion of Canada and the Province of Manitoba and to introduce a Soviet system of government". This strange charge was made to stick against all but one of the accused, and after trials that lasted over a year, one received a two-year sentence, five received one year, and one got six months.

The pattern of bringing in strikebreakers—ostensibly to uphold the law, but in reality to act as strikebreakers—was firmly established. What is more, it worked. In 1931, the RCMP—whose name was changed from the Royal North West in 1920—were brought in to help break a strike in the Souris coal mining area in southeast Saskatchewan, around the towns of Estevan and Bienfait. The causes of the strike were familiar — poor wages, which were driven downwards even further by Depression conditions to around $1.60 a day, unsafe working conditions, and terrible living conditions. The sixteen-year-old daughter of one Bienfait miner described her home to the Wylie Commission into the 1931 strike this way:

> One bedroom, two beds in there, dining room, no beds in there, kitchen, one bed, and eleven in the family. I think we need a bigger place than that. When it is raining the rain comes in the kitchen. There is only one ply of paper, cardboard paper nailed to about two inch wood board (on the walls) . . . . When the weather is frosty, when you wake up in the morning you cannot walk on the floor because it is all full of snow.

This house belonged to the mining company; some of the privately-owned shacks were worse. An inspection after the strike showed that of 113 houses and shacks, 53 had inadequate heat, 43 were leaky, 52 were dirty, and 25 were over-crowded. Almost all needed repairs.

In addition, the coal companies ran stores at which their employees had to trade, and to pay exorbitant prices. When the workers tried to organize, they were met by the familiar cry of "foreign agitators". An attempt to bring in an organizer from the One Big Union movement ended when he was kidnapped and threatened. The seven men responsible were acquitted by a local jury. They included a corporal in the Saskatchewan Provincial Police.

Finally, in 1931, the miners formed a local union of their own, and applied for membership in the radical Mine Workers' Union of Canada. An organizer came to the area and signed up most of the men, but the companies refused to recognize the union—connected, they said, with "The Red Internationale of Soviet Russia" — and a strike was called for September 7, 1931.

As soon as the workers went out, a dozen RCMP arrived in town, and joined a private force of thirteen special constables in the pay of the Saskatchewan Coal Operators' Association. Farm workers were brought in to work the mines, but a mass meeting of strikers descended on the new workers and persuaded them to seek employment elsewhere.

As the strike continued, the workers called a protest meeting for September 29, to be addressed by a communist, Anne Buller of the Workers' Unity League, in Estevan. The protest was to take the form of a parade, but the town council of Estevan, at a special meeting, passed a bylaw banning any demonstration. A letter was dispatched to the strikers to tell them of this bylaw, but did not arrive until too late. The strikers — either deliberately or by mischance — were told that what had been banned was a parade, so they changed their program to a motor caravan instead, and thought themselves very clever indeed.

Accordingly, when the caravan of 400 miners and their families arrived on the outskirts of Estevan in the early afternoon of September 30, and were met by a cordon of police, they were outraged. They decided to push on, and to hell with the cops. A bloody battle broke out, with the strikers using clubs and stones, and the police using guns and riot sticks. The arrival of police reinforcements turned the battle into a rout, and after about three hours of fighting, the streets were cleared, leaving two miners dead and one fatally injured. In addition, eight miners, four bystanders, and one Mountie were shot but not killed, and eight police received wounds from miners' weapons.

The strike was broken and the union smashed, and twenty-two strikers served jail terms for their part in the riot.

The pattern was repeated again in 1935, at a strike in Corbin, B.C., when 250 coal miners and their wives staged a protest parade to a struck mine. They were met by joined squads of police and strikebreakers on a narrow ledge on a mountain road. At this convenient location, with no easy exit off the side of the road, the police drove a bulldozer into the crowd, breaking the arms and legs of several of the women, who had formed a picket line in front of their husbands under the naive delusion that the cops wouldn't smash into a line of women. A pitched battle followed in which sixteen police and twenty-five strikers were injured before the workers were driven off and the strike broken.

The police played a major role, as we have already seen, in the Regina Riot later in 1935, helping to provoke a confrontation that turned into a major riot and ended with the smashing of the protest.

Then, in 1937, the Ontario Provincial Police were used to try to break the Oshawa autoworkers' strike. This time, it was the Committee for Industrial Organization (CIO) who were assigned the role of foreign devils. This U.S.-based union gave the Canadian workers organizing help that drove Ontario Premier Mitch Hepburn to near apoplexy. The Oshawa strike, said Hepburn, represented "only the first open attempt on the part of [United Mine Worker President John L.] Lewis and his CIO henchmen to assume the position of dominating and dictating to Canadian industry". Hepburn was widely supported in the press, with the Toronto *Telegram* thundering, "The time to check the foreign invasion is now", and the *Globe and Mail*, owned by Hepburn's friend and patron, George McCullagh, praising the premier for taking a firm stand against the CIO before "it can extend into all the major industries of Ontario and wreck havoc in its wake."

Hepburn wanted the RCMP ordered in to thump the strikers with truncheons and other instruments of industrial logic, but Prime Minister Mackenzie King was not fond of Hepburn, even though he was a fellow Liberal, and refused to comply. Besides, a tide of opinion was setting in against the use of police as strikebreakers, so King told Hepburn — with the suitable circumlocutions that marked everything King said — to go fly a kite. Policing the Oshawa strike fell on the shoulders of the Ontario Provincial Police. But this time, union discipline held; there were no major incidents of violence on the picket lines, and no excuse to beat strikers black and blue.

General Motors, the company against which the strike was directed, took the interesting stand—interesting, that is, for a wholly-U.S.-owned firm—that it would not deal with the autoworkers because they were contaminated. One of the members of the strike committee was a representative of the international union from Detroit, and GM was not going to deal with that kind of international riff-raff.

This piece of solemn guff was accepted; when the strike was eventually settled, the union did not get formal recognition. However, the company did give its workers a boost in pay and a cut in hours, from fifty-five to forty-four a week. More importantly, the Oshawa strike signalled the trend towards the domination of industrial—as opposed to craft—unions in a major Canadian industry.

Sometimes the police did not have to get into the act; another Ontario strike in 1937 was broken by the local citizens. That was at the Holmes Foundry in Sarnia, where seventy workers, most of them recent immigrants from Europe, staged a sit-down strike to back their demand for union recognition. A mob of about 300 Sarnians descended on the plant with clubs, sticks, and bottles, beat the hell out of the workers and evicted them, while the Sarnia police stood impassively by. Then the cops moved in and arrested the evicted strikebreakers for "trespassing".

The times, however, were a-changing. The use of the OPP in the Oshawa strike probably did more harm than good to the company cause, and the flying squads of Quebec Provincial Police who tried to break up the 1949 Asbestos strike had a major effect in swinging public opinion behind the strikers. That strike (perhaps the most-studied labour dispute in our history, so I don't propose to re-tell it here) turned on questions of health and safety as much as on wages and union recognition. It was fascinating to see, in the 1975 strike at the same spot, how the mine-owners keep right on saying that there is nothing the matter and the miners, between coughs, keep right on saying there is.

Quebec has had a generous helping of brutal strikes, from the textile battles of the 1920s and '30s (in August 1937, Dominion Textile workers went on strike to persuade their employers to improve on the sixty-four-hour week at $3.50 a week for women workers) to the prolonged and bloody battle at Murdochville, where copper miners and strikebreakers traded punches, charges, and threats in 1957. A squad of fifty provincial police were sent in to maintain "law and order". Their arrival, as usual, provoked widespread disturbances. In the climate of violence that had by now become *de rigueur* for major strikes, strikers dynamited company property, and one man was fatally injured by a dynamite explosion he may have helped to set. Company employees were seized and beaten, and the union hall was invaded and smashed up.

The strike was eventually broken, but not before the "foreign devils" routine had received a brisk work-out. The union seeking recognition was affiliated to the United Steel Workers of America. On August 19, 1957, a group of 400 Canadian labour leaders, with a sprinkling of American steel workers, came to Murdochville to picket in sympathy with the strikers. They were attacked by squads of hired goons and strikebreakers, who stood on a hillside and hurled rocks at them, while the QPP looked on. Then the police approached the strikers, not to offer protection, but to suggest that the Americans leave town. The Gaspé Copper Company sued the union for damage done to its property, and eventually won damages of over two million dollars.

Violence has also marked the major strikes in Atlantic Canada, in the coal mines and steel mills of Cape Breton, in the fish plants of all the Maritime provinces, in the lumber mills of Newfoundland. Newfoundland loggers went on strike on December 31, 1958, over conditions that included wages of $1,500 per year — for sixty-hour weeks — and crowded, filthy bunkhouses. The International Wood-workers of America had overwhelming support among the loggers, until Premier Joey Smallwood called for the formation of a company union, and brought in legislation to decertify the IWA.

On March 7, 1959, several busloads of strikebreakers were moving along the road to Badger, escorted by between 100 and 125 police, mostly RCMP, when they came upon a horde of picketers, determined not to let the scabs past. The police formed into columns of threes, and marched into the crowd, swinging lead-filled nightsticks; the strikers scrambled for safety, and the road was open. The police marched past, into Badger, then turned about and marched back again in a standard manoeuvre to keep the way cleared. This time, however, they suddenly wheeled off the main street and down into a sideroad where the loggers had bunched together. The snowbanks were high and packed; there was no place left to retreat, and, in the pitch dark, a bloody battle broke out, with the police using nightsticks and the loggers fists and sticks. In the mêlée, 24-year-old Constable William Moss was beaten to the ground and his skull fractured. He died the next day in hospital, without ever gaining consciousness. His killer was never found, but the usual dénouement followed swiftly; the strike was broken, the union smashed, and a number of strikers charged with assault.

In the 1960s and 1970s, as we all know, violence on the picket line has become almost accepted practice, whether it is Nova Scotia fishermen slashing each other's nets for the sake of solidarity, Toronto construction workers bombing each other for fun and profit, or Quebec construction workers going on a rampage and smashing several dozen heads and $2 million worth of equipment on a James Bay worksite to settle an issue of union jurisdiction. When aircraft workers at what was then the United Aircraft plant at Longueil (now Pratt and Whitney) went on strike in 1974, festivities were opened by a mob of strikers breaking through the main gate and chasing a guard, who panicked when he was cornered, grabbed a fire-axe and sunk it into the arm of one of his pursuers. From there it was all downhill, with truck burnings, car smashings, and the usual assortment of beatings, threats, and intimidation.

There certainly have been some changes down the years. Canada's early strikes were fought, mainly, for recognition, or to stave off wage cuts, or because workers who dared to organize were thrown out of their jobs. They were often ideological, a fact that company owners recognized and twisted out of all proportion, but a fact, nonetheless.

A lot of those old union chaps really believed in daft notions like the brotherhood of man, and working to better conditions for everyone. Most of today's strikes—and I say this as a sometime union executive and labour editor — seem to flow from a stronger, simpler, motive — naked greed.

When the U.S. labour boss of the 1930s and '40s Sam Gompers, was asked what he wanted for his workers, he replied with a single word—"More". We used to laugh at old Sam, but he holds an honoured place, now, in almost every picket line. When our plumbers lay down their tools because $10 an hour isn't enough, and they want $13.50, they are not rejecting the capitalist creed of their society, as their forefathers did, they are joining in. Our newspapers sound just as apoplectic about modern-day unions as they did about the Bolshies in the 1920s, and I can never understand that; if it is all right—indeed, sanctified by the deans of economics—for employers to give their greed fair play, and strive to make the utmost in profit, surely the savage grasping of the modern union should be embraced for what it is—final obeisance to the canons of free enterprise. Alas, there is no satisfying some folks, and today's newspapers are as full of denunciations of the working man as they were in the dear, dead days when we thought he was trying to slip a blade of communism between our ribs.

Our newspapers are also just as full — fuller — of strike

violence. Police are no longer the major cause; now that most police forces are organized into unions, and even the RCMP are flirting with the notion, they do not throw themselves body and soul into the job of strikebreaking as they did of yore. In their place have sprung up the professional strikebreakers, organized into companies and hired out by job lots, and the violence goes on.

That is because one thing that hasn't changed about our strikes is that violence still works. At the United Aircraft strike in Quebec, union organizers, while publicly deploring the brutality on the picket lines, admitted privately that it was the pictures of flying fists and smashed trucks, carried on TV and in the newspapers, that kept the strike alive by keeping it in the news. Violence has been used, time and again, to destroy strikes; sometimes the technique has backfired, more often it has succeeded. It has also been used to win strikes and, once more, the unsavoury fact seems to be that it succeeds more often that it fails.

A union needs only a very few pickets to inform the public that a strike is in progress—which, it is easy to forget these days, is what picketing is supposed to do. But the union that forgets to line up a mob outside the gate, to harass and threaten and maybe even jostle the non-strikers who cross the line, or to sabotage the company's shipping facilities and, if necessary, its plant, is in trouble once the strike passes the first few weeks. A union that can close down the plant, by fair means or foul, is headed for success.

I suggest that any reader can test this theory for himself in his daily newspaper; he can also see there that we are having more strikes, not fewer, that the collective bargaining process is failing more often, that we have yet to come up with any technique for sorting out industrial disputes more effective than that old Canadian standby, the punch in the eye.

CHAPTER 14:

IMPERIALISM (CANADA) LTD.

Turks and Canadians have this in common: the love of life; the
desire to live a little better day by day; the hope of the joy of
neither killing nor dying for foul imperialist profits.

Nazim Hikmet, Turkish poet, 1952.

There is a splendid display of Indian artifacts in the
museum at Fort Macleod, in southern Alberta, dominated
by a reconstruction of the meeting between Crowfoot and
James F. Macleod of the Royal North West Mounted Police.
The inscription begins, "On December 1, 1874, Chief Crowfoot of the Blackfoot Confederacy arrived at Fort Macleod to
meet Assistant Commissioner Macleod. Upon their meeting hung the peace and well-being of this part of the Canadian West." They are equally splendid figures, the impos-
ing, uniformed white man and the handsome chief in his
splendid tribal array. Local Indians who know their history
must find that display a source of bitter amusement; not
long after that historic meeting, Crowfoot's people had all
been herded onto reservations, most of his own children
were dead of tuberculosis, and the thought that whites and
Indians would meet as equal statesmen had become a sick
joke.

Crowfoot was a man of astonishing qualities; courageous
—yes, of course, he was fierce in battle, and once killed a
grizzly bear with a spear to save a child — intelligent,
certainly; generous, honest, and open—all that—but he
had in addition the indefinable quality of leadership. He
was a great talker, but the world is full of talkers; the point
about Crowfoot is that when he talked, people listened.
When the whites came pouring into the Indian lands,

249

Crowfoot held his people in check; he was shrewd enough to see ahead, smart enough to count, and he knew that in any pitched battle, the Indians would simply be massacred. When the depredations of the whiskey-traders brought drunkenness and disease, he welcomed the law-bringing North West Mounted. In 1884, he could easily have wiped out Macleod's tiny band, but he knew, and Macleod knew, that the police were bringing peace and justice, and a fair break for the Indians; after all, it was all written down that way.

When the Second Riel Rebellion broke out in 1885, and the Métis pestered Crowfoot to lead his people into joining the rebels in a great Crusade to drive out the whites, the Blackfoot refused to budge. He had seen the whites, seen their guns, counted their houses, watched their trains; the way to deal with that horde was to negotiate, not to fight. So he toured the prairie tribes and, even though his adopted son, Poundmaker, took up arms (it worked out about the way Crowfoot had it figured, with Poundmaker in penitentiary and most of his followers scattered or dead), even though his own life was threatened by Indians who resented his blathering about peace, Crowfoot kept his people in line. A remarkable chap.

There was one minor flaw in his reasoning, however. Macleod had not come to the West to bring peace (although he certainly thought that was his role); he had come to put down the whiskey-traders who worked the natives up with their rotgut, and to make the country safe for settlers and railwaymen. White settlers, white railwaymen. The deal Macleod and Crowfoot struck (which our school textbooks still record with approving mentions of how it led to lasting mutual respect between Indians and the NWMP) wasn't worth a dime; Crowfoot kept his end of the bargain, but he was soon reduced to the leadership of an impoverished, diseased, and puny band of Indians living on government handouts. Their land was gone, their livelihood was gone, many of their children were dead of malnutrition or of white man's illnesses. When Crowfoot made his last trip among his allies, the Assiniboines, women spat at him, and young warriors greeted him with rude gestures and threatened his life; even some of the old Indians jeered. He died the next year, ill, poor, and powerless; from statesman to bum in five years.

Thanks in part to Crowfoot, Canadian Indians did not experience much of the savagery that opened the American West; we have no Wounded Knee in our history, and no Battle of the Little Bighorn. Once, when the building of the CPR was held up by Indians defiantly camping at the end of steel, the Mounties literally kicked them out of the way. A nicer solution than U.S. Cavalry sabres—but with the same results. In fact, the results were about the same in the long run for Indians on both sides of the border; the land that was theirs became ours, their wealth was dissipated, their livelihood gone. They became squatters, drunks, and beggars on what used to be their territory. With or without massacres, the underlying imperialism was about the same.

Now "imperialism" is a rude word that I know will startle a lot of my readers in this context, so perhaps I should define it. My dictionary — Random House — says imperialism is "the policy of extending the rule or authority of an empire or nation over foreign countries, or of acquiring and holding colonies and dependencies."

Canadian history is marked by two kinds of imperialism, martial and economic. The way we acquired the country in the first place represented the first kind; we, as colonies of the English and French, in turn created colonies of our own in the West and North, and then simply gobbled them into the Canadian nation. That was our martial imperialism, although it was accomplished more with threats and posturing than with bullets and bombs. Our economic imperialism is quite different; it consists of reaching out with corporations and with government to put other people in thrall.

It has been one of the tenets of conventional economics that a nation can be either a colonist or a colonizer, but not both; in fact, as McGill economist R.T. Naylor has pointed out, Canada is a "striking exception" to this rule; we have been constructing our own little imperialist empires on the financial front since before Confederation. Even our struggles on behalf of the Mother Empire had a cash ring to them; Naylor, in his thesis on "Canada's International Commercial Expansion to 1914", which I caught up to in the magazine, *Our Generation*, quotes the president of the Canadian Bankers' Association, in 1898, on a practical note: "Of what use is the shedding of our best blood on the sands of Africa or on the snows of the Himalayas if nothing is to come of their sacrifice but military glory?" What was wanted were opportunities for trade and exploitation, for, in a word, imperialism.

Except in periodicals ranging from the respectably radical (like *Our Generation*) to the loony left, we don't talk about Canadian imperialism. We are quick to spot the imperialist machinations of those chaps below the border, whose grab, grab, grab began in the 1800s, flowered through the Mexican and Spanish-American wars, expanded into the Philippines and Puerto Rico and transmogrified itself, recently, into economic imperialism, led by the shock troops of IBM, General Motors, and ITT. We see that, and know it for what it is, imperialism as clear as anything the British raj brought to the unenlightened wogs when he took up the white man's burden. We can spot Soviet imperialism, too, not only in the swallowing of independent neighbours after World War II, not only in the brutal smashing of independence movements in Czechoslovakia and Hungary, but in Soviet interventions in the Middle East, the Far East, Africa, Latin America—indeed, anywhere a wrestling match can be worked up with Americans. We have the Russians taped. Canadian imperialism, however, is simply a phrase thrown out by kooks with long beards and dubious armpits who try to whip the populace into a frenzy fierce enough to set them stoning CIL headquarters on May Day. Alas, these nuts are right; imperialism is very much part of our make-up.

In our early years, some of us (French, some English, some Dutch) simply grabbed the eastern seaboard from the Indians. That was the work of our ancestors; they pointed the way, but we can hardly be blamed for what they did in the name of God and Glory. It was normal for their day. It was not normal, however, to turn the hunting of natives into a popular sport, as our forefathers did with the Beothuck Indians of Newfoundland. From 1613 to 1823 the Beothucks — a tall, fair, friendly people who were foolish enough to welcome white men to their island — were hunted down like rabbits, hunted into extinction, while the whites kept track with notches carved in their guns. One man, Noel Boss, killed ninety-nine men, women, and children; he wounded his hundredth, a little girl, but she escaped, dammit. The last Beothuck died in 1829. No white man was ever punished for killing a member of the tribe, even after the sport became illegal. It was simply the way we took over their land.

Well, maybe that was a hangover from Imperialist Britain; after all, it was the clash of two imperial policies that occupied much of our early history, and this clash was marked by much mutual murder and such episodes as the dispersal of the Acadians in 1755. At that time, with Britain and France continually clawing at each other, the Acadians were considered to represent a subversive element, situated as they were on the edge of an English colony. So Captain John Winslow was sent to them with a body of troops and a set of instructions which—although he did not agree with them — he read to the assembled populace at Grand Pré.

253

There is a tablet at the site, in the centre of a lovely national park, and you will find Winslow's message there: "That the inhabitants may not have it in their power to Return to this Province or to Join in the Strengthening of the French of Canada or Louisebourge, [the King] is resolved that they shall be dispersed Among His Majesty's Colonies upon the Continent of America." Winslow's instructions did not mention the convenient fact that Grand Pré (literally, "Large Meadow") was in the centre of some of the finest farmland in the Maritimes, and that the dispersal turned over this land, and the Acadians' houses, to the English.

All that, I say, was part of the clash of two empires, but after the dust had settled and we took control over our own affairs, the policy we adopted was effectively imperialist. It may not have looked that way to our side—we were simply protecting and enlightening the hapless heathens by grabbing off their land—but that's what it was. The westward sweep of the railway was an adventure that might have tickled Clive of India, and the puny attempts to strike back, in the two Riel rebellions, were handled, perhaps not as efficiently as Clive might have liked, but just as firmly.

So, too, in the North. There was nothing as dramatic as Caesar's "I came, I saw, I conquered", but that was because the Eskimos, like the Indians, have doubts and confusions about ownership of the land. They believe you can't own land; that it belongs to the generations before and those to come, that it must be kept for the use of everyone. Dumb bunnies, no wonder they had trouble. We simply moved into the North and took over. "I came, I saw, I wrote a memo" — it worked just as well as Caesar's way, and wasn't so rude.

It is only in the last few years that anyone has begun to see anything dubious about this method of acquisition. If I have a gun and you have a spear, it stands to reason that I now own the land that used to be yours. That was the way it went, and it wasn't until Mr. Justice Emmett Hall wrote his dissenting judgment in the Nishga case in 1972 that anyone even thought about the matter. In that famous case B.C. Indians sued for the return of 4,000 square miles of land along the Nass River. They lost, but Hall's dissent, which argued that, if they hadn't been licked, and hadn't been treatied with, and hadn't sold their land, it still belonged to them, was accepted in principle by Prime Minister Trudeau, for which he deserves much praise — providing there is a follow-up.

We also backed off — although only slightly — after the natives of the James Bay area in northern Quebec protested the destruction of their environment and livelihood for the construction of a huge hydro project that, in the words of the late Philip Sykes, author of *Sellout*, "makes no economic sense whatever". The Cree Indians brought a suit against the James Bay Development Corporation (the battle is outlined by Boyce Richardson in his book, *Strangers Devour the Land*). While it was under way, the construction crews went on happily tearing up the area (Sykes quoted an Indian trapper who told him, "They gave me some sugar and some tea and told me they were going to build an airstrip in my section"). When a judge found in favour of the hunters, and ordered a work stoppage, two things happened swiftly: (1) the press suddenly found it impossible to get near the site to see if work actually had stopped, and (2) the judge's finding was over-turned by a higher court in near-record time. Work went on, but the partial and temporary court victory did give the natives a bargaining weapon; they are still getting tromped on in James Bay, but at least they got a money settlement out of the Quebec government.

The Nishga case and the James Bay case indicate, I hope, that we have left the more naked kind of imperialism behind us. Our territorial ambitions are sated by the knowledge that we are having a hell of a time looking after the land already conquered. Every now and then, of course, one of our more imaginative statesmen will suggest some new venture—as MP Max Saltsman did when he wanted to bring the Turks and Caicos Islands into the Canadian fold in 1974—but, by and large, we are a reasonable people. A land-grab of 3.8 million square miles satisfies us.

Indeed, a good deal of our public energy is devoted to howling down imperialism, as we see it in the guise of American companies moving into our country to take a stranglehold on the Canadian economy. That has certainly happened; a modern nation that has more than sixty per cent of its manufacturing sector and even more of its natural resources in foreign hands has a just complaint about economic imperialism. But that doesn't alter the fact that we ourselves are in the imperialist game, that we have been for decades, and that, in many parts of the world, we stand in no better odour than the Americans and for the same reason — we own too damn much.

The question of how much we actually own abroad is a confused one, and it is possible to suspect that we are not anxious to have figures that are either too exact or up to date. When a Senate committee asked Mitchell Sharp, then External Affairs Minister, how much we had in the way of direct investment in the West Indies during a 1970 hearing, he replied that he thought it was perhaps $500 million, but maybe more, maybe less, he didn't really know. That was a curious answer for a man who, as former Vice President of Brazilian Traction (now Brascan), is something of an expert on foreign direct investment.

In the summer of 1975, I asked officials in the Department of Industry, Trade and Commerce how much investment Canada had abroad, and where, and they told me they hadn't the foggiest notion. But I finally obtained, from Statistics Canada, a rundown dated April 3, 1975, but which in fact covered only the period 1968–71, and embraced only direct investment (not the far larger, but harder to trace, indirect investment). That survey showed that we have large (and growing) investments in the developing countries. In 1971, direct investment amounted to $1,594,000,000, up from $844,000,000 in 1968 (a major share of the jump was accounted for by the reclassification of Brascan's South American holdings from portfolio to direct investment in 1970). We have $568 million directly invested in Mexico and the West Indies, $827 million in South and Central America, and $187 million in Africa, most of which ($111 million) is at work in South Africa.

You can't mount a saddle on the shoulders of another people without a certain amount of resentment, and we are now beginning to suffer from that sort of resentment. In April 1970, the city of Port of Spain, Trinidad, erupted in a series of riots, stormy Black Power demonstrations, and the beginnings of an army revolt. The revolt failed, the riots were put down, but things have never really been the same there for Canadians. For what the signs were blazing, and what the students were shouting, were the words "Canadians Go Home". (Trinidadians had not heard that bastard Yankee word, "Canucks".) Well, I mean! Canadian banks had to be boarded up against rock-throwing rioters, Canadian companies were besieged, Canadian homes, for pity's sake, had to be protected. Don't these people realize that we are their friends?

Well, no, they don't. They see us—most of the Caribbean islanders now see us — as people who have come in with large amounts of capital, carved out solid niches for ourselves, set up companies to drain off the resources of the area at bargain-basement prices, and cleaned up. They see us as the hordes who come pouring in every winter, waving fistfuls of dollars, drinking ourselves senseless, screwing ourselves bowlegged, and bitching about the prices, the insolence of the natives, and the fact that nobody loves us.

One day on a street in Kingston, Jamaica, I got into a shouting match with a young black militant; he kept on calling me names like Bloodsucker and imperialist and foreign pig. I was sure he had me mixed up with somebody else—an American, perhaps. No such luck; he knew who I was. The line that goes so well in Europe or the Far East—"but I'm not American, I'm *Canadian*"—means nothing in the West Indies. There, *we* are the Yankees. It is our banks that sprout on every corner, our managers who have their hands deep in the local economy's till, our companies, from Alcan to Manufacturers' Life, from Imperial Optical to Bata Shoes, who are regarded as usurpers and exploiters.

Canadian law does not permit any substantial foreign ownership in our financial sector—it is simply too crucial—but it is our banks that have made the deepest penetration in the Caribbean. At last count, there were forty-three branches of Canadian banks in Port of Spain, Trinidad (a city of some 170,000 people) alone. Throughout the British West Indies, the Canadian share of the bank industry runs from sixty to ninety per cent as it hops from island to island. The Bank of Nova Scotia, following the traditional triangle trade pattern—Maritimes–West Indies–England—set up business in Kingston, Jamaica, more than eighty-five years ago, and now has over 100 branches in the Caribbean. The Royal Bank began with a branch in Havana in 1899, and has eighty branches scattered across the islands today. Toronto-Dominion, Bank of Montreal, and Canadian-Imperial, though later into the field, also have substantial operations there.

In recent years, some steps have been taken to make our banks disgorge some of their holdings. In 1970, Trinidad and Tobago took over the local operations of the Bank of London and Montreal (which was partially owned by the Bank of Montreal), to form a national bank. Two years later, the Royal Bank and the Bank of Nova Scotia were incorporated in Trinidad (they had been offshore operations until then), the beginning of a move to gain control of their operations. Under Jamaican law, local citizens will acquire control of more than fifty per cent of all foreign banks there over the next few years. These minimal changes have been a long time coming, and we resisted them as bitterly as the Rockefellers battled during the mid-1960s to delay passage of the Canadian law that set foreign ownership limits here at twenty-five per cent in the banking industry, and forced the Canadianization of the Mercantile Bank.

It was the major role of our banking industry in the West Indies that led Canada, in 1919, to consider seriously taking the area off Britain's hands, and running it as our own colony. However, Sir Robert Borden, then Prime Minister, was cool to the idea because of the capital outlays involved and because of "The difficulty of dealing with the coloured population, who would probably be more restless under Canadian law than under British control and would desire and perhaps insist upon representation in Parliament." If the wogs were going to want the vote, to hell with them; we would keep our colonialism on a cash-flow basis.

Our colonizers—banks, insurance companies, extractive industries, manufacturers — have shown the same fine sensitivity to local wishes that we have discerned back home in the upper echelons of giant American-based corporations. The Aluminum Company of Canada, the largest foreign enterprise in the Caribbean, takes great pride in its behaviour as a corporate citizen there, but when the company president was questioned by a committee of the Canadian Senate in 1970, he sounded pretty much like Harold Geneen of ITT discussing his firm's good works in Canada. No, the company does no research in the West Indies; no, there were no shares, and no intention to offer shares, to the locals, and no, the company did not plan to use local help at the upper echelons: "We feel somewhat handicapped by the regulations which require the use of nationals in management positions if they are available."

The company, as of the time of this testimony, owned 48,000 acres of land in Jamaica, and its bauxite operation, worth $175 million — the largest single investment on the island — is used to extract the raw material, which is irreplaceable, ship it off to Canada for processing, and sell back finished products at extravagant prices. The Jamaicans don't like the process any better than we like the exploitation of our oil, pulp and paper, or iron ore. They are now moving to demand a greater share of the profits through abrupt royalty hikes.

Our firms are also playing an increasingly important and controversial role in Latin America, from Mexico to Argentina. Following the pattern of U.S. and British companies, most of the investments are held by a handful of giant corporations whose size and formidable economic clout make them a major force in local politics and economics. While there are 713 Canadian corporations with direct investments abroad, twelve of these account for two thirds of all such direct investment; these twelve have average foreign holdings of $264 million, so that, while total Canadian investment in developing lands is not impressive compared to, say, similar American investment, its concentration in a few hands makes us formidable beyond our worth, and leads to drastic effects not only on the local economy, but on Canadian foreign policy.

For example, Canada was clearly sympathetic to the overthrow of elected régimes in Chile and Brazil, and their replacement by dictatorships that have proved friendlier to our corporations. In Brazil, the giant Canadian conglomerate, Brascan (total assets, $1.7 billion), was one of several large foreign companies under the threat of nationalization when, on April 1, 1964, a military coup overthrew the elected government of Joao Goulart, and ushered in a military dictatorship.

For the ordinary workers of Brazil, the results have not been pleasant; the rich are getting richer and the poor poorer. In 1960, the top five per cent of the population received 27.4 per cent of Brazil's national income, and the bottom forty per cent received 11.2 per cent; by 1970, the top share had swollen to 36.3 per cent and the bottom share had shrunk to 9.0 per cent. The junta has allocated only one per cent of the national budget to health (the figure was four per cent in 1964), while 14 per cent goes to military spending. Brazilian infant mortality is rising steadily, life expectancy is down to thirty-five years, and tuberculosis is rampant; the government's reaction has been to forbid mention of health problems in the press. But while the poor of Brazil have suffered under the junta, Brascan has prospered mightily. The threat of nationalization was removed at once, and the company shares bounded from $1.95 to $3.60 within two days of the coup.

The Canadian government has shown itself both friendly and generous to the military dictatorship. The Export Development Corporation lent Brazil $40 million during 1974, $26.5 million of which went to the Sao Paulo Tramway, Light and Power Company, a Brascan subsidiary.

The EDC was not so forthcoming, of course, when Chile made the mistake of electing a Marxist, Salvador Allende, on September 4, 1970. In his twenty-one months of power, Allende's government took over 300 companies — most of them foreign-owned—and began a massive redistribution of income. The Americans began to work at once—through the CIA—on the overthrow of Allende, but Canada did its bit, too. The Export Development Corporation promptly cut off loans to Chile, and that contributed to the economic chaos that led the way to the military coup and Allende's murder in 1973. Once he was out of the way, and a dictatorship established, we gave instant recognition to the new régime (it took us twenty-three years to recognize the new régime in China) and went back to handing out EDC loans. The *Globe and Mail* noted on October 2, 1973, that "Concern for the completion of a deal worth more than $5 million between de Havilland Aircraft of Canada and Chile's domestic airline was a major factor in expediting Canada's recognition of Chile." The financing for that deal was arranged through the EDC, which had, a few months earlier, turned down a $4 million deal for logging equipment with the Allende régime.

My concern here is not with the swiftness or slowness of our recognition of new régimes (swift in Brazil, Greece, Chile, slow in China, North Korea, Vietnam), but with the pattern we seem to have established abroad. We have, time and again, supported régimes whose chief virtue is that they will allow a handful of our corporations free rein to exploit the native economy for the benefit of investors back in Canada. That is the traditional stance of an imperialist nation.

Nowhere is our policy clearer than in the Union of South Africa. Time was when we took a strong stand on the subject of racist exploitation in South Africa. In 1964, our government refused to allow Ford of Canada to sell trucks to that nation for use as para-military vehicles; in 1968 and 1969 we supported resolutions in the UN condemning Portugal for its treatment of African colonies; at the same time, we committed ourselves to economic sanctions against the breakaway Smith régime in Southern Rhodesia and supported the vote to end South Africa's control over the territory of Namibia.

After 1970, however, we became increasingly attuned to the white régimes in control of the areas where we have major investments. Perhaps it is only coincidence that our investment in the Union of South Africa nearly doubled (from $58 million to $111 million in direct investment) during the 1968–71 period while we were undergoing this change of heart. Although South Africa left the Commonwealth in 1960 — and we helped to push her out — that nation still operates under Commonwealth Preference in trade matters. If our aim is to bring the white racists to heel — in accord with our stated position in the UN — we are certainly going about it in a peculiar way. We have stepped up our trade missions to South Africa, allowed Canadian companies to make deals for the mineral exploitation of Namibia (the U.S. will not let its companies do this) and turned a blind eye to Canadian investment in Southern Rhodesia, where it is not supposed to be.

When Hugh Nangle of the Montreal *Gazette* visited Southern Rhodesia in 1973, he reported that the Bata Shoe Company and Falconbridge Nickel were operating subsidiaries in Southern Rhodesia. Order-in-Council regulations passed to conform with a UN resolution appeared to make this illegal, so MP Gordon Fairweather (P.C.—Fundy Royal) put a question on the House of Commons Order Paper to ask about it. He was told, "The Canadian government has received no evidence that Canadian incorporated companies have branch plants in Rhodesia. Our position on this is quite clear. Canadian companies are not permitted to invest in Rhodesia, nor are Rhodesian exports allowed entry into Canada." It appeared that Nangle's going there and finding out what was going on, and then keeping his discovery a discreet secret between him and the readers of the Montreal *Gazette*, simply didn't count.

I was so fascinated by this bland reply that I wrote Thomas Bata, President of Bata Shoes Limited, to ask about his company's position. He replied that the company involved had been incorporated long before the sanctions were applied, and assured me that everything was legal and above board. Presumably Falconbridge, too, has found a legal way around the law; it must be a great comfort to the blacks of Rhodesia to know that the conditions under which we work them are perfectly regular and proper.

Actually, the *Gazette*'s reporter found that the Bata company was more liberal in its treatment of Rhodesian workers than some others. Falconbridge, for example, was paying beginners in its gold mine near Gwanda fifty-six cents a day when Nangle visited. "A few black mineworkers at the Blanket Mine, some with as many as twenty years service, earn between twenty-seven and thirty Rhodesian dollars per month" (which comes to between $43.74 and $48.60 Canadian per month). The eleven white miners there were paid up to $810 a month, and lived in comfortable houses with their families; the blacks lived in crowded shacks made of asbestos corrugated sheeting.

What has the Canadian reaction been? Well, the government doesn't recognize that Falconbridge exists in Rhodesia. When the Study and Action Committee of the YWCA wrote to the Department of Industry, Trade and Commerce, the department replied that it was not aware of "any Canadian-controlled investment in Rhodesia".

I had a long talk about this with a Canadian desk officer at UN headquarters in New York, who made two points worth considering. The first was that it is harder to obtain legal proof than journalistic assertion. "Some of these firms have devised incredibly elaborate schemes for disguising who they are. We do our best to track them down, but you have to remember that we are going to have to prove our case in a court of law. Often we know what is happening, but by the time we get a case together, the company has switched operations." The second was that there has been a distinct change in Canadian policy since the emergence of the New Majority of developing nations in the UN. "You talk about a coming shift of power," I was told. "Hell, it has already happened, and we are responding to it. South Africa is moving against what it calls 'petty' discrimination—water fountains for whites only, that sort of thing. South Africa and Rhodesia are getting tired of being insulted and boycotted; they're beginning to get tired of being leaned on, and Canada is doing some of the leaning."

I am the soul of optimism, and I would like to believe that this is happening. When Prime Minister Trudeau refused to attend the international plowing match at Oshawa, Ontario, in September 1975, because entrants from the illegal Rhodesian régime were on hand, my heart leapt up. I think it is obvious that a message has been transmitted from the UN Assembly to our Permanent Mission at 866 United Nations Plaza, half a block down the street. I think, too, that word has percolated up to Ottawa about the value of symbolic gestures. I am less optimistic that the corporations involved are ready to make changes.

A number of concerned Canadian shareholders tried to raise the issue of exploitation at the Falconbridge annual meeting in Toronto in April 1975, but they were banged out of order by company president Marsh A. Cooper. He said that "Falconbridge may not be comfortable with conditions it finds in an operating location [but] it adjusts to the prevailing business climate, assumes the inherent risks, and through its operations attempts to effect improvements".

This line—which was Thomas Bata's explanation to me, too — holds that Canadian firms exercise a liberalizing influence. We are such nice guys that our investments are not exploitative, but reforming. We lead the way, fifty-six cents in hand, to a better tomorrow.

This argument would make more sense if it were not for the coincidence that increased outside investment in Africa has historically gone hand-in-hand with ever stricter enforcement of apartheid and ever stronger repressive measures. Don't mistake me; I'm not arguing that foreign investment has itself added to the savagery of repression—I don't know whether it has or not—but it sure as hell hasn't eased the pain any. Indeed, as Hugh Nangle argues, "South African society—and thus South African industry —has institutionalized policies in favour of whites against blacks. Without exception, Canadian subsidiaries in Southern Africa accept and operate within the system."

The proportion of the national income going to whites in the area has gone up, and that to blacks has gone down, in recent years. The YWCA-funded study, *Investment in Oppression*, concluded in its 1973 report, "Historical analysis in no way suggests that foreign investment has been a liberalizing force. Rather, it suggests that this investment is content to coexist with a pattern of repression which has intensified during the very years that this investment has increased most rapidly."

The YWCA enlisted a number of experts to probe into Canada's South African adventure, and wrote letters to the heads of some companies active there. W. I. M. Turner, President of Consolidated Bathurst, replied in a letter, reading the investigators a little lecture on interfering with South Africa: "If the main objective of the exercise is to see the Republic of South Africa evolve into a more racially equitable society then I would argue that any program designed to put pressure on the government of the day simply hastens [sic] their resolves." If you translate "hastens" to "hardens", which is what Turner must have meant, you will see that he is saying you shouldn't try to influence the whites of South Africa; you will only make them worse. Anyone waiting for people with attitudes like that to bring a liberalizing influence to bear in Africa will still be waiting when Capetown freezes over.

When Canadian firms pay exploitative wages to blacks— or any natives, in Africa, or Latin America, or the West Indies—they are not "adjusting to the prevailing business climate", they are taking advantage of it; they are—sorry, Nazim Hikmet, you idealistic Turkish poet—collecting foul imperialist profits.

Well, why shouldn't they? The government itself appears to be striking an imperialist stance in the debate to establish dominion over the sea. The Law of the Sea Conference, which has worked through two sessions in the last two years without getting anywhere much, has been marked by a display of grabbiness on Canada's part that I thought had disappeared when we finished snitching the socks and underwear off our Indians.

The issue is one of the most important ever to come

before a world body. Who will control the mammoth re-sources of the oceans? Will they be used for all mankind, or just for the states bordering on them, or just for those rich enough, tough enough, and well-equipped enough to en-force their claims? We have reached a state of civilization in which flying at the table with knees up and elbows pump-ing is considered bad form, and most nations appeared ready, at the conference in Caracas during 1974, to accept the notion that coastal states could establish an "economic zone"—that is, a zone in which the state would have rights to mineral and marine exploitation—of 200 miles. But not Canada.

We argued instead for an extension to "the natural pro-longation of our land mass", a zone that would include all the continental shelf and the slope down to the deep sea-bed. We were pushing for an economic zone that would reach 600 miles into the ocean off our east coast. Some of the landlocked states suggested that, well, if we were going to demand so much, at least we should offer to share some of the revenue from the area beyond the 200-mile limit with other nations (i.e., them). It was suggested that there should be an international commission, operating through the UN, which would collect a royalty on exploitation of the extended zone, and distribute it among nations that don't have a bathing-zone, much less an economic one. Even Britain, which has taken a tough stand on the economic zone issue, indicated a willingness to share revenues beyond the 200-mile mark, but we replied, through then Energy Minister Donald Macdonald, "Canada has no in-tention of conceding any part of its margin."

We produced an entrancing argument to buttress this position, namely that it is in the world's interests that we should get even richer. Or, in the jargon of our experts, "Self-interest requires the betterment of Canada and it implies a world order which is favourable to or compatible with such betterment. The promotion of national self-interest fuses the planes on which government objectives are pursued."

The Robber Barons of an earlier age would have recognized the sentiment, although they weren't much for fusing planes. It is the old "trickle down" theory of Victorian economics, under which, as the rich get richer, the quality of crumbs dropping off the table to the bums beneath improves with each passing year.

Canadian intransigence helped to break up the first two Law of the Sea Conferences without any substantial agreement. God knows what will happen at the next conference; we may claim everything east to the Canary Islands and offer to fight all comers.

When British bumptiousness became a joke, the Empire was slowly giggled out of existence; we may be the first nation to try to assert gunboat diplomacy without any gunboats. It should be a load of laughs.

CHAPTER 15:

STANDING BY

Friendship is selfishness, half the time.

T.C. Haliburton, 1844.

It was warm and sunny that Sunday afternoon; in the park close by our Ottawa house, a squirrel scampered overhead, cursing, while a handful of youngsters dangled fishing-lines in the canal, and two young lovers strolled hand-in-hand across the grass. The setting was idyllic, except for the young woman who sat in the lower branches of a tree, shrieking her heart out. She was a profanity; her wild screams, high, piercing, strident, wordless, were an affront to nature; they froze us in our places; we hunched like rabbits beneath a stooping hawk, then, when she paused for breath, went our various ways. A young couple, canoe-ing in the canal, paddled over beneath the tree, looked up, smiled at each other, and paddled away again.

Our kids were among the line of fishermen, and I asked my daughter how long the screaming had been going on. "Oh, all day. She was lying on the ground for a while, hitting it. Then she climbed up into the tree."

I was for calling the cops; my wife said, no, she was going to see what this was all about. My son rolled his eyes. Joan went over to the tree, held up her hand, and, in the no-nonsense tone she uses on recalcitrant kids and erring dogs, told the girl to come down out of the tree. She came down. She was a very ordinary-looking girl in her early twenties, slender, plain, with thick glasses that were al-most opaque now with tears. My wife took her hand, and we went home.

Over coffee, when the sobs stopped, she told us that she

knew she was suffering from a mental breakdown. It happened sometimes like that, on the weekends, when there was nothing to do, when her room-mate, as usual, had a date and she did not, when there was no one to see, no one to talk to, and life became too much. Her mother lived nearby; they didn't get along, hadn't for years, but when these wild crying fits came, she nearly always found herself somewhere near her old home. She had spent some time in the Ottawa Sanitorium and thought she should go back there now. The trouble was, you could only go crazy between nine and five on weekdays in Ottawa; nights and weekends, the admitting office was closed. When this had happened to her once before, some people had called the police, and they had put her in jail until the hospital opened again. I said "oh".

I telephoned a doctor friend in Ottawa and asked him how to go about getting a girl admitted to the San in off hours. He said, "You want my advice on what to do? My medical, professional advice?" I said yes. He said, "Open the door, put her on the porch, close the door firmly behind her, and forget it." I said thanks. His wife was more helpful; she said that if we could get the girl admitted to Ottawa Civic Hospital, they could refer her to the San right away.

We all got into the car and drove over to the Civic, and marched into the Emergency Department. They were not happy to see us, and they had miles and miles of forms and lots and lots of questions. The girl was getting upset again; it looked as if we were going to be there all day; she was going to crack up, right there, and lawsy me, it was going to be embarrassing. Joan got her hand on an intern, and told him she wasn't going to let go until that girl was in the hospital. He was harassed, poor chap, with a dozen things to do, but that got to him. He said, "You really mean it, don't you?" And Joan said damn right. Five minutes later, the girl was admitted, transferred to the San, and bedded down.

She was there for about a week. We saw her a few times after that, then we moved from Ottawa. God knows what happened to her, and I doubt if anybody else cares.

Remember how we all shook our heads at that scene in the movie *Midnight Cowboy* where New York pedestrians calmly step over a man lying prostrate on the sidewalk? Ah, those Americans. Well, I don't accept that Canadians are a more caring and concerned people than Americans. I know my own reaction was to get rid of that girl as fast as possible; I know a whole park-full of Ottawans agreed with me; I know my doctor friend was following the first rule of medicine—don't get involved—(the Hippocratic Oath is the second rule) and that he was in good company. It was my wife who took action, and everybody knows she's a busybody.

Most of us are not. In Toronto, one night in February 1974, an elderly cripple lay in the slush of a downtown gutter, where he had slipped and fallen, for more than twenty minutes, while scores of people walked past, ignoring his feeble gestures and cries for help. Finally, a mother and daughter (on their way to choir practice, yet) got him up and to hospital. In Toronto, in April 1975, four youths beat up a bus driver and robbed him while a busload of passengers looked on impassively. He asked them to help, and they looked out the windows and at their watches until the robbers left the bus.

We are not wicked, we just don't want to get involved. We live in a society that spends much of its energy teaching us to be alien, to fight for privacy, to demand to be left alone. That's all we ask — don't bring me your troubles. I have been told that this is the outcome of big-city living, that people in the boondocks behave better. Perhaps so; but then, people in the boondocks know each other — it's not like having to help a *stranger*, for heaven's sake. What generally happens is that we wait for officialdom to take over. That's what they're for, officialdom. The trouble is that sometimes they don't take over. I remember the *Jane and Judy*.

On November 30, 1964, chill winds out of the north-north-east were battering the South Shore of Nova Scotia. It was cloudy, and there were occasional bursts of near-freezing rain. In the village of Stoney Island, on the east flank of Cape Sable Island, Stillman Quinlan — "Riggley" to his friends — rolled out of bed at 5:45 a.m. He dressed, ate a big breakfast, and, in the lightening dawn, strolled down to the shore, a few yards from his front door, to cast a wary eye on the weather. It looked like a rough one. Well, he'd been out in dirty weather before, in forty years of fishing. Tomorrow was the first day of the lobster season, which meant that today the fishermen could put out their traps. The first day's catch was always the big one; it could bring as much as $600. A little wind and wet wouldn't keep Riggley on shore today.

He began loading lobster traps in the *Jane and Judy*, his Cape Island fishing boat, a sturdy, thirty-eight-foot craft, built for weather rather than comfort or beauty. Soon he was joined by Jimmy Smith, a local man hired to help him for the day. Smith was young, just twenty-six, and his wife was pregnant; they could use the fifteen dollars — plus the catch from twelve traps — that he'd get for this day's work. The men worked quickly, talking little. They checked lines and weights, cut bait, loaded traps. By ten, they were part of a fleet bucking a stiff breeze across Barrington Bay on their way to the lobster grounds, four miles off shore. The trip went smoothly enough, and they placed seventy-five traps in three hours; then, on the way back, the *Jane and Judy*'s motor began to smoke and cough. Finally, it gave out, and the boat began to drift downwind. Quinlan fumbled over the engine; it caught again, roared into life, but continued to smoke as they staggered in to shore. There, Quinlan's son, Bob, who had his own boat, came over to ask about the trouble.

"Forgot to oil 'er," Quinlan grinned sheepishly. By the time he had lunch, rounded up seven quarts of oil, and started out with a fresh load of traps, they were a good hour behind the other fishermen. As the *Jane and Judy* chugged out just after 2 p.m., he shouted back to his wife on shore, "We should be back by seven. If we ain't, we're in trouble."

Quinlan and Smith worked hard all afternoon, exchanging occasional shouted greetings with other boats nearby, as the weather grew steadily worse, with rain and snow lacing the chill air under the thrust of mounting winds that swung from northeast to northwest. At 6 p.m., most of the other fishermen struck for home, grateful to duck out of the gathering storm, while Quinlan and Smith laboured on. It must have been about seven when the *Jane and Judy* — behind schedule—turned into the wind and began to batter her way home.

About a mile out, she cut across a submerged net, instantly severing a nylon line that snaked around the propellor and choked it into silence. One minute the motor's gruff roar rumbled defiance to the storm; the next, there was no sound but the slap of waves and the howl of wind. It took only a moment to clear the boat's anchor and drop it overboard. With luck, it would hold them from being pounded to pieces on the rocks. The anchor caught and held; the boat pitched badly, and occasionally took some water, but she was sound, she would do. It was dark now, and there was no chance that they would be seen out here. There was nothing to do but shelter as best they could, and bail, and wait.

On shore, seven o'clock passed, then eight and nine; obviously something had gone wrong with the *Jane and Judy*. At Clark's Harbour, two miles along the shore, Mervin Atkinson, the fish buyer to whom Quinlan normally sold his catch, began to worry about the missing boat. He drove to the B.C. Packers Plant, to call on Manager William Moffatt, and see if anything could be done. Moffatt called a

273

friend who had a fifty-foot long-liner, more seaworthy than the open Cape Islanders, but he was told there was no point in going out on a black night like that. Moffatt drove from Clark's Harbour to The Hawk, a fist of rock that thrusts out into Barrington Bay, and shone his headlights out to sea, but it was black, black as hell. After half an hour of peering into the howling wet dark, he went back to his office and called the Rescue Co-ordination Centre in Halifax.

The RCC is the focal point of search-and-rescue operations in Canada, which are primarily the responsibility of the armed forces. For sea searches, the RCC calls in the coast guard, the navy, government ships, and private merchant men in the area. Moffatt's call, at 12:05 a.m. on December 1, came to an air force officer, who promised to "get right on it". At 12:58 a.m., the RCC issued an All Ships Broadcast, to advise every craft in the area of the *Jane and Judy*'s last known position. Then a quick check was made to locate the nearest government vessel to the scene. The RCC files showed that the closest ships were two Coast Guard buoy-layers, the *Sir William Alexander*, at Lockport, about thirty miles east of Cape Sable Island, and the *Walter E. Foster*, at Yarmouth, fifty miles northwest. Four futile hours were spent trying to locate these ships, until the *Foster* was found in Saint John, New Brunswick, and the *Alexander* in Halifax —both 150 miles away. In fact, the closest ship to the *Jane and Judy* was the *Cygnus*, a Fisheries Department vessel, 153 feet long, snugged in at Shelburne, thirty-two miles away. But the RCC thought the *Cygnus* was in Halifax, and the *Cygnus* either missed the All Ships Broadcast or ignored it.

When dawn broke on December 1, the wind had risen to forty-two knots (about 47 miles an hour), and the steady rain was being driven almost horizontal to the sea. In the grey morning light, a woman peered out into the ocean off The Hawk, and saw the *Jane and Judy* bucking in the surf. She was stern-on to land, and the two men were crouched in the cabin; from there, they could see their homes, less than a mile away on shore. The RCC was called and asked to send a helicopter, but the wind was too rough.

By 11 a.m., sixty cars jammed the narrow side-road and 200 villagers peered across the wind-whipped waves to where the Cape Islander pitched. The fishermen attempted to launch a dory, but it swamped almost at once. Then Captain Merrill Rogerson of Port La Tour tried to bring up his sixty-five-foot long-liner, but the waves beat him back.

Then, suddenly about 1 p.m. the wind died, the snow and rain stopped as abruptly as if they had been turned off at a master switch. The Hawk was in the eye of the storm. For nearly two hours the wind was still, and, although the waves continued to pound in, pinning small fishing boats ashore, the chances of rescue by helicopter seemed bright. Sylvia Smith, who was about to leave home for the beach to greet her husband, decided not to go because, "I was expecting Jim would be home soon, and I wanted to have his dinner ready."

But nothing happened. There were no more rescue attempts. The people on shore were sure the authorities had the situation in hand; they were expecting, at any moment, to see a helicopter swoop down on the *Jane and Judy*. But the RCC had no way of knowing that there was a temporary, local calm. By the time someone thought to phone and they got a plane off, just before 3 p.m., it was too late.

Shortly after 1 p.m. the storm had closed in again; the wind rose to sixty-five knots, whirling away the wavetops, spinning them to freezing spray. The *Jane and Judy* became a dancing dot in the blinding bursts of snow and rain. Then she was gone. The anchor rope, strained by the constant tugging through the night, gave way at last, and the tiny ship was at the sea's mercy.

At 2 p.m., a Fisheries Department employee suddenly remembered that the *Cygnus* was lying at Shelburne; she started out, but turned back before she even cleared harbour. At 4.30 p.m. a scallop-dragger beating for shore steamed back and forth looking for the drifting boat, then came in.

Two days later, a watchkeeper on the HMCS *Cap de la Madeleine* spotted the overturned *Jane and Judy* in the water twenty-two miles east of Cape Sable Island. The bodies of Smith and Quinlan were never found. Quinlan left a wife and four children, supported by $70 a month in welfare, and a meagre store of savings; Smith's widow, and their baby — born a month after the father's death — lived in a tiny trailer, without running water, on $60 a month in welfare.

There was a good deal of rage in the village, directed mostly at the RCC and the Coast Guard, but there was no attempt to help the bereaved families. The crew of the navy ship that found the overturned wreck got up a collection — $100 for each of the families, "to add to whatever the local people had gathered," as a navy spokesman said. But the local people hadn't gathered anything.

There was no insurance for the dead men, either. At a South Shore fishermen's meeting, called mainly to bitch about the Coast Guard, I asked about this; wouldn't it be a good idea if the locals got together to take out a group insurance policy on all the fishermen? "Are you crazy?" one man asked, "You think I'm going to pay good money to cover some bum who can't even handle a boat?" That drew a lot of vigorous nods. I wondered, too, if the fishermen wouldn't be better to pool their resources, and put up a decent boat; they said nuts to that, they were going to stand on their own two feet. I wondered if they had thought of banding together for purposes of bargaining with the packing company that bought their catch, and they wondered if I was a commie, or something. I told them that it was an education for me, a city slicker, to see how the smalltown folk cling together, and help each other, and I left.

There were about a dozen times when resolute action by somebody—anybody—might have saved the *Jane and Judy*.

Even the most minimal neighbourliness—pairing up with another boat, for safety's sake—might have ensured that the men would be taken off as soon as they ran into trouble. But neighbourliness, saluted in song and story, is not much honoured in practice in Canada. I remember Ricky Lozecki.

Ricky was beaten to death one sunny afternoon in a quiet apartment building in downtown Hamilton, Ontario. He was killed ten days after his second birthday in 1966. He was hit so hard that his mesentary — a thick membrane attached to the wall of the stomach—was torn by the force of the blows. He was covered with bruises, and suffered a brain hemmorhage. About one third of his body blood was found in his stomach; splashes of blood were also found on the wall and floor of the bathroom. The man who did this was his father, Raymond Lozecki, who was sentenced to fifteen years in jail for manslaughter—expiation for insanity.

He had battered the boy before, quite often, and quite brutally. Almost everyone who knew the family knew about the beatings. The police and Crown Attorney had been called about one beating four months earlier; a neighbour heard the sounds of several batterings, and saw the beaten child; a baby-sitter noticed bruises on the boy and called in a friend to show her five marks, in the shape of four fingers and a thumb, imprinted on either side of Ricky's ribcage. A barber who cut the boy's hair saw an ugly bruise behind his ear and asked about it; in reply, Raymond Lozecki showed him Ricky's private parts, bruised and swollen. The barber told Lozecki he should be locked up, but left it at that. A friend, who often came to call, noticed that Ricky cringed and whimpered whenever the father came into the room, but he never cried, not even when Raymond hit him. She thought that was kind of strange. In all, twelve people saw or heard evidence of the regular, brutal battering of this two-year-old boy over a period of months, and none of them did a damn thing.

Ricky's mother knew what was happening, of course, but she was terrified of her husband, who beat her, too. She once brought an assault charge against him, after her family doctor—who was convinced that Lozecki was mad—urged her to do so. But she dropped the charge, and the police, who had been called by the doctor, were reluctant to interfere in a family matter. Nobody ever called the Children's Aid Society, although it was within a ten-minute walk of the Lozecki home. Oh, they talked about it, the beatings were a common subject of conversation in the apartment building and in the neighbourhood, but nobody wanted to mention them to the mother, and she was convinced, because everybody avoided the subject in polite Canadian style, that she was truly alone.

So, after four months of merely brutal beatings, Raymond Lozecki killed his baby boy. He later kept Ricky's picture in his jail cell.

The mother was a little bitter. She blamed herself for the weeks and months when she did nothing while her child was being terrorized, but she blamed others, too. "I was frozen. I was terrified. I think I was out of my mind. But what about all those other people who knew what was going on?"

They were all — all except the family doctor, who had tried to do something — upset and defiant. They kept on asking me, "What the hell did you want us to do? What would you have done?" And I kept saying I didn't know. Nothing much, I guess. Just like anybody else.

Just like, for example, all the people who stood around sucking their thumbs while Dr. Gustave Gingras fought to get a rehabilitation hospital for the war-wounded children of South Vietnam. Gingras is a remarkable man, executive director of the Rehabilitation Institute of Montreal, perhaps the world's most respected authority on disaster aid. In 1959, he was called in when nearly 10,000 Moroccans became paralysed after eating food cooked in adulterated oil.

In 1962, he directed the long battle to put some semblance of normality into the lives of the thirty-four babies in Quebec and the Maritimes afflicted in the thalidomide disaster. In 1965, he was called, by External Affairs Minister Paul Martin, to help the children of Vietnam.

Canada had been asked to start a rehabilitation program in South Vietnam; would Gingras take on the job? Of course he would. On September 28, 1965, he flew to Saigon, and what he found there saddened and angered him. "I saw wards and wards of children with an arm gone, a leg gone, terrible scars across the face from burns. . . . I saw hundreds of children and I don't remember seeing one of them smile."

He hurled himself at his task, located a building in Saigon, obtained government clearances, and checked supplies. To save time, he dictated notes and orders as he walked and worked each day, and mailed the tapes home every night, and his Montreal staff began the mammoth organization job long before he left Vietnam. He arrived back in Canada on October 14, 1965, drew up a detailed report, complete with such details as an insurance scheme for volunteer workers, then flew to Ottawa to deliver the report in person. The government official he had an appointment with was too busy to see him; an underling told him nothing except, "Don't talk to the press", accepted the report, and waved him goodbye. Gingras returned to Montreal and began rounding up volunteers while he awaited an official go-ahead.

It never came. South Vietnam, on due reflection, realized that a rehabilitation centre was bound to produce pictures of war-mutilated babies and napalmed children. They began to stall. The Canadian government was aware of the stall, but refused to press for action, or even to ask why Saigon had turned cool to a project it had suggested in the first place. Gingras kept up a steady barrage of pestering letters and phone calls, but they were ignored, so he went

279

charging down to Ottawa again, and buttonholed Martin. The External Affairs Minister smothered him with clichés, buttered him with flattery, promised everything, and did nothing. Britain, the U.S., and Sweden all mounted rehabilitation schemes of their own, over, under, and around the Saigon government. Canada, with the world's leading expert on tap, did nothing.

On December 16, 1966, fourteen months after Gingras had rushed home with his report, Martin told reporters in Paris that the project was off. The reason finally passed to Gingras by a civil servant was that Canada and South Vietnam could not agree on who should pay for such items as the electric bill for the centre. "My God!" Gingras snorted, "Here is a house on fire and a man is trying to get his kids out and up comes the milkman and says, 'Hey, you owe me for last Tuesday.'"

In the House of Commons, under questioning, Martin said there was no question of the centre being reconsidered. It was finished. But Gingras refused to accept the verdict. "This meant I had failed, and I am not accustomed to fail."

He decided to ignore the only firm word he had ever received from the government — don't talk to the press — and began a publicity campaign to change the government's mind. Reports began to appear in the newspapers; the *Star Weekly* carried a long article, accompanied by pictures of wounded children. Soon, Martin was under fire; in Toronto, housewives formed a citizens' committee; in Ottawa, the External Affairs department was bombarded with letters and phone calls; in Montreal, Gingras received more offers for medical volunteers than he could use. (This positive response argues that Canadians will, on occasion, get involved, but the occasions are rare.)

In January 1967, the rehabilitation centre was a closed issue; in April, it was on again. An official from the Canadian International Development Agency flew to Saigon (no one had actually been to check up on why the project had been killed until that time). Diplomatic pressure, polite but insistent, was brought to bear. A six-man team headed by another Montreal doctor, Michel Dupuis, was dispatched to draw up a new report. Finally, in May of 1969, nearly four years after the idea was broached, a Canadian rehabilitation centre for children was opened in South Vietnam. It was not built because Canadians are a sympathetic people led by a responsive government; it was built because Gustave Gingras is a stubborn cuss who doesn't know when to quit.

Vietnam has surely, for all time, dispelled the myth of Canadian neighbourliness. Although we were members of the International Control Commission, charged with blocking the flow of weapons into Vietnam, we sold nearly $3 billion worth of arms—from fill for land mines to jackets for bullets, from complex electronic gear and bombsights to the green berets worn so proudly through many a smashed hamlet. Throughout the war, we took the view that we were merely shipping the stuff to the Americans, and what they did with it was none of our business. We learned to accept the notion that our responsibility ended at the exit door of Canadian munitions plants.

Learning to accept is one of the things we did best in Vietnam; we learned to accept not only the U.S. view of the war, but the huge profits that flowed to us through the Canada–U.S. Defence Production Sharing Agreement. We even accepted the role of informant—or spy—for the U.S. in Vietnam, with our ICC officers passing on military information. (The Poles passed on similar information to the Viet Cong, but that doesn't make it right.)

Even at the very end, when the war was lost and the North Vietnamese and Viet Cong were marching into Saigon, and our Vietnamese friends, allies, and employees were clamouring for space on the Canadian planes, we showed the stuff we are made of. Our embassy staff loaded the waiting aircraft with furniture and personal effects, told the natives to come back the next day, and fled into the night, leaving behind hundreds of people to whom we had issued perfectly valid visas. While other nations slashed red tape to help refugees, Canada went by all the rules and filled in all the forms, and got away with having to take only a few.

We had learned to accept that we are not our brother's keeper. And to hell with him.

AFTERWORD

Advancing quietly; old differences settling down and being fast forgotten; public feeling and private enterprise alike in a sound and wholesome state; nothing of flush or fever in its system, but health and vigour throbbing in its steady pulse; it is full of hope and promise.

Charles Dickens,
describing Canada, in 1842.

It would be quite possible, and quite legitimate, to turn a book like this one on its head. Because I have argued, in the way a journalist likes to argue, from examples, it would be possible to find other examples to make other points, even diametrically opposed points. Canadian tolerance could be shown in the case of a white family who adopted an Indian child, Canadian justice in a case that went right, for a change, Canadian responsibility in our Suez role of 1956. But it is not my purpose to show that we are a brutal, venal, violent, bigoted people, who are rotten to the core. Rather, I have attempted to show that we are a people: the same admixture of intolerance, fairness, savagery, gentleness, authoritarianism, and sweet reasonableness that marks any other collection of humans in like circumstances.

I am not seeking to build a myth, but to offset one — the myth that we, of all peoples under the sun, have been magically endowed with qualities refused all others, especially those bastard Americans. It is a dangerous myth, because it blinds us to the reality we face in the coming decade. We are not, despite what we like to think, any longer accepted as peaceful intermediaries in the Third World. We are regarded as just as selfish, just as racist, just as imperialist as anyone else.

283

It is a crippling myth, because it prevents us from making the changes in our laws and institutions that must be made if we are to become the kind of nation we already think we are. Prime Minister Trudeau once suggested that we should have a constitutional Bill of Rights, to embed guarantees of personal freedom into our law beyond the reach of ordinary legislative change. He received almost no support for his idea. Most Canadians dwell in the delusion that they have all the rights they need; that justice, equity, tolerance, and fair play are already entrenched in this nation's heritage and enforced by her courts. They yawned Trudeau's notion out of existence. That's a pity, because, had he succeeded in framing a constitutional Bill of Rights, the Prime Minister would certainly have been blocked from plunging the nation into the War Measures Act in October 1970, without a lot more explanation than we ever got. That's a pity because, for a great many Canadians, this is a nation of inequity, callousness, carelessness, misery, and abject poverty. We don't mean it to be that way, any more than Americans do, or Afghans, or Ukrainians; it's just the way things work out. And things work out that way, in part, because we don't know it, and don't want to know it.

We are, again, not unique in this. There was a time when Romans considered that to be a Roman was to partake of perfection, a time when Britons sang lustily that Britons never, never, shall be slaves, even while some Britons were just that, in the mines and sooty factories of Wales and Scotland and northern England. There was a time — and not long ago, either — when American bumptiousness embraced the notion that to be a U.S. citizen was the most precious thing in the world.

In other words, self-delusion is the one international sport that has stood the test of centuries; only the names of the players change. Our capacity to kid ourselves is no more highly developed than was the Americans', before brutal reality began to break over that country, beginning in about 1949, but we have the advantage of the experience of those who went before us down this path.

What this book has attempted to do is to learn from that experience, to measure some of the distance between our self-image and reality. The reality does not show us to be any more wicked, venal, violent, or tyrannical than other peoples, it merely indicates that we are not any less so. That is useful information, I hope. We are not likely to reform our gun laws when we see ourselves as placid folk, or to give ourselves a badly-needed constitutional Bill of Rights as long as we think our legal system is free of flaws. And so I end as I began, affirming—probably in vain—that the sour notes I have struck on these pages do not signal my contempt for my native land, but my love.